'A Week in the Life of MAF *takes us*  *the maintenance shops, the homes and the Fellowship staff worldwide. As well, we* *serving God in locations far beyond the reach of normal transportation and communication links who depend on Mission Aviation Fellowship for their very survival as they minister. This is a fast paced, week-long snapshot of one of the most exciting ministries in existence today.*

Whether it is Africa, Asia, Latin America or Australia, this book invites you to join with the pilots, engineers, administrators, radio technicians and their families on a globe circling adventure with Mission Aviation Fellowship. You will experience the challenges of living in an undeveloped country where resourcefulness and creativity get the job done. You will join with indigenous Christians who literally had the Gospel brought to them "on wings from above". Get ready to ride along on a life-saving air ambulance flight as a critically ill patient is transported to a modern hospital to receive the medical care they so desperately need.'

Kevin Swanson – President/CEO – MAF-US

'Along with documenting the many details and skills necessary to ensure the success of MAF's ministry, A Week in the Life of MAF *gives readers a view of the hearts and minds of MAF staff members around the world. As they provide aviation and related services, these dedicated men and women, with their families, make daily sacrifices because they love God with all their heart and their neighbours as themselves. The tremendous impact of their ministry on those they serve is evident throughout this book.*

This lively account of their daily tasks has produced a fascinating and enlightening story that will inform, encourage, and amaze readers who are interested in the work of modern missions. Those who experience MAF through the pages of this book will be both entertained and blessed.

This work also provides an excellent account of the development of Mission Aviation Fellowship over time as it has adapted to new technologies and challenges, and will be of interest to those who are new to MAF as well as missionary veterans.

Mark Outerbridge – President/CEO – MAF Canada

'A Week in the Life of MAF *gives a behind-the-scenes look of a vibrant global ministry reaching out to people in need. In it you will meet an eclectic group of people from many different countries and backgrounds and with a variety of specialisms, skills and talents. These people have all linked together through a joint desire to share God's love with people in isolated areas through aviation and other technologies. Both as an organisation and as individuals in it, we can truly testify of God's tremendous faithfulness and provision in our service to Him.'*

Chris Lukkien – CEO – MAF Europe Operations

I read the transcript of Irene's wonderful book A Week in the Life of MAF *on a flight to Nairobi and the memories came flooding back, along with the tears and the laughter of days past.*

When on deputation I always tried to remove the MAF worker from the pedestal others had placed them on by 'saying it as it is' – the anger, frustrations, tears, yes as well as the blessings. But this was not always well received as it seemed to betray the image we in the west have of 'the missionary'. Where I failed, Irene has succeeded and for that I applaud her. Her book removes the glamour while keeping the sense of hard work and total commitment to the Gospel, often in the face of adversity, by showing MAF's missionaries to be no different to any other Christian. Each one with their own personal struggles but with a common purpose - to serve the Lord Jesus Christ wherever and in whatever circumstances.

I am so grateful to Irene, and the many contributors, for being prepared and willing to risk saying it as it is and what it is really like to be a missionary in today's world – warts and all.

Keith Jones – CEO – MAF UK

My own journey with Mission Aviation Fellowship has taken my family from New Zealand to Tanzania, Kenya to England, and now Australia. This journey is not unusual. Many 'MAFers' move from base to base and even country to country a number of times whilst serving in MAF.

The journey that you will go on as you read around the world in A Week in the Life of MAF *highlights for me, the diversity of our organisation – every story is different. Yet it also highlights our unity – for we all serve the Lord through our unique ministry, using aviation and technology to share God's love.*

The MAF journey that started around 60 years ago with committed pilots who had a vision to use their aviation skills for the Lord, continues today because of men and women like those you will read about in A Week in the Life of MAF *people who have given up comfort and security to give wings to the gospel. Be encouraged, challenged and inspired by their stories as you journey around the MAF world with them.*

Bill Harding – CEO – MAF Australia

A
Week
in the
Life of MAF

IRENE HOWAT

CHRISTIAN FOCUS

Copyright © Christian Focus Publications 2006

ISBN 1-85792-940-3

10 9 8 7 6 5 4 3 2 1

Published in 2006
by
Christian Focus Publications,
Geanies House, Fearn,
Ross-shire, IV20 1TW Scotland

www.christianfocus.com

Cover design by Alister MacInnes

Printed and bound
by
Nørhaven Paperback A/S, Denmark

CONTENTS

Acknowledgements

Compiling a Week in the Life of Mission Aviation Fellowship was only possible because the Mission's staff were willing to take time in their busy lives to keep the diaries I asked for. I want to thank them most sincerely. Their honesty makes the book worthwhile.

MAF Europe allowed Max Gove, MAF Europe's Manager of Research & Development, to act as a conduit between MAF staff and me. His help in doing so was invaluable. But that was not all Max did. He answered query after query, checked and rechecked the manuscript, compiled the glossary, organised the photographs and much else besides. Without his gracious assistance this book would be a pale shadow of itself.

And I wish to thank Keith Jones, MAF CEO UK. Keith, a friend for over three decades, opened the door for the book to be written. My interest in Mission Aviation Fellowship stems from our friendship.

Irene Howat

2006

Foreword

For more than fifty years I have been closely linked with MAF and its story.

It began for me in January 1956 when, aged eight years, I listened avidly with my parents to the daily BBC radio reports of five young American missionaries who had gone missing in the Ecuadorean jungle while trying to contact an unreached tribe of Indians. After five days their bodies were discovered; killed by those they had gone to help. It made a huge impression upon me as I thought of the sacrifice these men had made to share the love of Jesus with people who had never heard.

It continued for me as a fourteen year old, when I read the biography of Nate Saint, one of those same five missionaries, and realised that he been a pilot with an organisation called Mission Aviation Fellowship, and had flown the other four men on their fateful mission. God spoke to me through Nate's life and clearly challenged me to also become a missionary pilot.

In 1971 my wife Susan and I joined MAF. Over the next 13 years we worked in Ethiopia and Kenya, where I flew as a pilot. Since 1984, I have fulfilled a number of management and leadership roles and have been privileged to visit more than 30 countries for MAF. I have seen firsthand the myriad ways that MAF is serving and have also witnessed the significant changes which have affected every aspect of the work.

When MAF began flying in the 1940s and 1950s it was mainly to support western missionaries in their role of "speeding the gospel to the ends of the earth". By the time we went as a family to Africa in early 1972, the church was already growing exponentially as a result of those pioneer efforts. Today we see that a major shift has taken place so that national church leaders, pastors and evangelists are increasingly the ones using the aircraft to visit their congregations and to open up remote and inaccessible areas. MAF staff are also changing as more nationals join as technicians, managers, administrators etc. This is exciting and rightly reflects how God has been building His church in today's environment.

Today MAF also works in many places where it has been able to bring relief and help in disaster and long-term development situations. Often these tragic situations bring opportunities to be witnesses to God's love especially in countries where Christianity is a minority faith.

Looking ahead, we see that the era of missionary aviation is far from over and that it is not exclusively a ministry in the tribal areas of the world. We will need to remain flexible and focused on our task if we are to adapt to a world that is increasingly wracked by political turmoil, economic upheaval, natural and man-made catastrophes and yet, sometimes paradoxically, often offers greater freedom to God's people to demonstrate and share His love and the good news of the gospel.

As a Christian aviation organisation, MAF has always had a glamorous and exciting image that frequently does not reflect the sheer difficulty and tedium of the task – running an exceedingly complicated, highly-regulated, technical organisation while operating in some of the harshest and most remote locations of the world. I have therefore been thrilled to be part of Irene Howat's vision to share the routine, the complexity, the hardship and yet the great joy of operating such a vital support ministry.

Irene's idea to produce a diary which would give a modern snapshot of MAF activities around the world is very timely. We have many supporters who have grown up, as I did, on the stories of Nate Saint and other pioneers. This has been right and proper. But it is also important to acknowledge that this is no longer the norm. The original vision and purpose of MAF in 1945 is very little changed today but technology, the political environment, the people we serve and so many other aspects of MAF's work are significantly different.

Irene's book will give you a wider understanding of what MAF is doing in today's world. It will help you to see the changing face of many of our programs. You will be challenged by the incredible commitment of MAF staff working in difficult situations but also amazed at their cheerfulness as they happily live and serve in remote and trying locations without the benefits of everyday life that most of us take for granted.

After 34 years working with MAF you would think that I know everything about MAF and its people but the diary week has given me a new insight into MAF's ministry. I have been challenged about my own commitment in serving God as I have read through the contributions from around the world and pray that you will be too.

Max Gove
Manager of Research and Development
MAF Europe

AT THE HEART OF THE MISSION

For over half a century Mission Aviation Fellowship has facilitated the work of Christian mission and supported Christians in remote areas, that being what it set out to do. But the world changes with the passage of time. When MAF was founded much that we take for granted today had not been invented. There were no satellite Global Positioning Systems, and none of the hi-tech instruments that today's pilots and passengers take for granted. Nor was communication easy. The Internet was unborn, e-mails were in the far distant future, and news spread in an altogether slower fashion. While it can be uncomfortable running to keep up with the world, Mission Aviation Fellowship has done just that. And there are many remote and isolated places where MAF has been the agent of change, the means by which technology and instant communication have become available. Today MAF is involved in a whole list of activities and services. But should anyone worry that the Mission's initial reason for being has been lost in the mists of history, this book will reassure that the work has extended rather than diverted. Mission and the support of local Christians is still at the heart of MAF, and MAF is certainly right at the heart of mission, and much else besides.

A Mission Aviation Fellowship aircraft takes off or lands somewhere in the world on average every three minutes, day and night, week in and week out, throughout the year. In order to give a snapshot of the Mission's ministry, members of staff were invited to keep diaries of their activities for a week in September 2004, and what follows is a digest of their diaries. The diaries came in a wide variety of forms, and they have been altered as little as possible in order that they reflect the personalities of the writers. Many names occur in the text and, as a rule, only MAF missionaries are given their surnames; Christian names are used for others, although there are exceptions where MAF's national employees contributed their own diaries.

But where to begin? Dimitry Mustafin, a member of the Moscow Camp of Gideons International, says that it gives him great pleasure to think that, because of the vast distance between the western and eastern borders of Russia, Bible distribution is a twenty-four-hour-a-day activity. When he and his friends in Moscow pack up for the night, their fellow Gideons are beginning their distribution work in far off Vladivostok. It is even more so with Mission Aviation Fellowship. Russia stretches halfway round the world, but

MAF, working in thirty-nine poor and remote countries, operates right round the globe. Not all MAF programmes were able to provide diaries of their activities during the week. Had they done, the amount of material would have been quite unmanageable!

The sun's first rays of each new day shine down on the Chatham Islands to the east of New Zealand. It is very shortly afterwards that the day the Lord has made, and in which we rejoice and are glad, dawns on Australia. MAF Australia is one of the Mission's four main operations: MAF Australia, MAF Canada, MAF Europe and MAF US. A number of national MAFs function within their own countries. Each of these four has its geographical area of work that reflects its history and development. MAF Australia works in Arnhem Land (an Aboriginy Northern Australia in the north-east of the Northern Territory) Papua New Guinea and Cambodia. It has also carried out temporary relief work in Ache in Sumatra, Indonesia. MAF Canada's activities are carried out in Angola. MAF Europe has work in Africa, Bangladesh and Mongolia, and the focus of MAF USA's activities is in South and Central America, South East and Central Asia and Africa.

PART ONE

MAF AUSTRALIA

NORTHERN AUSTRALIA

✈

PAPUA NEW GUINEA

✈

CAMBODIA

1.

CAIRNS, EASTERN AUSTRALIA

The week in 2004 in which the snapshot of MAF's work was taken started with the rising of the sun on Sunday, 5 September, and the first operation on which it shed its light was in Eastern Australia, in Cairns, where MAF's Head Office is. The staff there provide managerial and administrative support to its operational and engineering branches, and they also wrote full diaries that give a real insight into the workings of MAF's administration. As the book traces the work of MAF worldwide, the Cairns office will be taken as typical of others. So who was there, and what were they doing?

New Zealander Bill Harding, Chief Executive Officer, had a busy diary for the week. Staffing needs, and the possibility of staff moves to cover current shortages, were a priority. But other things also needed his attention. Chief among them was the situation in Cambodia, where MAF's aircraft is the only one of its type, and the only one using Avgas, resulting in the fuel being rare and expensive. Thursday saw him helping to finalise the sale of an aircraft, with a view to the proceeds giving a much-needed boost to the aircraft replacement fund. But it also brought concerning news of a fire in the cockpit of one of the fleet serving in Papua New Guinea. Such is the area that he serves, that the CEO's mind has to be in several places at once. During the week he had discussions regarding a conference he was to attend in Thailand, made preparations for meetings with Aboriginal leaders in North Australia—and last week he was in Papua New Guinea. One of his pleasant duties is to respond to major donors, and towards the end of the week in question a donation of A$10,000 arrived in the office at Cairns.

In the Projects Department, Brad Sinclair was involved with pilots and engineers regarding work on a Cessna 206. Cambodia was on his mind too, and a suggestion that a container with fuel in drums might might better solve the problem there. On Wednesday, MAF was probably very far from his thoughts, as his wife delivered their second child. Donors were the focus of Brad's attention later in the week as he wrote a report for a potential donor, explaining the Mission's work and the need to replace the ageing aircraft fleet.

Mark Emerson, Papua New Guinea General Manager, who is based in Cairns, was involved in approving a new pilot (from MAF Canada). Although his e-mail server was down one day in the week, Mark's computer was much in use: editing the monthly newsletter for PNG (Papua New

Guinea) staff, highlighting stories illustrating the difference that MAF made during the last four weeks, writing his MAF Australia Board report, preparing next year's budget and editing the MAF PNG prayer points that are distributed to Papua New Guinea staff members and numerous others. While a mission needs to be efficient, none can operate to the glory of God unless it is backed by the prayers of God's people. Prayer notes are seen as a priority.

The other departments in Cairns are Human Resources, Information Technology, Finance and Accounting, and Support/Administration. Because of the distances involved in the work of MAF, conference calls are in regular use. On Monday, Laurence Whitehead, in the Human Resources Department, was involved in three conference calls. One related to safety and the early introduction of new 406 MHz Emergency Locator Transmitters on the aircraft, another was a candidate committee meeting where the MAF Canada candidate was considered and accepted for work with MAF Australia. A third involved a discussion about future managers. Mission Aviation Fellowship is at the forefront of technology, in that it helps provide high-tech services to remote and isolated places, but it also uses up-to-date technology for the smooth and efficient running of the Mission. While one day of the week found Laurence thinking about a new member of staff, the following day he turned his mind to those who are completing their time with MAF, as he prepared material for a three day 're-entry' course to help staff who have worked in a different culture reintegrate into their home environment. Culture shock can be a two-way experience.

In the Finance and Accounts Department Ruby, Ting, Dael, John and Patrick beavered away at their various jobs: from keeping an eye on cash flow, checking cost centre reports, writing cheques and sending invoices, preparing financial reports and organising flight training centre accounts to arranging the leasing of cars to MAF staff and fixing the photocopier! While operating MAF's financial arrangements does not have the glamour of flying their aircraft, every flight costs money and is totally dependent on the careful administration of the Mission's finances.

Terry and Glenn work in the Information Technology Department. While they can and do plan their work ahead, they are also there to respond to the blips that every IT system throws up. Monday saw them working on one such blip. MAF North Australia's nearly-empty computer hard-drive indicated that it was full. Such are the wonders of technology that Glenn was able to sort the problem remotely from Cairns. Most of their week was spent working on the PNG flight manifest system and dealing with software problems. One member of the IT team, Neil, was in Papua New Guinea in the week in which diaries were kept; he was sorting out computer issues there.

Cassy, Wendy and Bev in Support/Administration made up the Cairns team. Alison joined them who, along with her husband, was awaiting a visa to start work with MAF in Papua New Guinea. They were the oil that kept the wheels running smoothly in all the day-to-day office jobs. Besides that, they provided hospitality for visitors who called in and arranged travel for MAF staff, mostly to and from Papua New Guinea.

On Friday the PNG General Manager in Cairns was helping out MAF US – he was able to source 1,500 anti-malarial tablets for them.

2.

MAREEBA

West of Cairns is the MAF Mareeba base of the Atherton Tablelands, where farewell had just been said to an old friend, a Cessna 206 that was being pensioned off after a long and productive life. For thirty-one years it had served remote aboriginal communities in the top end of Australia's Northern Territory. It could have told countless stories of comings and goings from the Homeland Centres: medical flights, pastors' visits, the transporting of government agencies, supplies, and all the general movements of the communities. During the wet season, when roads were cut off for months on end, the aircraft had been particularly valued. However, the time had come to say farewell to the old lady and she had been brought to Mareeba in preparation for sale.

MAF Mareeba exists as an engineering support base for the MAF operational areas of Papua New Guinea, the Northern Territory and Cambodia. Routine maintenance is done on the fields, but for major work the Cessna aircraft in the fleet are ferried to Mareeba where twenty engineers and support staff apply vital expertise and commitment to the task. Of course, their families also make a valuable contribution to the community.

⚹ *Sunday*

Belinda and Trevor Gaulke were on leave, visiting family and friends in the Southern States of Australia and undertaking mission deputation. Today they spoke at two Lutheran churches in Melbourne. The response was, in their words 'awesome, encouraging and humbling. ... The prayer support is even more overwhelming. It is exciting to have people praying for MAF. It will be even more exciting seeing its effect, especially in the Kingdom of God.'

Meanwhile Howard Andrews led worship at the Atherton Baptist Church. Phil and Donna Andrews were received into membership during the service - dual membership, as they are keen to maintain membership of their home church in Melbourne, which continues to support them in their work with MAF. Grant Dixon presented a mission's focus during the morning service at the Uniting Church. Nicole, Karen and Jenny taught Sunday school or led Kid's Church in various churches around town. Paul delighted Aboriginal children by putting out five cartons of second-hand items for them to help themselves to after church in Mareeba.

Since MAF moved north from its former base at Ballarat three years ago, churches in Mareeba and nearby Atherton have given staff an enthusiastic welcome. Local churches have appreciated the input of this group of enthusiastic and committed Christians with a missionary perspective. The wider community has also taken note. The ministry may be focused primarily on service to the MAF operational branches, but it includes significant witness in the local area.

The first Sunday in September is Father's Day in Australia. Most MAF families enjoyed spoiling Dad with a special breakfast or other celebration. Some enjoyed Sunday afternoon relaxing at scenic locations such as the beautiful crater lakes not far from Atherton. Ed Hawthorn arrived back from Papua New Guinea. Ed is Manager of MAF Mareeba, and also Engineering Manager for MAF Australia – a task that often takes him away from home.

The primary focus of his week in PNG was a meeting of Christian aviation organisations. Representatives of MAF, Wycliffe/JAARS (Jungle Aviation And Radio Services – the flight arm of Wycliffe/Summer Institute of Linguistics), and New Tribes Mission participated. Such conferences have, in the past, proved valuable for mutual encouragement, sharing of expertise and ideas, and a joint approach to government on relevant matters. There was also an opportunity for Ed to speak with MAF engineering staff in Papua New Guinea, and even to apply his expertise briefly to aircraft avionics problems.

Nicole Wilson and her seven-year-old daughter, Mikaela, enjoyed a special time together just before bedtime. They read about Miriam and Aaron criticising Moses and how Miriam had leprosy and was out of the camp for a week because of this sin. Nicole writes, 'We had a good talk, both of us recognising that we say bad things about others at times. I think it's a big lesson for me, but I'm encouraged that Mikaela can recognise that these are the areas in which God wants us to grow, even as a child.'

✈ Monday

First priority in the morning was the arrival of an engineering auditor from the Australian Government's Civil Aviation Safety Authority (CASA). With his usual thoroughness, Darren Lydeamore, the Chief Engineer, had endeavoured to ensure that all procedures were in place and adhered to, technical records up to date, and the hangar and workshop neat and workmanlike.

Another priority was the departure of Cessna 206 VH–AEE, returning to service after a 2,400–hour inspection. This scheduled major maintenance, carried out approximately every four years, sees the aircraft stripped down for a detailed inspection and, where necessary, renewal of major systems or components. The aircraft had been in the hangar for seven weeks, requiring 686 engineer-hours of work done on it.

Phil Andrews received an e-mail from Mt Hagen (PNG) asking him to approve a design for a compressor wash ring for the PT6A-34 engines in the Twin Otters. This ring will make washing the engines more efficient and effective and will improve their reliability even more. He also received a request to approve a design for a camera hatch in VH-WOC, the Cessna 206 destined for Cambodia. Emil Kundig in Cambodia will be able to charter the 206 for aerial survey work now that it has a camera hatch. Unusually, Phil arrived home in time to help Caitlyn with her homework. They both enjoyed that.

Tim and Anita Young celebrated the first meal in their unit in Mareeba, after spending much of Saturday setting up home. Having been here only a week, Tim is learning the routines and responsibilities of the engineering parts store. Meanwhile Anita is looking into possible involvement in youth ministry.

✈ *Tuesday*

The working day began, as each one does, with devotions— Bible reading, a meditation from *The Word for Today*, and prayer for the work of MAF, family needs, and other matters of concern.

The women gathered for their Tuesday fellowship that usually meets in the morning after children have been dropped off at school. A devotional followed by sharing and prayer is the general format, but social occasions are also held from time to time. Support for one another in prayer, friendship and in practical ways is strong.

Jung-Sik Park's Work Permit was granted by the Papua New Guinea government today – another step towards his long awaited visa. Jung-Sik, an aircraft engineer from Korea, is visiting at Mareeba until his visa arrives. He and his family have worked with MAF in Tanzania and are looking forward to becoming part of the team in PNG.

MAF Aeronautical Engineer, Philip Andrews, worked on a number of design projects. One is for the camera hatch in the aircraft being prepared for Cambodia; another is for the compressor wash ring for more effective and efficient cleaning of the engines used in Twin Otters. Repair jobs on some of the older aircraft also occupied a considerable amount of his time. Phil received a request to design an access hole on the inside of the Cessna 402C (VH-AII) lower airstair door. This would enable access to the hinge that needs replacing. Relaxing in the evening, Phil's soccer team only lost by two points to the top team. It was a good game!

Peter Diprose carried out radio work on a helicopter on behalf of another maintenance organisation at the airport. Good relationships have been built up with staff in neighbouring hangars, and opportunities for witness present themselves.

✦ *Wednesday*

Today volunteers supplemented the ranks. Joe, a retired civil engineer and administrator, puts in an average of two days a week in the engineering parts store. Meanwhile Frank, another retiree, is undertaking some minor building maintenance tasks. Such voluntary assistance from individuals and church groups has been a great blessing. During the setting up of the Mareeba facilities, MAF staff welcomed a stream of folk who undertook a multiplicity of tasks. A side benefit was the relationships that were built with local churches and the increasing awareness it created within their ranks of the work of MAF.

The engineering audit progressed well. There are always little things picked up, but the generally favourable comments thus far are encouraging. A good working relationship is enjoyed with the government regulators. CASA (the Civil Aviation Safety Authority) and others in the industry have paid compliments to MAF. The audit inspector's visit provided an opportunity to further the application for approval of Mareeba's avionics workshop. It has already been recognised by the Papua New Guinea aviation authority, but has yet to be approved by the Australian regulator for overhaul of Australian aircraft radios and electronic equipment.

Ed Hawthorn (Engineering Manager) had lengthy discussions today with the manufacturer of a new aircraft type recently introduced into the MAF fleet. The GA8

Airvan has been developed for short airstrip/bush flying and is proving a popular replacement for some of the older aircraft. Dialogue from the development stage enabled MAF to have early input. Recently Phil spent several weeks working with the manufacturer on various design matters. Today Ed discussed work towards fitting a turbo-charged engine (necessary for higher altitude work in Papua New Guinea) and a turbine option for locations where Avgas is not readily available. Jet fuel is much more generally available than the Avgas required for piston engines. Provision for a patient stretcher system in the aircraft is also under consideration. Grant Dixon (Engineering Quality Assurance) has been completing engineering manuals for the GA8 Airvan's operation in the Northern Territory of Australia, in consultation with CASA. Training programme development is also currently occupying Grant's attention.

Community involvement and opportunities for outreach are important for many MAF families. Anita Young is a volunteer at Mareeba High School, working in conjunction with the school chaplain and a local pastor. Nicole Wilson spent the day as a volunteer at her children's school, listening to reading, working in the tuckshop, and watching a class presentation. In the evening she was involved with a Scout Group awards' night.

Phil Andrews spent most of the day working on the camera hatch design. After work his son, Josh, showed him an aeroplane he'd made at preschool out of bits of wood, nails and craft things. He loves making aeroplanes. His parents are already wondering what his future occupation might be!

'What is the Second Coming? I've never heard of it.' Jonathan and Natalie Brown were delighted to be able to answer the questioning of a relatively new Christian after their home Bible study group, going deeper into the Word of God with her. Another Bible study took place at Ed and Liz Hawthorn's home.

✦ Thursday

Paul and Connie Jones drove to Cairns airport at 2am to say farewell to 17-year-old Alex, who was returning to New Zealand to work. Alex recently completed an agricultural skills course. Educated primarily through home schooling, he is now taking up a position as groundsman at the headquarters of his former school. Part of the cost to many MAF families is seeing their teenagers not only leaving home but also scattering far and wide. Young people who have grown up cross-culturally often become citizens of the world, at home anywhere and everywhere – or perhaps nowhere! They are usually richer for their experience, but as adults they may live very far away from parents and siblings.

Ian Wilson's wife, Nicole, volunteers a few hours each Thursday morning to help with receiving of stock in the parts store. She says, 'I love this job. I learn more about our work in MAF and gain more understanding as to what life at the hangar is like.'

A group of mostly young adults met, as they do each Thursday evening, for a Bible study at the Andrews' house. Phil usually leads, but tonight Donna had another go and it went really well. Phil and Donna say, 'We love being able to encourage those who come along, and they encourage us.'

✦ Friday

The Engine Shop Supervisor, Ian Wilson, was busy with paperwork and supervision of two on-going jobs: a cylinder repair for MAF in the Indonesian province of Papua and an engine overhaul for Papua New Guinea. Training is often incorporated into the supervisory role, particularly with Andrew Locke, who is in his first year on the job. Profoundly deaf, Andrew has done well to complete engineering training through the Bible College of Victoria's Mission Aviation Course, and he is now building his engineering experience.

In the administration office, Chris Hitchcock has been preparing to take over some accounting functions from Head Office in Cairns. The budget for the coming year is also being formulated. The Finance Manager from Head Office met with the local management team to work on this. Ed Hawthorn completed a report to the MAF Board on engineering activities and progress over the past two months. He is also working with an aircraft broker on the sale of a surplus Cessna 402C, an older aircraft which is no longer viable as far as MAF operations are concerned.

Jung-Sik Park and family were advised today that their visas for Papua New Guinea have been approved. They still don't have them in hand, but it should be close now.

✈ *Saturday*

Stirring military music, the throb of World War II aircraft engines and the hum of voices provided a background to stocktaking in the MAF engineering parts store this morning. A group of enthusiasts for warbirds regularly rebuild, maintain and fly the collection of vintage aircraft housed in a hangar across the tarmac. An open day was being held there for service cadets from around North Queensland, including drill competitions, displays and a fly past.

It was a reminder of the airport's World War II heritage. Up to 100,000 military personnel were based on the Tablelands en route to or from the battles in wartime New Guinea. Many servicemen, mainly from Australia and the

USA, were repatriated to a military hospital here; some are buried in the war graves section in a local cemetery. A more peaceful purpose is pursued here now. Aircraft, maintained and refurbished by MAF engineers, return to the now independent nation of Papua New Guinea for Kingdom use. Apart from those involved in stocktaking, MAF staff enjoyed the weekend's respite from work to spend time with their families, including a parents versus kids soccer game. But Grant Dixon spent most of the day in study while Sharon and Joy looked around Cairns.

3.

MELBOURNE

Most Melbourne staff work for MAF on a part-time basis. Not long before our September week, MAF took over the management of Christian Radio Missionary Fellowship. They share an office and some staff, though their functions are quite different. CRMF's role is to provide and maintain radio, computer and e-mail services to missionaries and villagers living in remote locations throughout Papua New Guinea. A vital spin-off from this service is the provision of actual weather reports for MAF pilots; another is access to emergency evacuations by air for those living in these remote spots.

The week saw a team of nine (Cath, Daina, David, Denis, John Quay and John Wall, Laurie, Petra and Sheila) involved in a wide variety of tasks, from reviewing the first round of alterations to the Spring *MAF News* and sending photo captions to the magazine designer, through organising participation in an airshow, to being involved by video conferencing with others in MAF Australia on matters already mentioned in the Cairns' diary. And that was just *Monday*!

Raising finance for MAF is an ongoing job. The work can only be done if the finance is there to pay for it. Direct mailing is one way in which MAF raises financial support, and part of *Tuesday* was spent on that. The following day, *Wednesday*, was very forward looking, as David and Petra planned the photo selection for the MAF 2005 calendar. One advantage of using a calendar is that it is often looked at and referred to, consequently the work of the Mission is brought into supporters' minds, and hopefully also into their prayers on a very regular basis.

Thursday was different, and the kind of day that everyone needs from time to time. The server was down, and staff members were unable to send or receive e-mails or access network drives. On recovering from their initial frustration, they spent the day doing some of the things that just wait for a day like that to be done! By *Friday* people were beginning to be stressed by not being hooked up to the technological world, but normality was restored at lunchtime and it was all hands to the keyboards, especially those whose job it was to reply to the e-mails that had accumulated. John Wall finished the week a happy man, as he spent part of Friday discussing the position of Northern Territories' Aviation Safety Officer with a pilot who was on holiday in Victoria. John noted, 'He agreed to take on the role—which is great.'

4.

NORTHERN AUSTRALIA

Arnhem Land is the northern extremity of Australia's Northern Territory, the remote and lightly populated area that stretches east of Darwin and the Kakadu National Park to the Gulf of Carpentaria. Although it covers 96,917 sq. km it has a population of only about 16,000 people. Arnhem Land is one of Australia's last strongholds of Aboriginal culture. The main airport from which MAF works is situated on the Gove Peninsula, the most northeasterly point of Arnhem Land. In World War II the Gove Peninsula was pivotal to Australia's defence, and many relics of the war remain in the area. MAF has permanent bases at

Milingimbi, Ramingining and Numbulwar. It also supplies management and staff for Aboriginal-owned airlines at Elcho Island, Gove and Lake Evella.

Mission Aviation Fellowship provides a regular public transport service from Gove, flying timetabled flights on established routes that link the main communities of eastern Arnhem Land. Flights transport medical personnel to outlying communities and take patients to hospital. They also transport essential supplies, particularly perishable goods, to the remote communities in the region. As in other areas of MAF's operations, pastors and church personnel as well as education, health and government staff are carried to and from isolated communities. From time to time Mission staff are involved with search and rescue operations, and these might involve boats, aircraft or people lost on land.

In the week beginning Sunday, 5 September 2004 many members of MAF's staff in Northern Australia kept diaries of their activities. The pilots among them were Philip Agg (and his wife Linda), David Leek (with Amanda), Chris Maher, Brad Rule (and Belinda), Andrew Herweynen (with Sally), Ken Mack (and Angela) and pilot/engineer Russell (and Heather) Dunkin. Engineers Kevin (with Carol) Kraak, Glenn Childs, and Brian (and Alison) Creek kept notes of their activities. Brian is the Hangar Supervisor at Gove. Others who contributed were Marree Cross, Operations Manager at Nhulunbuy, Doug (with Yvonne) Miles and John and Nicole Strickling and Ben (with Lauren) Fleming.

Philip and Linda Agg served in Elcho Island and Ramingining before moving to Gove in 2004. He is a MAF pilot. During our week, Philip flew regular public transport flights—as well as helping to clean the hangar and staff quarters. One turnaround at Elcho Island gave him the opportunity to try to encourage a young Yolngu

(Aboriginal) refueller/baggage loader. Back home he and his wife engaged in the ministry of hospitality, something for which MAFers are well known!

✦✦✦✦✦

Glenn Childs works as an engineer based at Gove. As well as his regular work and study, he made the most of an opportunity to share about the work of Mission Aviation Fellowship with a woman whose son hopes to be a pilot. Glenn makes the most of his hobbies to share the gospel with those he meets. This is especially true of his membership of Christian Rods and Customs—his car club! The Hangar Supervisor at Gove is Brian Creek, who serves the Lord there with his wife Alison and their two children. Their week started in a campsite where they had spent some relaxing time with three other MAF families. Sunday saw them involved in their church service, with Brian helping the Yolngu ladies to lead worship. His working week found him toiling hard in the engine bay: removing the engine of a Cessna 402 and preparing a new engine.

MAF staff don't only work together, they pray together. On Wednesday, Brian and two other MAF engineers spent time praying together on the beach. Continuing education is a feature of Brian's work, and he spent part of the week studying for his next engineering exam. Alison 'burnt down Sodom and Gomorrah' with her class of children on Sunday. The class is half Yolngu children and half white. The following day saw her walking with a friend round the local community praying for those whose homes they passed. Many MAF wives, like Alison, are involved in local schools; sometimes they are the only Christian presence in a school.

✦✦✦✦✦

Also very involved in the local community is Amanda Leek, fitting that around home-schooling two children. She has many friends among the indigenous people. This was a sad week for them as David's mother died. It is hard for missionaries working away from home when they are not there for their loved ones at times of family crisis. Amanda, however, had difficulties of her own. 'A man got angry and slung rocks at the car I was driving. He hit the windscreen and it cracked; slivers of glass flew into the car. The windscreen didn't break all over. He tried to sling more shots at the car before I could drive away. Thankfully no one was hurt.'

✈ ✈ ✈ ✈ ✈

Normally Sunday is a no-fly day for Chris Maher, but at 2pm on September 5 he received a phone call at home from the local clinic where there was an emergency. He was told that Baby Jerome, the son of a local woman, was suffering from pneumonia. His lungs had filled up with fluid and breathing was not possible without the aid of oxygen. The little boy needed to get to hospital as soon as possible as he was dehydrating. Chris, who works from Lake Evella, knew he had to help, as the Medair King Air Aircraft, which would normally have done the medical evacuation, was unable to operate because the runway was being upgraded. The only alternative was for Jerome to be taken a three-hour drive to Gove.

Within half an hour of receiving the call, Baby Jerome and his mother were on board the MAF plane, and his oxygen was secured to the back row of seats. By then he was in a very critical condition and most distressed. From Chris's point of view the flight was uneventful, though it was carried out at a lower level than normal in order that the baby's oxygen would flow at a normal rate. By 3.15pm Jerome was in an ambulance at Gove airport, where he had an intravenous antibiotic drip attached. When Chris enquired two days later, Jerome was doing well and was expected to make a full recovery.

That same day Pilot Brad Rule was also involved in an emergency visit to hospital as his wife was hurt by a ceiling fan – a very necessary piece of home equipment in the heat of Northern Australia. Thankfully the damage was not as severe as it first seemed. Brad's regular passenger transport flights that week took him to Gove, Groote Eylandt, Lake Evella, Elcho Island, Numbulwar, Baniyala, Gurrumuru, Dhoyndji and Gan Gan. That included a flight for Laynha Aviation, one of the Aboriginal-owned airlines. Brad's wife was fully occupied caring for him, and their small daughter, and her involvement in Mothers of Pre-Schoolers and the MAF ladies' meeting.

Being a pilot involves much more than just flying. During the week in question, Andrew Herweynen spent time supervising a new pilot and working in a management capacity at his base in Elcho Island. The island has been described as an elongated paradise. Lying off Australia's northernmost coast, it is 50km long and 6km wide. Elcho Island is part of Arnhem Land, which was set aside as Aboriginal land in 1931, and it cannot be visited without a permit. The main community in Elcho Island is Galiwin'ku, which is home to 1500 Yolngu from several different language groups. There are many small villages dotted around the island. MAF staff are very involved in the local community, and when one Yolngu staff member was in a bad car accident, Andrew was able to sit with her until a medevac (medical evacuation) was arranged.

Organising time off was causing Andrew concern, as he noted in his diary, and that must have been even more the case during the following two weeks when he and a pilot in training were the only two available to fly. Andrew and Sally had three children then, though a fourth was expected. The children are being home-schooled by their mother, which is a huge commitment, and a necessary one for many missionary families. On Saturday of diary week, Sally noted that they had their adopted Aboriginal brother and cousin to tea. The children no doubt enjoyed that greatly!

✦ ✦ ✦ ✦ ✦

Russell Dunken is a pilot/engineer and his wife Heather works part time in a a local Aboriginal school with children with special needs thus making good use of her training as a physiotherapist. The week saw Russell putting both his skills to work. On Monday he was involved in a 100-hourly inspection of a Cessna 402 engine, while the next day he was in the air en route to Elcho Island to pick up patients who needed transporting to hospital. From there he flew to Banyala to collect homelands (village) residents who were going to Nhulunbuy for shopping. Later in the week he transported teachers, more shoppers, and took mourners to and from a funeral. The homelands are dependent on MAF for transport for all but the most basic needs. Russell and Heather have three teenagers who no doubt attended the youth group their parents help to run.

✦ ✦ ✦ ✦ ✦

Base engineer at Gove, Kevin Kraak, is the son of missionary parents and lived in Elcho Island until he was nine years old. His wife, Carol, was also raised in a Christian family. Their four children are in their teens and twenties, and one is married. The Kraak's time with MAF has extended over twenty years, with service in Ballarat, Papua New Guinea and Central Australia prior to them coming to Gove in 2003.

The day begins early for Kevin, as the bus that collects him calls at 6.25am. Work starts at 6.50 with a time of prayer. As well as routine engineering in Gove, Kevin had to attend a meeting in Darwin. While the engineers are concerned for the smooth running of the fleet, they are also concerned for the souls of those with whom they work. Kevin noted in his diary that he spoke with a young Aboriginal aircraft engineer, laying out the plan of salvation as well as trying to answer his questions. Carol had several meetings and activities during the week, including praying with a group of friends, preparing a Bible study, balancing their bank statement and completing their annual tax return. Such things have to be done even on the mission field!

✦ ✦ ✦ ✦ ✦

The Operations Manager in Nhulunbuy is Maree Cross, whose husband works for a local mining company. Both are very involved in Christian work locally, and Maree also plays in the Nhulunbuy Town Band. Maree's work that week included organising charters to cover regular flights and coverage for a base as the pilot there had to accompany his wife to hospital, arranging a schedule of maintenance for engineering, and helping to finalise details for forty Yolngu who were travelling to Gove to attend an Indigenous Christian conference. Often when Maree's phone rings it is to do with operational detail, but one day it was with an altogether different request. She received a call asking for help to find a missing fishing boat. This turned out to be a false alarm.

✦ ✦ ✦ ✦ ✦

The Base Manger at Milingimbi is Ken Mack, who had a full week of flying. His wife, Angela, sells Bibles and other Christian resources, including music CDs, as well as caring for her family and home. Some of Ken's flights were regular timetabled ones, others were health charters. One was to Mooroonga to collect a teacher and another to Currumorru to bring people back home from a funeral. For those who think that being a pilot must be the most glamorous job in the world, that thought may be dispelled by noting that when someone was sick in flight it was part of Ken's job to clear up afterwards!

✈ ✈ ✈ ✈

John and Nicole Strickling work as a man and wife team for MAF. They are based in Gove where she is Reservations Manager and he is Engineering Stores Manager. Previously John was a MAF pilot. While he is Australian, Nicole was raised in a Christian home in Canada. She noted that she 'came to Bible College in Australia and met my man'. They have been serving the Lord together ever since. Keeping the stores running smoothly is what keeps the fleet flying smoothly. Most things are routine, but sometimes John finds himself sourcing little-used parts from wherever he can find them. He always has a mind for finance, and looks for the best price for the parts he needs. MAF is a tight ship, and the money that is donated to the Mission is used carefully, with an eye both to efficiency and to the wise use of the Lord's money. In any set-up such as the one in which John works safety is very much an issue. Half of a day in our chosen week John spent at Nhulunbuy Fire Station learning the theory of fire, different classes of fire, fire containment and the details of various fire extinguishers. Though it is hoped that such expertise will never be called into use, it needs to be kept up-to-date in case it is.

Nicole was a little nervous as she set out to work one day because she was due to interview an employee and review his work. This was her first experience of a review and it went well. Another day she was dealing with a larger number of people, all of whom were on standby for the Gove to Elcho Island flight. The regular flight, however, was full and she had to find alternative travel options for them. Not all local staff members are Christians, and Nicole makes a point of being there for them. Everyone needs to relax sometime, and Nicole's idea of unwinding is to read a Laura Inglis Wilder book. A good book is a good book wherever in the world it's read!

MAF staff need to keep their skills up-to-date, and in our snapshot week Ben Fleming, Aircraft Co-ordinator, was doing just that. He spent several days studying for exams, and the remainder of the week engineering. Nor were his studies limited to technical matters, as Monday evening saw him proof-reading Bible study material that his wife, Lauren, had prepared. Lauren's Bible study was for use with her 'Chics' group—six girls studying the passion of Christ in the Gospel of Mark. She was also involved in a number of other meetings as well as one-to-one conversations. On Wednesday Ben took time off work to go with his five-year-old son to a physiotherapy appointment. The little one has a medical condition that necessitates continuing treatment. Missionaries and their families are not immune to health and other problems, though often prayer is made for them that concentrates more on their ministry situations. It is good to be reminded that they are real people, living in real families, and sometimes with real problems to face.

The work in Northern Australia needs a manager to oversee its smooth operation, and the one to whom that job is entrusted is Doug Miles. Doug and his wife, Yvonne, have been in Arnhem Land for fourteen years and both work for MAF; Yvonne is the Technical Records Officer. Their three daughters are growing or grown up, and two are away from home. Although it was just September, Yvonne had Christmas in mind, but she was determined to keep Christ in Christmas as she gave some thought to how to write her testimony in a way that would challenge friends and acquaintances who might be given it as a gift. Doug's week was certainly varied. Many might have 'put up shelves' in their diaries, but few will follow it by 'arrange a replacement aeroplane, organise the acquisition of building materials for a house in Elcho Island and write a Board Report', not to mention other administrative work including dealing with a customer complaint.

It is a tribute to the work of Mission Aviation Fellowship that in all the many diaries that were kept in September 2004, this was the only mention of dissatisfaction. The day on which Doug dealt with the complaint, the MAF women were meeting together. Reading through the diaries, it is quite remarkable how many mentions are made of MAF staff and their wives or husbands at prayer for the work of the Mission. Paul's injunction to 'Pray continually' (1 Thess. 5:17) does seem to have been taken to heart. Perhaps that is why MAF is so singularly blessed and used.

As supporters pray for the work we visualise flights bearing pastors to remote communities, food to areas afflicted by famine, teachers, doctors, nurses and all the rest. And that is very much MAF's work and it needs prayer. But, having read through the diaries of the MAF staff who work in Australia, I deliberately chose to conclude with Yvonne's record of her week as it shows the practical hands-on helpfulness of a Christian woman wherever in the world she is. 'Did Meals on Wheels and spent half an hour listening to one of the old ladies… Visited a mum new to the town… Encouraging those at the Bible study.' While MAFers fly high in the sky they also hold out hands of Christian friendship to those they meet day by day on terra firma.

5.

PAPUA NEW GUINEA

Papua New Guinea is made up of the eastern half of the second largest island in the world, and the islands that surround it. It lies north of Australia. The western half of the island is part of Indonesia. One of the neediest countries on earth, Papua New Guinea is also one of the most inaccessible. A spine of high mountains runs along the middle of the island, rising to over 4000 metres, and due to the high rainfall many of the mountains are forested right to the top of their cloud-clad summits. Nearly eighty-five per cent of the land is covered with tropical rain forest.

Mission Aviation Fellowship started work in Papua New Guinea in 1951, and has provided essential air services to communities so isolated that until the twentieth century many were unaware of villages just a few miles distant. The Huli are the largest of PNG's ethnic groups, and it was only in 1954 that their territory in the Lavani Valley was discovered. To give an idea how lightly populated Papua New Guinea is, between 4.5 and 5 million people live in its 462,840 sq. km compared to the UK where about 59 million live in half that area.

The most rugged mountains in the world are sliced by some of the most spectacular gorges. Consequently, flights need only be a few minutes long to link communities that are separated by insurmountable geographical features. Among the services MAF provides in Papua New Guinea are free mail deliveries to remote communities and an e-mail hub that is available to all Christian mission groups. It also works closely with Christian Radio Missionary Fellowship in providing a high frequency radio network.

✦ ✦ ✦ ✦ ✦

Pilot Thomas K Keindip is based at Wewak. He describes the kind of problem that can occur when landing in a remote airfield. His report is from a few days before the diary week, but is such a good example of what sometimes happens that it deserves inclusion.

Maprik station, in the East Sepik Province, has a medical stores centre for its outstations under the Maprik District Health Division. The Australian Aid programme funds flights out of Hayfield, which is Maprik's airstrip, to deliver medical supplies to Nungwaia and Torembi. We had an Internal Notam (Notices to Airmen) that Torembi had long grass and that their windsock needed repair or replacement. However, the people at the station came on the radio saying that they had already commenced work on the airstrip.

I went into Hayfield and the health workers there were very helpful in loading the aircraft though I had to leave the seats with the hospital staff to make room for all the cargo. I flew out of Hayfield for Nungwaia with 225kg of medical supplies. The flight time was only fourteen minutes, but Nungwaia is inaccessible by road. Unfortunately, because of new regulations, I cannot carry a 45kg gas bottle lying down in the aircraft, so they said they would arrange for the people at Nungwaia to come and pick it up at the nearest village. The people and the health workers at Nungwaia were much relieved to receive the badly needed supplies, and were thankful that MAF had helped.

Back at Hayfield I got help from the Maprik hospital staff to load the aircraft with the seats that were left behind because I was supposed to go back to Wewak after Torembi. Twelve minutes flight from Hayfield, I arrived overhead the airstrip and had a hard time trying to confirm that the windsock was on the pole. After doing a low-level flight, I finally confirmed that it was in rags and that the airstrip was not cut after all. The grass was still long, and the windsock gave no indication of wind speed and direction. After doing three low-level flights, I decided the airstrip was not suitable for a safe landing and diverted to Wewak with their supplies after talking with the base there about the condition of the airstrip. We agreed that we would bring in their supplies when they had completed the work.

✈ ✈ ✈ ✈ ✈

The following day started as usual for Thomas, until he received a call from Klauhau that there was a need for a medical evacuation out of Yemin.

As the people at Yemin do not have a radio they had to walk for a good number of hours to Klauhau to inform us about the medevac. The last time I went into Yemin was three weeks ago with a Route and Strip Check Pilot and we closed the airstrip because of long grass. However, they said that the grass had been cut and the strip's surface was firm. I had my Base Team Leader request approval from Flight Operations Office in Mt Hagen to do the landing and the medevac at the same time.

I did one drop off at Arkosame before continuing to Yemin for the medevac, then flew over the airstrip at low-level before setting the aircraft up for the normal approach for landing. The strip was cut to the full length and width and the surface was firm. The patient, a woman suffering from gum cancer, was losing her teeth. Apparently the grass cutting at the airstrip was done partly because of her situation. The woman, her son and a guardian were then airlifted to Nuku to seek medical attention.

Two days later he responded to another medical emergency.

Today was the West Sepik programmes' day. I had ten airstrips to call into, but because of weather I departed forty minutes later than planned so knew I would have to skip a landing as my flight plan for the day would have gone twenty-five minutes over my curfew. My flights were into Angugunak (a Christian Brethren Church station) from nearby airstrips, mainly picking up teachers to go there for their Teachers' Retreat. About 40 teachers attended the retreat. During my turn-arounds on the ground I caught up with my original expected times of arrival and departure.

After doing one extra landing because of loadings, I departed Nuku for my last bush airstrip, Mirsey, before heading off to Wewak. At Mirsey I picked up two nursing officers who were going to Wewak for a Nurses' Retreat. Having started the engines and done checks before take off, I called up Flight Service for my taxi report. On receiving my report, Flight Service told me to call up Wewak Base. Wewak Base, and any base with a telephone for that matter, can telephone Flight Service and get the pilots to call back to the base in an emergency. Because I had less than 250 hours in command on the C-206, under company regulations I was required to be back at my base before 5:00pm. An extra landing would have put me over that.

Wewak Base told me that they had received a call for a medevac out of Nagri, six miles from where I was. A woman there was experiencing labour difficulties. From Mirsey to Wewak is about thirty-five minutes flight time and it was 4.20pm. I told Wewak Base to call up Flight Operations Office in Mt Hagen and get the senior Cessna 206 pilot to give me an okay to arrive back after the 5.00pm curfew. The weather was fine in the afternoon and, having been given approval from the Chief Pilot himself, I departed for Nagri. On arriving I had to wait on the ground for 15 minutes before the woman arrived. It was a good thing having two nursing officers present because they handled the woman and helped her into the aircraft. They told me that she might need a caesarean.

On the way back I called up Wewak Base and gave them my ETA, telling them to ask the hospital to send an ambulance down to the airport. I ended up arriving in Wewak at 5.40pm, five minutes before my extended curfew time ended! The woman and nursing officers all went in the ambulance that was waiting when we arrived. God was in it all. He placed me in the right place at the right time to carry out the medevac.

✈ ✈ ✈ ✈ ✈

Another pilot, Chris Bubb (who serves in PNG with his wife Narelle) spent the week prior to our snapshot in Mount Hagen, the capital of the Western Highland Provence.

About 4.30 in the afternoon of my first day back we received a Selcall from CRMF, letting us know that Kamusi, a logging company airstrip some forty miles to the north, was trying to get in contact concerning a medevac. There were actually two patients, a woman in labour having difficulties, and a man who had been run over by a logging truck!

I did a flight plan, but could not pick them up in time to get them to Daru, the closest hospital with a doctor (140 miles to the south of Kawito) before nightfall. We arranged for a first light departure. Having risen at 5.00am, and finished the daily inspection of the aircraft, I tried to talk to Kamusi on the radio to confirm whether the medevac was still on. However, due to atmospheric conditions, I was unable to make contact with them until after 7.00am. As both patients were still alive, I picked them up and dropped them off at Daru.

Thursday and Friday were days out of the usual for Chris, and they deserve to be told in full.

✦ *Thursday*

Weather not so good today. Organised a Tari programme. Tari is the centre of the PNG Highlands, and we are often able to link up with flights that go in and out of Tari to other destinations in the highlands. I flew to Awaba and picked up two passengers in addition to the mother and infant that were on board from Kawito. Fifty miles to the North of Awaba, and approaching our destination Musula, (which is at the base of a small range called the Woolie Hills) I encountered low cloud, light to medium rain and very poor visibility. After trying for a while to find a break in the conditions to be able to continue, I elected to divert to one of the other nearby strips, but conditions at these places were no better.

I then spent some time trying to obtain updated weather reports in the Tari area, which is on the north side of the range, but was unable to raise anyone. The safest option was to return home and try again another day.

That night I received a call on the HF radio to say that there was a woman with a retained placenta at Kirowa. The missionary who was there at the time had been assisting, and in consultation with the doctor at Rumginae Hospital was asking if we could do a medevac the following morning. As it turned out I was to pick up this missionary and her family to bring them to Kawito the next day for the Pioneers Lower Fly River Team Meetings, before taking them on to Aiyura via Mt Hagen, where they were going to spend a year as house parents in the boarding school there.

This family required the whole plane to be able to move all of them in one go. Kirowa is an hour's flight away in a remote part of the Province in which we serve. It would require a special flight. To help it pay, I then (at 9 o'clock at night!) loaded two drums of Avgas into the plane to drop off at Kirowa. We normally keep a few drums there for emergency use, and this meant that the family only had to pay for one way.

✈ Friday

I was able to depart at first light and was at Kirowa by 7:30am. To make the best use of the space available, I had organised to take a passenger and as much of his cargo as possible (including his Alsatian dog!) to Kawito on the same flight. That freed up space on the afternoon flight which meant I'd have space for another passenger, should the need arise.

After removing the back and one of the middle seats, we carried the woman patient and placed her on the floor of the aircraft. One of her daughters came as guardian to help look after the newborn baby, and to care for her mother. We arrived in Balimo about 9.00am and the patient was loaded on the back of a utility truck for the ride into the hospital in town. After a short seven-minute flight we were back at Kawito, ready to start our normal day's programme!

I had completed several landings and was on my way to Daru when I made the mistake of thinking that everything was just starting to fall into place nicely. As I shut down the engine at Daru, the engine began chuffing like a chaff cutter! It sounded like a cracked cylinder. After helping the passengers who were on board unload their things from the aircraft, I then had to explain to the agent and my new set of passengers why I was pulling the cowls off, peering intently at the cylinders and listening to the sound of escaping air as I slowly turned the propeller by hand. Unfortunately I was not able to see the crack and therefore confirm that was my problem, but I knew something wasn't right.

When I tried to radio Kawito, and the engineering base at Mt Hagen, the HF radio decided it was going to play games. They couldn't hear me at all, yet another MAF base at Telefomin was able to hear me crystal clear. So they became the go-between, relaying messages back and forth with me shouting into the microphone desperately trying to be understood.

Hitching a ride into town, I set out to find a phone. The only one that was available was at the local post office and, after waiting twenty minutes or so, the manager finally agreed to let me call Mt Hagen Base. No joy there. There were no engineers or aircraft available until the following Tuesday! As the prospect of spending four days in Daru did not fill me with too much enthusiasm, I began to think of other alternatives. First I went to a little trade store to buy a torch and some sort of mirror to inspect the engine a bit more closely. The first two torches I bought broke even before I left the counter; the third seemed to be okay.

I broke the mirror to get a piece small enough to allow me to look up underneath the cylinders then turned the torch on. That enabled me to inspect where I thought the crack was for about 30 seconds before that torch broke as well! Still unable to confirm the actual problem, I was beginning to resign myself to a forced vacation in Daru. The ripple effects of this began to dawn on me - two families were stranded where they didn't want to be.

Then I learned that there was a helicopter pilot at Daru on his way to a village out near the Papuan border. I was able to talk to him and hitch a ride back to Kawito that night! It was quite a diversion for the helicopter pilot, and we were able to assist him several days later with some operational concerns as he came back through on his return to Port Moresby. I shook my head in amazement at the way the Lord is able to pull some things together. When I took off that morning I did not expect to be returning in a helicopter!

Saturday brought a sad end to his Thursday medevac.

The lady whom I had brought in from Kirowa to Balimo died. Even though the placenta was successfully removed, there was obviously internal bleeding, and sadly she didn't make it. Her family back at Kirowa obviously wanted her back to be able to bury her, only the plane was broken down at Daru. To add to our concerns, Balimo Hospital was getting very low on diesel and would not be able to run the mortuary for more than a couple of days. Another lady died at Kirowa and the local people became even more distressed. There had been a lot of talk of magic being performed on people, and in the surrounding communities in the previous week or so something like six people had died. Thankfully, there were some mature Christian men in the village who were able to give sound teaching on the matter, and things were brought back in hand.

✈ ✈ ✈ ✈ ✈

Pilot Manfred Hanicke gave a blow-by-blow account of a day in his week. It highlights one of the problems of living in a tropical climate.

07:00 I did one round of flying to get a tourist group into the Sepik area to buy art craft. In talking to them after the landing it came out that they didn't know that MAF is not an ordinary charter company. I had the opportunity of telling them that we are really here for the missions and churches but do some commercial flying also, because no one else is providing the service and most of the area doesn't have any roads.

11:00 Our second pilot, Thomas, took over the flying and I set up the e-mailing on our new computer in the office.

14:00 Hospital: I have a bad skin irritation and waited two-and-a-half hours to see the doctor. I was diagnosed of having a heat rash from literally sticking to the aeroplane seat. The doctor recommended having a shower and rest in the shade after each landing! That would wreck our daily programme big time.

17:30 Went home to a house full of national children from our compound. There are up to twelve children who spend around five, seven, or more hours with my wife Karin (we don't have children ourselves). They do drawing, colouring, games, handcraft, music, Bible stories, and so on. Some of them go to school and join in after school. This is Karin's opportunity to teach them social behaviour, conflict management and God's ways in all that. It is nice, and sometimes big fun, to watch them discovering new things and skills. Within this last year we have seen tremendous improvements in their work.

✈ ✈ ✈ ✈ ✈

The two reports that follow were written by pilots Chris Hansen and Richard West, both of whom were based in Telefomin in September 2004. Chris was there with his wife, Janice, and their children Rochelle, Jessica and Simeon. Richard served the Lord with his wife, Cherie, and their children, Larissa and Marcus. Just a few months after they wrote their diaries, Chris and Richard were called to make the ultimate sacrifice when they were killed in an accident. Their ten passengers and national crew member escaped with minor injuries. The communities they served mourned the loss of 'their pilots' and 'their aircraft'. MAF pilots and crew face real dangers, especially in the more inhospitable areas of the Mission's service. And the price that some, like the Hansen and West families, have paid to serve the Lord and to serve the people whom they love is very great indeed.

Chris Hansen
✈ Tuesday

My day started with the usual beep, beep, beep of the alarm at 5.40am. Up to read my Bible and have a quiet time for 20 minutes under the 12-volt fluorescent tube. Following that came breakfast (cereal and a glass of water) while putting the ingredients in the breadmaker bucket. This will be switched on to start the bread-making process at 8am after Janice cranks up the generator for the first half of our ten hours of power a day. The kids start to get up between 6.40 and 7am ready for home-schooling in their classroom in our house at 8am.

I was at the MAF base at 7am to do my part in getting the aircraft (De Havilland Twin Otter) ready for an 8am departure. There was light fog all around, coming and going, no doubt from the heavy rain we had last night. At 7.45am the Base staff and two pilots gathered together to discuss a few issues for the day, and to pray before we departed for Tekin. We left at 8.10am with two passengers on board (both for Tabubil) as we were expecting a full load out of Tekin.

Tekin is 5,500ft above sea level. It has a short steep airstrip, pretty typical of the ones we land on. This round was for passengers. Yesterday we picked up 1800kg of vegetables out of there. 'Everyone' wants to travel plus 2,500kg of vegetables yet to go. We didn't fly in this area last week due to fuel shortages, hence the backlog of passengers and freight. Loaded up with 19 passengers, we headed off down to Tabubil.

Tabubil is the airstrip for the Ok Tedi mine. Most of our flying is done in and out of there. Our first turn-around at Tabubil for the day is always busy—we have paperwork to fax through to Headquarters in Mt Hagen, e-mails to transfer off disk on to the computer to send and receive. As we have no phones in Telefomin, these phone things are done while on the ground at Tabubil.

Today I rang around a few people looking for a power-line terminator. A week and a half ago we had a big storm at Telefomin that took roofs off houses, felled trees and downed power lines. This part is needed by Pastor Yanga (who asked me to get it) in order that he can finish repairing the lines associated with the local hydropower system. When they are repaired it won't be long until we get hydropower again.

Back to Tekin again with passengers out and a full load of vegetables on the return: cabbages, broccoli, carrots, bok choi, lettuce, spring onions etc. – all good food for the many mine workers at Tabubil, and all good income for the people in the bush. This in turn leads to community development: health centres, schools, churches, better housing and living conditions plus money to spend on store goods.

From Tabubil we went back out west to Bak (next valley over from Tekin). This time our cargo was trade store goods out and a full load of vegetables in. The weather held well. We made more phone calls while on the ground at Tabubil. Still no joy with the power-line part—try again tomorrow. Aircraft loaded, drum refuelling complete, passengers on and we took off to Tifalmin. Tifalmin is only eight minutes away according to the flight plan, but it usually takes around thirteen minutes. We have to climb from 1,500ft above sea level – Tabubil, up and over the Hindenburg Wall at over 10,000ft and back down to Tifalmin at 4,500ft. Today there was a lot of cloud so we had to climb higher. Tifalmin is situated at the western end of the Telefomin Valley.

At Tifalmin we unloaded our passengers and freight. One of our passengers to Tabubil was a medevac—a five-year-old boy with one of his legs broken between the hip and knee. He was sitting on his father's shoulder, his good leg at the front and his broken leg, all swollen, hanging down his father's back. The boy sat there silently enduring the pain, leaning on his dad's head. I think he was in shock. He sure screamed in pain when his dad went into the plane and removed him from his shoulders to put him on the seat. Poor boy.

We flew back down to Tabubil. On arrival the weather had `gone off'. There was heavy rain and reduced visibility. Following the river valley, we made our way up to the airstrip and landed in the rain. The ambulance arrived not long afterwards to take our passenger away. We had a long turn-around due to the rain. I got wet helping with refuelling and loading for the next round back to Tifalmin—should have taken my umbrella! The rain eventually stopped and off we went. It was just a drop-off this time, and we were only on the ground for ten minutes. Headed back to Tabubil. There I cleared e-mails again and transferred incoming ones to disk to read tonight before flying back to Telefomin with passengers and trade store goods. Surprise, surprise, it was raining! Got home okay. My daughter and Richard's daughter came down to greet us on our arrival. That was 4.15 hours of flying, 11 landings, 10.5 duty hours and 1 hour of instrument flight time (time spent flying in cloud).

✦ Wednesday

Richard and I are flying together again today. As he is a new captain on the Otter, and is in a new area in PNG, I need to fly with him a lot to check him into the area before he can fly with the other two pilots who are based here.

Passengers were slow to arrive this morning, but that was not such a big deal as weather reports from the various bush airstrips were showing fog that was slowly lifting. We gathered together for our usual information time and prayer before heading off. Our first stop for a full load of passengers was Okisai in the lowlands. The strip has been open around two years. Not long after it opened a local villager found gold in the hills behind the village. The man didn't tell anyone, he just 'disappeared'. He was found several days later gathering as much gold as he could. We flew him to Tabubil not realising he had 52kg of the stuff on his person! From then on there has been a gold rush there. It has been relatively peaceful with very few disputes over newfound riches. It is good to see money going back into the community with portable sawmills milling timber, timber houses, schools and a new health centre all being built.

From Okisai we went up to Mianmin with passengers, four of them health workers out of Telefomin. They were going to run clinics plus check up on how things were going health-wise in that area. We went back down to Okisai with another nineteen passengers, then passengers from there to Eliptamin, which is the next valley to the north of Telefomin. Out of Eliptamin we had a full load of passengers to Telefomin and Tabubil, including a pastor and his family who were returning home from a funeral. Having stopped off in Telefomin to drop off passengers and pick more up, we carried on down to Tabubil.

We were running about forty-five minutes behind time at that stage, but thought we might catch up with quick turn-arounds at these 'south of the ranges' airstrips. But we arrived at Tabubil to find trolleys laden with building materials—there went the quick turn around! While the men loaded, I sat in the office and caught up on paperwork, checked e-mails and made a few phone calls regarding the power-line parts. Still no joy.

As we departed to Golgobip with the Catholic Mission building materials on board, the weather was just starting to go off at our destination. But we managed to get in before it went off altogether. It started to rain as we were finishing off-loading the timber and roofing iron. Then it was out of there and back to Tabubil. We went to Olsobip next with a full load of passengers. There was still an ongoing backlog due to us not flying in our area last week because of a fuel shortage. Everyone is happy that we are finally up and flying again.

On our departure out of Olsobip we looked up the narrow valley towards Kiyol, which was going to be on our next round out of Tabubil. The weather in that confined valley didn't look too good. As it had deteriorated since landing at Olsobip, we decided to cancel that round. We arrived at Tabubil ten minutes later to find rain there too. And while we were on the ground it got heavier and heavier. Our ground staff loaded the aircraft with drums of jet fuel for us to take up to Telefomin, battery acid for the Telefomin High School and topped the load up with food for the school. After my paperwork was finished, I headed off down the road in the pouring rain to pick up the hydro-part/power-line part, having had a message that it was there to be picked up. On arrival at the electrical workshop I was told that the man wasn't around and his office was locked!

From there we went back to the airport to find that the weather at Telefomin had gone off big time and we were not to bother departing. I made use of the time by going to the local supermarket though I didn't buy anything. Their stocks were low due to the Fly River being too low for the barges to come up to Kiunga—hence the fuel shortage too. It was an uneventful flight home where I finished the day's paperwork off.

The rest of Chris's day was spent with his wife and family. And the remainder of his week was just as busy as the beginning. On Saturday he did sixteen landings and watched an airshow on DVD in the evening for relaxation. Something of a busman's holiday!

✈ ✈ ✈ ✈ ✈

Chris's colleague, Richard West, wrote about his Sunday before the working week began.

Sunday is pancake breakfast day in the West household, a little treat we try to maintain no matter where we are. After breakfast we actually made it to the local community church on time; in fact, the doors were still closed. No matter how hard we try, it seems that we are often late for church. This is not usually a problem as time is fairly flexible in this Melanesian culture.

After church, along with the Hansens, we decided it would be nice to take a picnic lunch to 'the race' (part of the hydro power-supply project that diverts water from the river to the holding dam). As the name suggests, this is an open concrete shoot that doubles as a splendid water slide. The kids had a great time in the water while I watched over them and Cherie did the BBQ. Last time I did such a bad job of the BBQ that Cherie told me to step aside and let her show me how a Girl Guide did it!

Monday was a busy day for Richard.

Today we made eleven flights and carried ten passengers, 4,800kg of vegetables from the bush for the local supermarket and mine caterers at Tabubil, 3,000kg of trade store goods out to bush communities, and 1,600kg of building supplies for a new teacher's house in the bush. All of that took 11 hours of work, 4.8 hours of flying and used 1,500 litres of fuel.

Contact with home and supporting churches was on his mind too.

I had an urgent e-mail to get off to Mum for a Baptist Missionary Fellowship meeting that she has tomorrow with a group at our home church in New Zealand. Today of all days either my e-mail was down, or the server had decided it couldn't recognise me. I tried every time that I was on the ground between flights, but it was no use. Today the Internet was not working in Papua New Guinea.

The following day Richard had more success.

The Internet lives in PNG today and I got my now very urgent, if not already too late, e-mail off to Mum. I hope she gets it in time, but I suspect that it will have arrived too late.

Today we made ten flights and carried 60 passengers, 2,100kg of vegetables to Tabubil and another 3,000kg of trade store goods to the bush. It took 10.5 hours of work, 4.4 hours of flying and used another 1,300 litres of fuel. In the Telefomin area MAF uses approximately 500,000 litres of Jet A each year.

Richard's wife and children, along with a young friend, were also in the air as there was necessary shopping to be done in Tabubil. On his day off Richard found himself with more to do than he bargained for.

Today I was planning to write this diary, catch up on reading and replying to e-mails, put the finishing touches on a video that I am working on for our supporting churches, start our regular three-monthly newsletter and, of course, there is still all of that study waiting in the background should I feel like I need a change of scenery. Things were going reasonably to plan until Cherie had the misfortune of overloading the generator and causing it to stall under the extra pressure. Then the fun started. It doesn't like to start after being stalled. We discovered this when it stopped for no apparent reason the other day. It turned out that it has a low oil cut-out switch installed, and this is activating early when there is still quite a bit of oil in the engine. Anyway, easily fixed, I put more oil in. But it didn't want to start even then. While trying to get it going again, the starter cord finally failed and came away in my hand! It was time to get out the tools, pull the starter apart and fit another piece of rope.

Talking of generators, we only have five hours of electricity in the mornings and five hours in the evenings. As I am writing this, the generator is off and now it is the turn of the laptop to fail as it is beeping at me that the battery is flat. Tonight I plan on just relaxing and recharging, as will my laptop when the generator comes back on again.

For Chris Hansen and Richard West all the problems and irritations of life are now over as they are in the presence of the Lord whom they loved and served. They have joined 'the great multitude that no-one could count, from every nation, tribe, people and language, standing before the throne in front of the Lamb' (Rev. 7:9). And MAF supporters continue to remember their wives and children in their prayers.

✦✦✦✦✦

Mike Jelliffe and his wife, Kathy, served with MAF in Papua New Guinea from 1977 to 1986 and returned in June 2004. He is Operations Coordinator/Pilot based at Mt Hagen's Kagamugu airport. His account of the Saturday before his 'official' diary began makes for interesting reading.

I have been assisting the pastor of the Evangelical Church of PNG Mt Hagen Church in a mentoring capacity and with some practical ideas and resources. This draws on our own previous experience in pastoral ministry some years ago in PNG's capital, Port Moresby. Part of this has been commencing a discipleship group with some of the newly converted young people, and I am team leading with Pastor Dulu. We arranged for the pastor to come for lunch at our house at 12.00 in order that we could prepare and pray, and feed the young people around 1.30pm.

At about 11.30am we heard familiar voices outside, and found the whole group had arrived! Kathy swung into her hospitality mode, which she does so naturally, and within a few minutes the table was spread with bread, peanut butter, pineapple, pawpaw (papaya) and other fresh fruit, peanuts and freshly made popcorn, always a favourite with Papua New Guinean visitors. After the group (with eight boys and girls, all teenagers) had eaten, we sang songs and started the discipleship lesson. As all have had some level of high school education, we are using English as our main language, with occasional lapses into Pidgin English. This week we looked at how to approach the Bible, understand its layout, and know where to find teaching: the story of Christ, beginnings, end times and so on. Their homework is to read a chapter from John each day and note down anything that strikes or appeals. I will build on this to do a study of John 15 in a couple of weeks, teaching how to let a passage of Scripture speak to you. Before the group left I asked them to prepare a drama with the rest of the youth on Matthew 22:1-14. They left about 3.00pm.

An hour later another group of PNG men and women turned up at our back door. They are part of a community group nearby in a Lutheran Church ministry that is being developed by Ben Angoranga, one of our Papua New Guinean senior engineers. The ministry is focusing on self-sustainable communities, and one of the goals is in housing. Between 1988 and 1991 I developed a low-cost housing project in Port Moresby, introducing earth-brick technology using a hand-operated machine that makes bricks from an earth and cement mix. I obtained a machine with which I hoped to encourage and train local people to build earth brick housing in Mt Hagen, especially as there is a need for accommodation for Pastor Dulu next year. As Ben's group had expressed interest in the technology, they came with some bags of dirt and cement to test and make a sample brick. When it started to rain we went under the veranda of his house (also on our MAF Kagamuga compound), got our hands dirty and made two sample bricks. One of these seems to have had a good combination of soil (clay) and cement and has impressed the group.

Around 6pm Kathy and I had supper and settled for a quiet evening. The day had gone well with a real sense that

God had ordered it even though it wasn't quite according to how we'd planned. The ministry with different people had been encouraging and uplifting, and we felt at peace. Our Internet connection has been unreliable and did not work tonight, so Kathy wrote some e-mails to our family to send later. I had been invited to go on the preaching roster once a month, and having been asked at short notice to swap for tomorrow, I spent some time preparing my message on Matthew 14, the wedding banquet. I have been preaching a series focusing on grace.

The following day found Mike and Kathy in church together.

We attend the Evangelical Church of PNG Mt Hagen, and in the few months we have been here have established a good rapport. Kathy sits on the floor to the left with the women, and most of the men on the right squeeze on to rough benches. The rented church building is covered on all sides with corrugated iron with no lining, but it does have some fluorescent lighting and electricity. The service is mostly in Pidgin English, though some musical items may be in a particular language. The service starts at 10am, with a variable finishing time between 12 and 1.30pm! A group of young men form the music group with acoustic guitars on one side of the table at the front, and a group of girls have a choreographed tambourine group on the other side. A couple of women sitting in the congregation provide a drum beat using kundu drums made of plastic piping and rubber tyre tubing drum skin. The singing is lively and harmonious. After the youth group did their drama on the wedding banquet, and did it very well, I preached in Pidgin English.

Reading Mike's diary gives the end of the story of Chris Bubb's engine trouble.

My work as MAF PNG Operations Coordinator (working under the Flight Operations Manager) involves liaison with the maintenance team and operational staff to allocate aircraft for scheduled maintenance, as well as coordinating operations when there is unscheduled maintenance. On Friday, a Cessna 206 P2-MFG was grounded at Daru, on the south-western coast of PNG, when the pilot reported a cylinder problem. Arrangements were made to send a mechanic down today on a scheduled airline flight, with a replacement cylinder and tools. Part of my morning was taken up in liaising with the Flight Operations Manager and Maintenance Controller arranging and monitoring the operation. The pilot was able to hitch a ride back to his base at Kawito on Friday on a helicopter that needed extra fuel we could supply, and he caught a scheduled flight back to Daru from a neighbouring airstrip. As the operation also affected other scheduling, I spent some time revising the fleet allocation of our fourteen aircraft around eight bases and then circulating it to all the base managers.

Another of my responsibilities concerns airstrips around the country. We have been negotiating with community leaders at Maramuni airstrip to reopen the strip to MAF operations. Over a year ago there was an incident where the pilot and crew of a MAF aircraft were threatened with weapons. This occurred during an election period when tensions were high, and a leader was not happy with some passengers who had boarded the aircraft. We closed the airstrip to operations. Apart from a number of items of correspondence and other operational issues, my afternoon included drawing up a security plan for the Maramuni leaders to put a structure in place that ensures only passengers and staff are able to access the airstrip boundaries.

I finished work between 4.30 and 5pm and walked home again, cutting through the market place which is usually crowded (unless it is raining) with people buying vegetables for supper. In the evening we tried the Internet again. On days when we have a good connection, having direct chatroom discussions with the children in Sydney gives us a cheap and effective way of two-way communications and makes the separation from them a little easier.

✈✈✈✈✈

On Tuesday Pilot Pierre Fasnacht, from Switzerland, had a few anxious moments.

Today I was rostered to fly to the Southern Highlands area. Outbound I had a combined load for Tiri and Mt Tawa. The pastor in Tiri would have liked to send his heavily pregnant wife into town for the birth, but our backload was already fully booked. I promised him that if my loadings changed, and they often do, I would come back and pick her up. Things did change. After Mt Tawa and Sopise I didn't have as full a load as expected and therefore went back via Tiri then on to Waluanda to pick up some missionaries from the Bible Missionary Church.

Let me tell you more about my Sopise landing. Sopise is the last airstrip to the south of that area, just before a large lightly-populated lowlands area. It is a very remote airstrip that often has bad weather. Today I had to circle down between the two ranges and fly a confined circuit for my approach. I was a little bit fast but touched down at the right spot on the 600m flat airstrip. But then I discovered I didn't have any braking; the surface was wet and slippery and even the slightest touch on the brakes made the wheels lock up and the aircraft just slide down the airstrip. The end with the fence seemed to come closer very quickly and there was nothing I could do. I headed for the left side as there was a small gap in the fence, and then – on the last 50m – there was bare ground and I got some braking and came to a halt just a few metres from the fence. Thank you Lord!

In the Cairns CEO's diary there was mention of a cockpit fire in a Papua New Guinea aircraft. Pierre explains what happened

Today was a Bosavi area day, but a circuit takes at least three hours flying and our C206 P2-MAJ didn't have enough hours left before the 100-hour maintenance. We therefore decided just to do an urgent flight to the close-by Bayer area. On my way back I got a message that our C206 in Madang had an electrical fire in the cockpit, thankfully while taxiing on the ground and not in the air! That meant that the Missions Director from the Evangelical Lutheran Church Germany, and his PNG pastor, were stuck in Kol and would not make it to Madang for their important meeting. I had just enough hours on the aircraft to divert to pick them up and take them to Mt Hagen. In the meantime our ground staff in Mt Hagen tried to book them on a commercial airline to Madang, and it all worked out! On arrival in Mt Hagen I was told that there was another missionary couple stuck at Koenambe who were supposed to be picked up by the Madang aircraft. As our Maintenance Controller told us that we could extend the hours on our C206 by another five hours, we were able to get the most urgent movements done.

✈ ✈ ✈ ✈ ✈

Rose Basokanu is a local woman employed by Mission Aviation Fellowship. She shares her thoughts on the work.

MAF is an organisation where we learn things so fast because of the good relationships that the staff develop with each other. Each person employed by the organisation is recognised as very important, and the efforts he or she puts in contribute to the success of the organisation. The very important thing is the person's relationship with Jesus.

Even though MAF is a Christian organisation, it is faced with problems just like any other. We are serving people in PNG who have different traditional beliefs, attitudes and personalities. Sometimes these people don't understand us and so cause problems between us. That's the time when we are faced with the challenge of whether to reveal the character of Jesus or show forth our human nature.

My observation throughout the week has made me realise that it is God's grace that sustains me and gives me success in each day's work. I've also realised that honesty and kindness are two very important things that enable us to find favour and respect for one another. Finally to those who are financially and prayerfully supporting MAF PNG, may the Lord extend the border of your provision through Jesus Christ.

All MAF staff in Papua New Guinea would no doubt say Amen to that.

6.

CAMBODIA

Over the western border of Papua New Guinea lies Papua, where MAF US has a large programme. However, as the work in PNG and Papua have certain similarities, we will travel right round the world before reading the reports from the MAF US staff.

Following the sun west and north from Papua New Guinea, the next MAF operation we reach is Cambodia, which is run by MAF Australia. It would be hard to find two countries more different than PNG and Cambodia. From a mountainous place with peaks rising to over 4,000m, we move to flat land, seventy-five per cent of which is less than 100m above sea level.

Cambodia's highest peak, in the Cardamon Mountains, rises to just 1,771m. In terms of communications, the country (with a land area of 181,040 sq. km) has less than 1000km of railway line, and about 14,000km of road, of which under 3,000km is of a good standard. About half of the country's roads are made up of crushed stone, gravel and earth. Cambodia shares borders with Thailand, Laos and Vietnam.

Mission Aviation Fellowship started its work in Cambodia in 1995 by teaching English to senior employees in the Civil Aviation Authority in Phnom Penh. Now it flies all over the country, even to the remote northern regions. Aid and development workers use MAF's services, as do translators, those engaged in mine clearing, and Christian humanitarian agencies. The United Nations and organisations involved in the care of the environment also use their services.

At the time over which MAF staff were asked to keep diaries for this book, Pilot Emil Kundig was having problems obtaining fuel for the aircraft. In fact, he had only a small quantity of fuel left and had been effectively grounded for a week. Emil kept a diary for two weeks, and as his situation was unusual in terms of MAF as a whole, both weeks are included.

✈ Saturday
There were no flights on Saturday, but the situation is looking more hopeful as we progress towards shipping our own fuel into the country. We went house hunting, as we have to leave where we are by the end of September.

✈ Sunday
We attended the Khmer morning service at the Faith in Christ Church on Sunday. I'm getting better at reading the

Khmer script from the overhead screen, and am now able to sing one or two lines of hymns. The sermon was on Philemon and Onesimus. With our teenagers, Tabitha and Tobias, we went to the afternoon service at the International Christian Fellowship in order that they could attend the Sunday school. Today I had to give my testimony to the church explaining why I believe in Jesus. In the evening we had a nice thunderstorm, but there was no flooding in the house.

✈ Monday

Monday found me getting final details on fuel shipment from Australia. The army wants to help us import fuel since we cannot do it ourselves. We have decided to use drum stock instead of bulk fuel due to our storage difficulties here at the airport. We went to see the new office, one week before the move. The premises will be shared with two other Christian Organisations. My wife, Margrit, interviewed two ladies to replace our house helper, Samoun, temporarily as she will go on maternity leave soon. We decided to take both ladies as we also need one for the office. They are on a trial period of three months. Nice rain again today. September and October are the rainiest months in Phnom Penh.

✈ Tuesday

A conference call with the other Managers of MAF Australia on Tuesday didn't work out again. The technology seems difficult to operate. We are waiting for a meeting with the General for final details of Avgas shipping. Spent part of the day organising materials for cleaning the new office.

✈ Wednesday

I went to see the people from our insurance company on Wednesday about workers' compensation insurance then checked on the new office. It looks possible that we'll move in next Monday, though it might not be one hundred percent finished. Today I received an e-mail saying that the ferry flight for the replacement Cessna 206 is about four weeks delayed. We expected the plane next week. Started again with a new language tutor, three times a week. It is necessary to keep on the ball or we'll forget the Khmer language we already know.

✈ *Thursday – Sunday*

Thursday, our secretary's husband's mother has passed away. They have to go to the Province to attend funeral procedures, and will be away for several days. Language learning is fun. Friday was a slow day, and I still haven't had my meeting with the General. I really want to go ahead and order the fuel now, but it is a good thing to be patient. Starting to pack up the office for the move on Monday. We spent Saturday packing up the office. Went to see some houses and decided where we would like to live. We are left with two choices and we'll pray about it. Ry, our secretary, called on Sunday. They are back from the Province, but their daughter has been admitted to hospital with a high fever and convulsions. It doesn't sound good. That's another matter for prayer.

✈ *Monday*

I haven't flown for two weeks. We have only three drums of fuel left, and that is not a good prospect. The last fuel we got was more than two months ago. This situation is starting to wear me down a little. At least it means that there is less pressure to move the office. My office still needs painting, but the rest is okay, albeit horrendously dirty. Would you believe it, in the meeting-room upstairs they are still grinding away on stones? What a mess!

✈ *Tuesday*

The General called today, Tuesday, to say that the army is no longer willing to help us import fuel. What a blow! That puts us back to square one. Ry called to say that her daughter is still in intensive care at the hospital. The doctors are not sure what she has. Dengue fever? Meningitis? Who knows?

✈ *Wednesday*

Wednesday was Samoun's last day before she takes her maternity leave. She is our house helper, and she'll be away for three months. The baby is due in two weeks. The rule in Cambodia is that the employer has to pay a 50 percent salary during that time. This is okay, but actually we have to spend another salary on a replacement. Signed a contract for a new house for us. We can move in now, but will wait until next week. One thing at a time.

✈ *Thursday*

My new desk has arrived on Thursday; it looks really nice. But it would be nicer if we had fuel to fly. The army called and said we can now buy fuel from them as before. However, they will have to order it from Thailand. I wonder if that means the crisis over there is finished. I wondered if I could write to the Thai fuel company myself, and mentioned the possibility to our assistant mechanic. I heard him call the General right away (my Khmer is improving!) and tell him what I'd said! I was shocked; why did he tell this to the General? And of course the General was not happy and would not give us fuel, ever, if we did it our own way. I had to talk to my assistant mechanic, telling him that I expected loyalty to MAF in the future.

Had a call from Samoun's husband, Borah. He said that his wife gave birth to a healthy baby daughter early in the morning. Good! She stopped working just yesterday!

✈ *Friday*

On Friday we had our first devotions with the three parties who share the new office: Christian Pace Building Services, Christian Care for Cambodia and MAF. It was all in the Khmer language, of course, and we were glad we could read our English Bibles. But it is good to be together and pray together. Finally I am able to unpack my stuff in the new office. At least we are progressing on the administrative side of things. I hope the plane is still at the airport! On the bright side, I had an enquiry for a forest survey flight for next week. We can do just the one flight on the fuel we have. Ry called and said that her daughter is recovering and will be released from the hospital today. Thank you Lord! They've had it rough over the last few months. First her husband's father died, then his mother, and now this sickness with their first daughter. To add to that, Ry is seven months pregnant with a new baby.

✈ *Saturday*

Today, Saturday, I was happy I had time to help my wife pack up our household and prepare for the move next Monday. It will be good when this is over and we are all settled again. It was good to stretch my legs in the evening. Thank you, Lord, for the strength to do all this with joy, even if it is not flying. But I am confident we will find a way to have our own fuel. I shall write to the Thai fuel company on Monday…

PART TWO

MAF EUROPE

AFRICA

✈

BANGLADESH

✈

MONGOLIA

7.

MONGOLIA

Mongolia, which lies north of China, covers a total of 1,565,000 sq. km, approximately three times the size of Spain. Ninety percent of this is pasture or desert wasteland, eight to nine per cent is forested, and just one per cent is arable. The Gobi desert stretches 1,610km from east to west across South-east Mongolia and Northern China, much of it on a plateau around 1000m high. It is one of the world's largest deserts.

The population of Mongolia is just over two-and-three-quarter million, therefore there are on average just 1.75 persons per square kilometre. Of course, populations do not spread themselves evenly over a country, but that figure gives some idea of the remoteness of small communities from one another. Transport in Mongolia is very inadequate, with only 1,810km of railway lines and under 9,000km of roads with a finished surface in the whole vast land. In some areas there is limited fresh water. Deforestation, overgrazing and soil erosion are real problems in many parts of the country. The weather varies enormously, with a short hot summer followed by a severely cold winter, cold enough to kill the livestock on which much of the rural population depends.

In that land of many needs, MAF Pilot Jan Tore Kjær Foldøy serves the Lord through Blue Sky Aviation, a joint venture between MAF and a local Christian Company.

In Ulaanbaatar (records Jan Tore Kjær Foldøy) there is one Christian Fellowship that provides an opportunity for the worship of God in English. The congregation is mainly made up of people living or working in Mongolia, tourists and visitors. It was there recently that we were fortunate to meet up with Jibek, a little girl who was evacuated by BSA last May from Bayanolgi in the far North-west of Mongolia. Bayanolgi is a 1,000 mile, five-day jeep journey, from Ulaanbaatar.

Jibek, who was then eighteen months old, was having breathing difficulties due to pneumonia in both her lungs. She was breathing at three to four times the normal rate. From their home, where her parents Chris and Sarah serve the Lord amongst the Kazak people, the Bayanolgi airfield was a 5.5-hour jeep trip through a snowstorm to get her to the Millennium Messenger (MAF's aircraft) and the care of Dr Rita Browning. Jibek was put on oxygen and Dr Rita accompanied her and her mother on the 4.5-hour flight to Ulaanbaatar via Tosontsengel for medical treatment. It is hoped that in the future an old airstrip closer to their location may become one of those regional airstrips that Blue Sky Aviation will see reopened in order to serve the countryside of Mongolia better, and increase the effectiveness of those that minister there.

The family recently returned to Mongolia after an extended time in the USA. They had hoped to get out to their home before winter in order to insulate a house that they are building. However, they have agreed that they will remain in Ulaanbaatar until spring so that Jibek can spend her first Mongolian winter since her medevac in the city. Jibek is now a bubbling, healthy three-year-old, and watching her playing happily, and hearing her folks speak eagerly of their awaiting home in the countryside amongst the local people, underline the essence of why Blue Sky Aviation exists and how we seek to be facilitators. But now to the diary week.

✈ Monday
We had a request to fly a dead person from one of the *soums* into Ulaanbaatar, but we had to decline, as we are not allowed to fly dead bodies.

✈ Tuesday
We flew for the Norwegian Lutheran Mission from Ulaanbaatar to Harhorrind, approximately one hour away. The purpose of their flight was to make a movie of Mongolia, that they will use in their work back in Norway. It was nice to fly for them since this is the mission which supports my wife and me and has suconded us to MAF. Unfortunately they had problems with the car they rented down in Harhorrind and were delayed. If they had been fifteen minutes earlier we would have made it back to Ulaanbaatar before the latest landing time. But we had to spend the night in Harhorrind, and found a nice Ger Camp close by.

✈ *Wednesday*

We were up one-and-a-half hours before sunrise because we had to depart just after sunrise back to Ulaanbaatar. We flew from Harhorrind back to Ulaanbaatar, where I said goodbye to my Norwegian friends, and found my next customer already waiting. After refuelling we flew to Moren, approximately two hours away. We had to refuel, because I needed more fuel for the return flight the next day, and at our destination, approximately 1.5 hours away, we could not get fuel. After flying from Moren to Barrunturun I parked the aircraft for the night. The customer on this flight, and for the rest of the week, was the Adventist Development & Relief Agency. They have a vegetable project in Barrunturun, which I saw last week when I had a flight up there. They are also building a school in the little village that is home to one of the Summer Olympic medallists. We were there to collect people we had flown up the previous week. They were students from Japan, who had volunteered to help ADRA build the school. As there were eighteen students, plus leaders, we needed to do two flights from Barrunturun to Ulaanbaatar to get everybody back. The time these people had in Mongolia was limited. Had we been unable to fly them it would not have been worth their while coming. Nobody else flies to this place, and travelling by car would have taken approximately three days—not allowing any time at all to stop and rest, day or night!

✈ *Thursday*

I was up just before sunrise to get the plane ready for the flight. The customer arrived and we flew to Moren for refuelling before going back to Ulaanbaatar. I didn't have passengers on the next flight to Totsontsengel, where I stopped for the night. The flight time to Totsontsengel is approximately two-and-a-quarter hours. It is always nice to go to places like Totsontsengel. The man in the tower wanted to practice his English and I taught him some new phrases. I asked them how the temperature was during the night, and he told me that it might be below 0 degrees. I decided to put on the wing covers in order not to have any problems the next day because of ice on the plane. So, after refuelling, five men helped me with the wing covers. Although it was pretty windy we got them on fairly fast and I took the bus into town. My reason for going to Totsontsengel was that ADRA was missing a box with some equipment for the school they are building. Since I was on my way there again I could collect the box, which they thought was in Totsontsengel. When I talked to the ADRA people there the leader smiled and said that I should not worry about the box as he had sent it back to Ulaanbaatar again! In Totsontsengel ADRA is teaching the people how to keep hens and use the eggs they produce to earn some money. We flew 960 chickens up to Totsontsengel two months ago.

✈ Friday

This morning I was glad that I had put covers on the plane as it was minus three degrees, and the covers were covered with frost. I took them off and was airborne just after sunrise. One-and-a-quarter hours later I landed in Barrunturun, where I picked up the remaining members of the Japanese group. We flew via Muren for refuelling. Back in Ulaanbaatar I parked the aircraft in front of our hangar, which I left on Tuesday morning. The plane is now due for Phase 7 inspection, and our maintenance personnel will do that. I can now have some days off!

8.

BANGLADESH

Mongolia is one of the least densely populated countries in the world. From there we travel south to Bangladesh, which is quite the opposite. Bangladesh, which suffers from great poverty, is also subject to natural disasters, particularly flooding, as it lies in the delta and floodplains of the Ganges and Brahmaputra rivers. Unemployment stands at over fifty percent, and over fifty-five per cent of the population live below the poverty line. Many Bangladeshi people are only able to survive because of the generosity of family members who live and work overseas. When Bangladesh separated from Pakistan in 1971 it was declared to be a secular state. However, seventeen years later, Islam became the state religion. Officially there is religious freedom, but this is not always observed, as some Christians have found to their cost.

Mission Aviation Fellowship Europe has been working in Bangladesh since the beginning of 2002, and the nature of the land makes a turbine Beaver, an amphibious aircraft, a most useful aircraft for the mix of land and water landings. A week's work for Pilot Marco Koffeman gives a snapshot of MAF's activities there. But first he provides some background information regarding the situation in Bangladesh at the time of writing. Marco serves the Lord along with his wife, Anneke.

Although floods are normal in the monsoon season (July/August), this year they were early, and much more severe than usual. Despite this, the relief work from the big organisations was late because the government was reluctant to ask for help. By the time the UN collected money from donor countries something else happened that affected the image of Bangladesh and, as a side effect, had a negative impact on flood relief work. During a gathering of the Awami League (the previous ruling party) in the city centre, there was an attack with hand grenades. The main target was the opposition leader, Seikh Hasina. At least twenty people died, but she was uninjured. It was not the first attempt on her life according to a newspaper article that listed numerous others. Politics is a dangerous business in Bangladesh. The result of this horrific attack was a series of general strikes (*hartals*) called by the opposition party in an attempt to unseat the government. During these *hartals* the whole country was at a standstill, no public transport other than rickshaws was available and going into the city centre was asking for big trouble! The situation in Bangladesh is tense these days.

✈ Sunday

The official working week starts today, Sunday, as the weekend here is Friday and Saturday. An enormous low weather system in the Bay of Bengal was determined to stick around. It was so bad that we were not able to fly today. In fact, it looks like we are going to have at least three days of continuous downpour, low clouds and bad visibility. Of course that is just looking at it as a pilot. For the people in Dhaka the rains have already filled up the poor drainage systems, and the roads in our neighbourhood are flooded knee high.

In the morning Anders Korswing, Programme Manager, and Joseph, Office Manager/Finance Controller, and I had our weekly meeting, discussing ongoing things in the programme. Anders is Swedish and Joseph is a local man. After the meeting I did some training on the simulator, and spent the rest of the day doing office work at home. The training we provide for Masood, a trainee in our training programme for Bangladeshi pilots, is still 'under construction' and many things have to be worked out. Working with us should help these pilots to get operational experience as well as some understanding of turbine operations and a greater appreciation of safety consciousness. We hope it will help them when they move on to a 'real' job with one of the local airlines. It is also a great way of getting to know these young men on a personal level while investing in their future.

✈ Monday

We had no flights today, which was just as well as the weather was horrible. Flying would have been impossible anyway. At 6am I attended a Promise Keepers' meeting in the American Club. About six of us (all men) come together every week to discuss a chapter from a book that we all read. It is great fellowship despite the early hour. Anders had a meeting with World Vision this morning.

There is a flight request for Tuesday for a flight to an orphanage in Bauphal. I worked with Joseph on the required request letter for getting our clearances. There were a few things missing, naturally, since SO much information is required by the security agencies. Joseph was able to fix it, and later in the morning he sent out Ashim our maintenance and office assistant, to deliver the request letter to the necessary offices at Civil Aviation Authority Bangladesh (CAAB). Because the weather forecast was still not good for Tuesday, the passengers cancelled the flight later that day. The rest of the afternoon was spent preparing for training I am about to do in the US. I'll have to hit the books a bit before I leave!

We received a call from Grace School, which our boys attend. The roads were flooded so badly that several school buses had broken down or were stuck. Thankful for our big car, I headed out for the school and picked up one of our sons and a few of his friends who live close by. They were very excited by all the spray when I drove the car through the high water. More and more cars were getting stuck on the roads, and when I arrived home I advised my wife to keep our son home from his usual Dutch lesson in the afternoon. It's really important that children of missionaries working overseas keep up with their own language and culture, though it does mean they have more 'schoolwork' to do than their friends.

✈ Tuesday

We had a flight today, Tuesday, for Stichting Land Ontwikkelings Project Bangladesh, a Dutch NGO (nongovernmental organisation), that has two orphanages in Bauphal, near Patuakali in the south. It is a great project, set up by a man who was adopted as a young boy by a Dutch couple. When he was around twenty, he went back to Bangladesh to see the area where he was born, and find out if there was any family left. Touched by the problems in the area, he started an NGO to address some of the many needs of the people. The organisation is doing some great projects now and many people benefit. A group of Dutch supporters wanted to visit the project, but because of the weather their visit had to be postponed to another day. In the newspaper we read that we had a new all time record: 371mm of rain in 24 hours!

Anneke, my wife, taught English this morning at the Asha Project. The Project provides a day programme for street girls: helping to educate them, teaching them skills that will enable them to earn money and, if possible, prevent the very early marriages that are a common problem in Bangladesh. About 240 girls attend daily. Anneke works three mornings a week. Since the girls know little or no English she has to be very creative in her approach. My wife tries to base the lessons on what is reported in the newspapers. This helps the girls to be more aware of what is going on in the world and to learn more about their own country. Each week they have the opportunity to choose a subject on which Anneke will base a lesson. These girls and their families, who live in slums, were severely affected by the floods. With the help of MAF, many were provided with emergency supplies like rice, water purification tablets and basic medicines.

✈ *Wednesday*

The weather was still bad this morning, but at least it had improved slightly. Anders informed me that he had received a call from someone about a possible flood due to a tidal wave.

We have different types of tidal waves; this one would be due to a long period of hard wind pushing water up the Bay of Bengal into the top corner where Bangladesh lies. This can build up exceptionally high tides, resulting in flooding in the river deltas far into Bangladesh. The news had not been confirmed, but Anders tried to find out more. Later contact with the Red Cross/Crescent put us on standby for flights to two areas to do aerial inspection. However, the Red Cross seemed to be hesitant to use the aircraft, and because some key persons are not in the country the flights were put on hold. It takes some time before people actually understand the advantages of flying an amphibious aircraft, and the concept is still unusual.

⊀ *Thursday*

We do quite a lot of medical evacuations in Bangladesh. The nature of these flights is that they are unexpected. Even when we get a call it can take time to gather all the right information about the patient, and know whether or not the flight is confirmed. Often there is also a problem with local doctors who do not want to release certain patients for transport to Dhaka, because that means loss of income for them. This morning we were on standby for a medical flight from Khulna, but soon afterwards we received another call via the Danish embassy for a medevac out of Barisal.

Barisal is not too far away, and there is an airport there, which makes it a very easy flight. We decided to do that flight first while things were sorted out in Khulna. It turned out that the patient was actually a doctor with heart problems. His condition was not too bad, but he definitely needed medical attention in Dhaka. Despite being on a stretcher, he retained a very dignified manner and more or less kept control of the situation. An hour later he was in our private ambulance on his way from the airport to the hospital in Dhaka.

Within an hour we had refuelled and taken a quick lunch. By then the medevac from Khulna had been confirmed, and the case seemed serious. We took off from Dhaka, leaving a bad weather system behind us. When I looked in the direction of Barisal I was glad I was not going there! But closer to Khulna another system hung just outside the river where I had to land. When I circled for landing the turbulence was quite unsettling, making it difficult to inspect the landing area. Many ocean-going vessels were anchored out in the middle of the river, since Khulna is a large harbour city. Big power lines go across the river, taking away some of my landing options. Eventually I turned in, in front of the power lines, over a big ocean steamer, and landed between two other vessels while the wind whipped me around. All went well, considering the circumstances, and we found a good spot of grassy shoreline alongside which to park the plane. While my co-pilot contacted the passengers to inform them of our location the rain started to come down again. At least it kept the crowd away a bit, although some curious people came swimming from the other side of the river and were obviously not concerned about getting wet! Forty minutes later the local ambulance arrived. The crowd that survived the rain had turned the shore into a slippery mud bath. However, the same people were very willing to help get the patient on board, and some went down on their knees into the mud to do this.

The patient was a union leader, a very important position in Bangladesh. Such was his political status that he was shot several times. He was in a bad condition, and I took off quickly from between the boats as the crowd waved me goodbye. The rain had gone and so had most of the turbulence. While we flew back to Dhaka the visibility was good and we had no problem landing safely on ZIA airport in Dhaka. Alam had cleaned the ambulance from the morning flight and was waiting, together with some political people, to drive the patient speedily to the hospital. When I taxied back to our new hangar I was thankful and satisfied at having accomplished the day's flights.

✈ Friday

No flying today. Friday is our 'Sunday'. As we live in a Muslim country, our church services are on Fridays. The official weekend has changed several times, depending on the government of the day. At present, our offices close on Thursday afternoon and open again on Saturday. However, Saturday for most people is still considered part of the weekend. We go to an Assemblies of God church, where there is an English service on the Friday morning, and I am involved in the worship team. On Sunday afternoons we usually go as a family to Dhaka International Christian Church, an international church/fellowship. About 200 people attend, from more than fifty nationalities! This church is a real encouragement because of the great Bible-study type preaching. We need such encouragement.

9.

MADAGASCAR

The world's fourth largest island, Madagascar, lies 600km off the coast of Mozambique. The Malagasy people, who make up over 98 percent of the population, are of mixed African, Indonesian and Arab stock. Less than 50 per cent of the population is literate, and that figure is in decline. Having been annexed to France from 1896 until 1960, French is widely spoken, sharing the status of official language with Malagasy.

Poor farming techniques have resulted in soil erosion, and Madagascar is not able to produce enough food for its people, which is bad news in a subsistence agricultural economy. Malnutrition is endemic, as is malaria. Inadequate communications, and a remarkably inhospitable terrain, do not help the situation. It is against that background that MAF Europe does its work for the Lord and for the people of Madagascar.

Sunday was a family day for the Madagascar MAF staff. The Tippers were actively involved in their Vision Valley Church and the Wagbrants in the English Chapel. The Adolfs, who had been away for a short break, returned home. Paul Folkart, Madagascar's short-term Chief Engineer, prepared to return to the UK for a funeral. It was a sad day for him, but he was looking forward to seeing his wife who had remained at home. Sometimes three different members of the MAF staff preach in three different churches on a Sunday! They certainly make an active contribution to the local Christian fellowships. On Sunday evenings the missionary community, from all missions and several countries, meet together for a meal and for a time of worship, fellowship, praise and prayer.

The staff combined in their account of their week's activities.

✈ Monday

The Viator left empty at 6am from the Antananarivo Base to collect the Director of the Norwegian Mission Society, the Country Director for Madagascar, and their spouses, from a conference with the Malagasy church leaders in Manakara. We had dropped them last week. Pilot Fredrik Wagbrant brought them to Antsirabe for their next meeting that was scheduled at 9am. The journey would have taken them two days by car. Meanwhile, at 7am Lionel, from UNICEF, called Jakob Adolf to ask for four bookings for this week, one as soon as possible. A representative of the Ministry of Health had to go to Marolambo to inspect preparations for the island-wide measles campaign that is due to start in one week's time. A flight was scheduled for 10am, after the airplane returned from its first flight. The distribution of the vaccines, and of the fridges needed to keep them cool, has kept us busy for the last forty days. Last minute preparation flights are booked for this week thirty minutes before the office opens! At 7.30am our staff arrived in a van that stays overnight in town, 25km away. A prayer meeting was held at 8.30am.

Jakob prepared the flight plan and his material for the upcoming flight. Marolambo is the shortest airstrip on the island into which MAF Madagascar operates. Early flights are difficult due to the fog, and towards lunchtime the wind increased from the east. It is a one-way runway, only 451m long, and facing west for landing. There is not a big time-window during which a landing is possible. Also after a landing accident (no injuries, thankfully) in 2001, the use of the Viator has been avoided. The Cessna Caravan is used instead as it copes better there. But the Caravan is in a big inspection all this week! With only one person to carry to Marolambo, weight can be kept to a minimum, thus a safe landing is assured. Our Caravan, Tilly, was donated by supporters last year! It has since proved to be the backbone of the programme.

On returning from Marolambo, we choose to overfly two new runway construction projects nearby. Both are a two-day walk away from Marolambo. Work had been started in both locations a few months ago, but progress was slow. This was mainly due to the fact that all the work is done by local volunteers; only the tools and the know-how is provided by MAF. The tools are basic: wheelbarrows, picks and shovels.

An eight-minute flight from Marolambo (two days' walk otherwise) found us overhead Sahakevo. To our great surprise we found a well-organised and well-planned construction site. Just four weeks ago the Mayor of Sahakevo went to town asking for a skilled person to build the runway. A decision to send someone there was postponed until the village people agreed to work more frequently than once a week on the project. From what we could see from the air, someone had been found within the community who knew how to do it! Although no one was actually working as we flew over, it was clear that this project would certainly be completed. We were not so sure about that four weeks ago.

The second runway, Ambodinonoka, is only two minutes by plane—or a four-hour walk away. There was not a big change visible compared to six weeks ago, but we could see about ten men actually working on the strip as we flew over. If they were half as encouraged by our overflight as we were at the sight of them this airstrip will also be completed.

Tina Adolf, Finance Manager, and Nick Hamilton, Finance Trainer from the UK, and Jakob spent the rest of the day working through the 2005 budget proposal with the goal of keeping the cost down in order to maximise efficiency.

The Line Staff prepared the Viator for the vaccine distribution flight for tomorrow. Haja, the Depute Operations Manager, worked on the flights for this week. More and more requests are coming in, but we only have one aircraft available. John Tipper worked out the details of overtime for a large number of staff. We are kept so busy! Kristina Tipper spent the day at the mission school in town where she is a teacher. Annie Wagbrant worked on a schedule for the English classes for our local staff that are about to restart after a short break. English has grown in popularity following a political change two years ago.

✈ *Tuesday*

At 7am the Viator, loaded with vaccines, was flown to Nosy Varika, only forty minutes away by plane on the east coast. The runway is just one large pasture. Every time we come we have to find a nice long track that is free of small holes and obstacles. As we have been here several times in the last month, the villagers knew we were bringing boxes for the hospital seven kilometres further up the coast.

After Jakob dropped two passengers and mail in Marolambo he collected Dr Felix, a Ministry of Health official, and three other officials of various town offices. Dr Felix continued on to Antananarivo, the capital city, and then, with Fredrik in the same plane, up to Manakara to carry out further pre-campaign inspections. Before departure from Marolambo, Jakob met the Mayor of Sahakevo, who was walking to his village. Jakob told him that he was happy about the progress at the one airstrip on his overflight on Monday morning. Meanwhile, at 10am, staff from Medair arrived in the hangar with freight and a passenger to be taken up to Maroantsetra. As it was obviously too much cargo, they spent about three hours weighing and sorting. It is mainly equipment necessary to drill and install new wells. They started to do this work in Maroantsetra right after Cyclone Gafilo earlier this year.

Technical problems often cause the Viator to be unfit for flight as it is very hard to find spare parts for it. But as the Caravan is still in the inspection, we have to use it. At the vehicle workshop Remi and Zo were working on a car trailer and a small cart on which to install our gas-welding equipment. Around lunchtime Paul Bruizeman arrived with another trailer and an old electric generator that we will bring back to life in the next few weeks. Power cuts are not a big problem but, when the power is off, work in the office becomes impossible as most is done on computer. By late afternoon the Caravan inspection was completed and it was tested without any problem. Annie Wagbrant took about nine other ladies from the airport side of town to the beginning of the Bible Study Fellowship classes. Today was the first class this term.

⊀ *Wednesday*

Early in the morning Lionel from UNICEF called to inform us that seventeen medical students, who are scheduled to go to Marolambo tomorrow to help vaccinating, were ready this morning, as were the vaccines for the north. Because cooled vaccines have priority we told him to have the staff ready tomorrow at 7.30am. Fredrik left with the Caravan early in the morning to deliver vaccines to Ambotondrazaka. That same destination also receives medicines for other nearby places with no useable airstrips. He then continued to Mananara to pick up Dr Felix and brought him a bit further up the coast to Maroantsetra. The bay they overflew was full of humpback whales! They passed south of the wettest spot in Madagascar. Dr Felix stayed in Maroantsetra for yet another inspection as preparation for the campaign. At the same time Fredrik left the material for Medair that could not go yesterday. After that, he continued to Mandritsara and Bealanana to drop more vaccines, and finally landed in Antsohihy in order to refuel the aircraft for the return flight.

From 9 to 10am Annie Wagbrant was teaching English as most of our staff want to learn the language. It is a third language for all of them, French being the second. Michel started the next inspection on the Viator. It is only a small inspection, but it will take a bit of time. Jakob and Michel looked at ways of increasing hangar floor space and office space – with a paper hangar and paper model aircraft.

The afternoon was spent on more English classes, an informal pilots' meeting and the repair of a washing machine. Paul Bruizeman, who repaired the machine, was only taken on-to a newly created job a few days ago. But he's busy eight hours a day. That gives the staff just a little bit of extra time as we used to do all the things that Paul now does.

✈ Thursday

There was an 8am start with ten medical students to Marolambo, where they will help with the vaccination campaign. On return Jakob took four people from Media Service Evangelique. MSE produces Christian audiotapes, and more recently have started to produce Christian video films. Mission Aviation Fellowship was instrumental in getting the necessary equipment for MSE when it was set up. MSE is part of the Malagasy Media Mission, which has a group of twenty-two people in Marolambo making a film about the importance of money. It is an evangelistic piece, and the climax of the movie will be inside the Caravan in flight on Monday morning when we get the rest of the crew. During the weekend they are showing previous projects in Marolambo as a thank you for the collaboration of the village during the two-week shoot. On the second rotation eight more medical students were flown to Marolambo.

Fredrik Wagbrant spent the day on the Internet searching for a better satellite phone contract and spare parts for various bits of electronic equipment. Jakob took the third flight of the day. His freight was mainly four-metre-long plastic tubes in three different sizes. It is an innovative kit to make wells and very simple water pump. It can't be too simple for the bush, as everything – absolutely everything – breaks really quickly in the harsh environment. The right front seat needed to be de-installed to load the pipes. Great care was taken securing the pipes down and back in order that they didn't slide into the flight controls, or even into the instrumentation! After flying the cyclone relief earlier this year, and now the measles campaign, I think we can say, we know how to do it. ... About 600kg of freight for Medair had to stay in Antananarivo as the plane was already loaded to the absolute maximum possible takeoff weight. An additional flight is pre-booked. By then other items that need to be taken to the cyclone affected area should have cleared Customs.

One hour and forty minutes later we delivered the 1000kg of freight to Medair in Maroantsetra, along with important mail to a Medical NGO. This group didn't fail to seize the chance and brought out 200kg of freight to return to Antananarivo! After collecting Dr Felix – who is our permanent passenger this week – we took off to Antalaha for refuelling. We went with minimum fuel because of being so heavily loaded. After a quick stop in Antalaha the aircraft still made it back to Ivato, the international airport where MAF is based in Antananarivo, before sunset.

What were the ground-based folk doing? Haja spent the day reorganising the next few days. UNICEF needed to rearrange the schedule for Monday, as there are still a few glitches to be taken care of regarding the vaccination campaign. Jakob discovered that he has to preach in two churches on Sunday morning. Good thing they are not far from each other and the services start one hour apart! Tina and Nick spent the day finalising the handover of the finances, and rearranging the furniture to give Tina enough space to work for the next couple of weeks.

While the Viator is undergoing its 50-hour check under Michel's supervision, Leonard used his spare time to rebuild the fibreglass engine cowling for the aircraft. Oil has weakened the structure from inside the turbine nacelle and it needed a 'cosmetic' touch up. Leonard, who is a pastor, works for us full time and works as a pastor after work hours. Many times he takes a week or two of unpaid vacation to go with some of his church members into the countryside to evangelise, or to help other churches in the bush. Though he is probably one of the best car and aircraft painters on the island, his main job with MAF is to help to prepare aircraft, freight and passengers for flight, and to secure the aircraft after flight. That's the job of the 'line man'.

One of the other two line men is Lova. Apart from helping us on the flight line he is very talented at repairing electronic equipment. More than once he has asked, after fixing something, 'What is it?' or 'How do you switch this on?' Lova starts the network in the mornings and attends to minor repairs when he is not working on the line. Late in the afternoons Fredrik does flight-following from the radio at home as our office staff leave around 3.30pm to avoid the worst traffic going into town, especially on Friday afternoons. Twenty-five kilometres can take up to a gruelling three hours in the worst case, but always at least one hour.

The Tipper Family is on a short vacation from last Monday until next Tuesday. After that Kristina will start teaching at the school in town, and John will take the second responsibility of Operations Manager next to Logistics.

✈ Friday

At 8am there were two flights to Marolambo taking medical students who will be helping with the campaign starting on Monday. Four hours later there was a departure for Maroantsetra with 1 tonne of goods for Medair, mainly plastic pipes that are needed to build 150 small water points.

After delivery, the aircraft continued to Antalaha to fill up for the return flight.

✈ Saturday

An 8am start again with one flight to Marolambo to pick up the remaining staff from the film crew. At about 12 noon four missionaries were brought to Analalava for a week-long language study project. On returning that night, we found a Malagasy couple standing in the hangar asking for a medevac to Antalaha. A terminally-ill elderly lady needed to go back to her family who live up in the north of the island, but it was too late to do it today. Jakob called Fredrik to ask if he would be willing to fly on a Sunday to make this possible. He agreed to take off at 7am tomorrow morning.

10.

MAF Europe

MAF Europe, the overseas operational arm of the 10 National MAF groups in Europe is based in Ashford in the South of England, though in the diary week some staff members were working in Kenya.

The Chief Executive Officer, Chris Lukkien, and Marjan Companjen, who is the Corporate Administrator, make up the MAF Europe CEO Department. Much of their work is done together, as their records show. On *Monday* they met with the person who coordinates EU-Cord, a conglomerate of European Christian NGOs based in Brussels. MAF Europe is considering becoming a member of EU-Cord. But while strategic planning took up much of the day, the personal touch was not forgotten. A former MAF staff member had just lost his wife, and it was Chris's privilege to send a message of condolence.

The following day, *Tuesday*, Chris and Marjan were engaged in strategic thinking. They are part of a task force that was set up by the European MAFs to review organisational statements (Statement of Belief, Calling, Purpose, Vision and Values). A variety of statements are used by various parts of the organisation, and the aim is to develop one set of statements that apply to all of MAF Europe. Marjan wrote to the international MAF groups requesting copies of their statements for the taskforce to consider.

That kept Marjan busy on *Wednesday* too as Chris applied himself to a draft Strategic Plan being prepared for a Senior Management Team meeting in October and the Board in December. On *Thursday* he had discussions with a senior management team member concerning a potential future position, and had a telephone conversation with MAF South Africa's Board Chairman in preparation for the MAF South Africa Board meeting on Saturday. Since January 2004, MAF Europe has been responsible for running the flight operations in South Africa. Marjan wrote and distributed *Prayer Connections*, the bi-weekly prayer letter containing news and prayer items from each base. It is an internal document that aims to increase the sense of community amongst the teams in Europe, Africa and Asia.

Friday saw both Chris and Marjan at Heathrow where they met with Arne Nordahl, MAF Europe's President (who represents the 10 European MAF groups), Stuart King (President Emeritus), Alan Devereux, the Chairman MAF UK, and Keith Jones, CEO MAF UK. They discussed the mandate given by MAF Europe's members at the Annual General meeting in Helsinki last June concerning their desire to increase centralisation and integration of MAF in Europe. The principle decision was made, but a plan of action now needs to be prepared for presentation at the next Members' Meeting in January 2005.

It was a week of thinking big and planning ahead. And with a worldwide organisation like Mission Aviation Fellowship, if such big thinking and forward planning were not done carefully and prayerfully, things would grind to a halt.

Meanwhile, on *Monday*, Max Gove, Manager of Research and Development, was researching a paper for use in MAF Europe on the subject of *Tentmaking*. This has become relevant as MAF opens programmes in countries where a traditional MAF service (for mission and church) are not possible or relevant. He also liaised with Keith Ketchum – MAF Aviation Services Department (ASD) Maintenance Coordinator – regarding an engine overhaul situation on a Cessna Caravan in Ethiopia belonging to our partner organisation, Abyssinian Flight Services (AFS). (Max is coordinator between MAF and AFS.) The next day, *Tuesday*, his mind moved from Ethiopia to East Timor as there is a proposal to provide high frequency radios for Youth with a Mission there. That led to contact with a Swiss company which produces modems that allow data e-mails to be transferred by HF radio.

Max's job does not bind him to a desk. *Wednesday* found him in London, along with a colleague from MAF UK, visiting the UK Department For International Development to discuss possible funding for projects involving MAF in Africa. It was with his passport in his pocket that he set out to work the following morning, *Thursday*, as he had a lengthy meeting with Medair's International Board of Trustees in Geneva, of which he is a member. Medair works in many of the world's trouble hotspots in relief and disaster situations. *Friday* saw him returning to Canterbury, and his office at home. Thinking ahead, Max finalised dates for an upcoming trip to Nepal. This was to be his second trip with two MAF US staff. They are keen to explore options for ways that MAF can assist the people of Nepal.

✈ ✈ ✈ ✈ ✈

Several other members of the MAF Europe staff spent the diary week in Nairobi. David Staveley, Aviation Services Department, explains why and describes the week.

All the members of the ASD travelled to Nairobi, Kenya for a team meeting and three days of Aviation Standards Committee meetings. Keith Ketchum (Maintenance Co-ordinator) and Geoff Hillier (Maintenance Quality Manager) are based in Nairobi and they were joined by William Nicol (Chief Training Captain) from Tanzania, Henk-Jan Muusse (ASD Manager) from Holland, and from the Operations Centre in England by Larry Heintz (Aviation Training and Safety Advisor), Trevor Phillips (Flight Operations Advisor) and me. Amanda Sotherden from the Kent office helped us with minute taking.

Larry led the team in a training session on *Tuesday*. This particularly focused on listening and communications skills. Several of us had not seen the others for a number of months, and it was a lively interchange of ideas as well as highlighting ways in which we could improve our communications and build rapport. Later we looked at the Department Team Charter in order that it could be tied in with the overall vision and strategy of the organisation. In view of the new legislation that we would be debating later in the week, we had to look carefully at how we could be flexible in an increasingly regulated environment. The day continued with a time of fellowship and discussion together.

✈✈✈✈✈

Geoff Hillier gives his own slant on the day. Unlike most others at the meetings, Geoff is based in Nairobi.

The ASD have an annual training conference. I led a short Bible study from Ecclesiastes on wanting to give up, against running the race and finishing—something that is quite pertinent to our work. We did some training in improving our communication skills and discussed how we can help the programmes to do their work most effectively. A profitable time of learning was followed by good fellowship and an evening meal together in a Chinese restaurant! I had to attend an emergency meeting at daugther Catherine's school as it has gone into receivership. It makes us feel a bit unsettled.

✈✈✈✈✈

Back to David Staveley.

Representatives of all the East Africa programmes joined the ASD team for an Aviation Standards Committee: Kenya, Tanzania and Uganda. Their principal task was to review the draft documents that had been prepared to meet the requirements of the new aviation legislation that is being introduced by these three countries. It was essential to have representatives from MAF's programmes in these countries at our discussions to ensure that the final proposals are workable. Ari Aho also joined us—he is an airline pilot from Finland, who is on the MAF Europe Board. The fourteen of us set about the mammoth task of going through pages and pages of detailed proposals—almost line by line. It was not exactly the most dramatic aspect of MAF's work, but absolutely essential for our safe operations in the future as well as satisfying the likely future requirements of the Civil Aviation Authorities in the countries where we work. Although this new legislation is imminent in the three East African countries, our plans will have to be adapted and widened for introduction in the other countries where MAF Europe works. The last session of the day finished a full twelve hours after the time we started and discussions still carried on over the (late) evening meal.

Thursday was another day of heavy meetings with our programme concentrating on Flight Operations legislation in particular. Despite being locked into discussions, the ubiquitous mobile phones continued to sound at various intervals – particularly for those in the local programmes who were juggling their regular responsibilities with the meetings. We finished a little earlier in the evening – a good thing since I was scheduled to meet with a MAF pilot who wanted to discuss some urgent operational flight safety matters. This meeting went on for over two hours, but I was very glad of the discussions since some areas of real concern had arisen. Bedtime at the MAF guesthouse was especially welcome, as I had to be up around 5am to catch my flight back to the UK.

The rest of the committee concentrated on maintenance legislation for much of *Friday* and the meeting finished in time for several of the members to catch their flights back to Europe or Tanzania and Uganda. My own flight to the UK was delayed by three hours, but that gave me time to write up some of my notes and action lists arising from the week's meetings. It was nineteen hours after getting up that I arrived back home in Kent—not really the best preparation for the week's cycling holiday in Suffolk that my wife had I had planned with her sister and brother-in-law!

✈✈✈✈✈

Henk-Jan Muusse, Manager of the Aviation Services Department, chaired the three days of meetings. But he had things to do before the meetings began.

Monday morning started with a meeting with Geoff Hillier to discuss some quality assurance issues that relate to the Tanzania programme. After that I met with Keith Ketchum, MAF Europe's Maintenance Adviser. We discussed how to handle the overhaul of an engine that we sent to an engine factory in Berlin. The price is much higher than we usually pay, and we discussed possible causes for this and what we could do to avoid similar expenses for aircraft in other programmes in the future.

That afternoon was spent with William Nicol, MAF Europe's Chief Training Captain. William is to ensure that the Check Pilots and Training Captain in each MAF programme receive regular training, and that the checklists and manuals that the pilots use are effective, efficient and guarantee a safe operation. He is also developing a training syllabus for new MAF pilots and we discussed several technical issues.

And Henk-Jan's thoughts on the three days of meetings?

The ASC meetings were long and intensive. We started at 8.30am and with only one hour break for lunch, we stopped around 7.30 in the evening. Although it was tiring, we all felt that these discussions were long overdue and we were pleased to make so much progress. The next step is to communicate the new aviation policies to the programmes and to ensure that they receive sufficient training and monitoring.

✈✈✈✈✈

Mike Chinneck, Infomration Services Department Manager,
arrived in Nairobi in advance of his colleagues. For him it was a
routine visit and, as usual, he stayed at the single-storey wooden
colonial house in the MAF compound that serves as guesthouse.
Sunday saw him at the Nairobi Vineyard Fellowship, where he
'enjoyed excellent teaching and worship'. Mike especially enjoyed
it as he is not often in Nairobi for weekends.

Monday was a busy day for Mike, but that's normal.

I devoted today to the aircraft maintenance software
system (SAMS) with MAF Kenya people. SAMS is the
commercial software package we use for keeping an inventory
of the stock in the hangar and its movement. To start with
I spent an hour with Wambui. She has had a difficult time
with SAMS, and she was able to explain her problems to
me. Many of them were easy to solve after seeing her work
the system—and understanding her real problem! At 10am
the provider of SAMS arrived. We spent the rest of the
morning (and lunch) going through a set of changes needed
to the software – detailed design work. After lunch we had
a meeting with three other users of the system to discuss
how we could save a lot of engineers' time by being able to
print out aircraft work documentation to submit to the local
government aviation inspectors. Getting the format and the
information right (and easy to use) will be a great benefit
– exactly what computer systems should be doing!

My last day in Nairobi, *Tuesday*, was spent with Fiona
and Theo discussing progress on the Wingman system,
which is a flight booking/aircraft loading/aircraft and pilot-
scheduling programme that also writes tickets and invoices
and keeps aircraft and pilot statistics. This was originally
started in 1998, and from 2000 Fiona Waugh has been doing
a great job keeping it going. Because of MAF's particular role

in mission flying, our flight planning and fare calculations are very different to a normal aviation business, hence the need to have our own product rather than something bought off the shelf. Fiona and Theo are nearly at the end of this project, but there is still a lot to do. We also need to plan the rollout of the software to all our other programmes-which includes retraining on the new facilities and training from scratch for three programmes that have to start using it for the first time. With just Fiona and Theo working on it there really aren't enough hours in the day. We need careful consideration and divine guidance on priorities for this work. I often carry back post for the UK staff in Kenya, but this trip only a single letter turned up for me to post when I arrived back in England.

Mike flew home on Wednesday, took a well-earned day off (he didn't even switch on his computer!) the next day, and worked from home at the end of the week.

✈ ✈ ✈ ✈

As Geoff Hillier remained in Nairobi when the others went back to the UK, he deserves the last word.

On *Friday* I spoke on why the manuals I have written for Tanzania will work, and how we can make double checks on certain maintenance procedures that I have compiled. Both of my manuals are approved and the Tanzanian men seem happy with what they have been given. This is the result of a year's work for many of us in ASD, and it's gratifying to see the work we do in an office making the transition to helping the men and women at the workface of MAF.

The following day Geoff went to a friend's house for worship practice.

We set the band up and I began to lead the others through a set of worship songs I have put together. I am still very excited from having visited Soul Survivor in the UK, and I am keen to really make this time of worship glorifying to God. We have a Kenyan on drums and lead guitar, an American on keyboard and myself on acoustic guitar with my wife Karen and daughter Catherine on vocals.

11.

KENYA

Having reached Kenya by way of an Aviation Standards Commitee, we remain there to meet the MAF staff. But what kind of land is it in which they live and work? Kenya is five-and-a-half times the size of England. The north and east are mainly desert; only the south and west – where most people live – are fertile. The economy is based on agriculture and light industry, though tourism is an important and growing source of income. Over 2000 missionaries work in Kenya, and around 700 Kenyans are missionaries elsewhere. MAF's Kenyan ministry extends back to 1959, and from there it flies to many parts of eastern Africa and the Congo as well as flying within the country.

During the fortnight 4 – 18 September (information was not given for just the diary week) MAF Kenya flew to a total of seventy destinations, operating six planes with nine pilots. Thirty-nine of the flights were to Sudan, one was to Tanzania and thirty were within Kenya. Three of the internal flights were for training purposes. Also within that time window, nine days of maintenance was carried out on four planes.

✈✈✈✈✈

It is to the MAF hangar we go to meet Ken Milligan, a Scot, who serves in Kenya with his wife, Alice. Ken is Chief Engineer.

Monday was quiet, mostly catching up with aircraft component and parts servicing. Peter Franz, a missionary who has his own private Cessna 182 aircraft, brings his plane to us for maintenance. The work we are doing on it is in preparation for its Certificate of Airworthiness renewal. One of our own fleet, a Cessna 210, was reported as having severe radio interference and heavy background noise. While we replaced the components that should set the matter right, we'll need a flight report to prove that the fault cleared. During the day we had an urgent prayer request from Angola. Lonnie, one of the staff there, was suffering from cerebral malaria and his son, Aaron, from malaria. There was some serious praying done over that serious news. Our minds weren't just in Angola as one of our Kenyan engineers, Sammy Kilonzo, started Non-Destructive Testing training in England today. This is a really big challenge for Sam, and we remembered him in our prayers also.

✈✈✈✈✈

John Meikle is an Avionics Engineer, and he provided his view of Monday in the hangar. He has given it in greater detail. John's wife, Jan, is with him in Nairobi.

6.45am. I arrived at the MAF hangar at Wilson Airport. It was quiet! Most people start at 8am though some are required to start at 7am and some at 10am to accommodate aircraft operations. I try to begin each day with Bible readings and prayers. I am presently using the McCheyne Bible Reading Plan that takes me through the Old Testament once and the Psalms and New Testament twice in one year.

8am. Morning prayers, then our Monday morning meeting on the hangar floor. This was an opportunity for Ken Milligan, our Chief Engineer, to welcome the engineering staff back to another week's service to God, and to brief them on the work agenda. We heard very sad news. Patrick Chege, who works in the Operations Department, lost his wife Susan to pneumonia on Sunday night. He is left with a 5-year-old daughter, Sarah.

Every Monday the Chief Engineer has a meeting with supervisors. Another busy week lies ahead. We carried out an investigation into a loud whine on the headset/intercommunication system on Cessna 210 5Y-MSW. When replacing the capacitor on the alternator made no difference, we suspected that it was internal alternator electrical noise. Joseph and Daniel replaced the alternator. We e-mailed our Cessna supplier about the unacceptable time taken to despatch a weather radar unit for Cessna Caravan 5Y-BRE. This problem is affecting the operational capability of the aircraft and we have already lost a flight as a result. Prepared engineering aids for use with the Pilatus PC12 aircraft.

One of the major problems encountered in mission is the fluid nature of staffing. Sometimes missionaries leave the field, and sometimes they relocate within the field. As very few engineers arrive at MAF with experience on the aircraft we operate, and because the maintenance manuals for these aircraft are far from explicit, I see it as one of my remits to produce engineering aids to assist new engineers/technicians, so another working lunch! Herman, who works on the bench, should have finished his holiday today, but he is ill in Tanzania! We have no details as yet but malaria or bad food poisoning has been suggested. Avionics training on the PC-12 for Joseph.

Prayers: Every Monday we select a few supporters, pray for them, and then send them a card. And each Tuesday night MAF international staff meet for an evening of prayer.

✈✈✈✈✈

On Wednesday there was news from Tanzania. Herman was in hospital in Dar es Salaam with malaria. There's never a shortage of prayer topics in a MAF base. A Cessna Caravan arrived from Tanzania to have special inspections carried out. That was programmemed for Wednesday, but the day had a surprise of its own. Ken's diary records it.

PC-12 in flight to Sudan radioed a problem with landing gear indication and requesting advice. Advised to return to base for engineering investigation and rectification. An attempted landing in Sudan with suspect landing gear is not an option. The PC-12 returned to Nairobi, the defect was found, repaired and returned to flight within one hour.

John Meikle explains what the problem was.

The PC-12 returned to the hangar after Aarno Alanne, the pilot, got a nose gear 'not up and locked' indication after takeoff. Contaminated sensor cleaned and landing gear checks carried out okay. Aircraft departed with no further problems.

✈✈✈✈✈

Thursdays start early, with a men's meeting at 6am at the Milligans' home, complete with coffee and homemade cake. They study a book together. On diary week the men started Christ-empowered Living *by Selwyn Hughes, having just finished* A call to Spiritual Reformation *by Don A Carson. As well as studying together they have a time of prayer before heading for the hangar to begin the working day with prayer.*

Thursday had its frustrations, as John noted.

We fitted the original HSI (Horizontal Situation Indicator – rather like an artificial horizon, and used in instrument flying) back into the PC12, post-repair carried out by our repair shop on Wilson airport. Sadly, they have not rectified the unit and the fault is still very apparent—typical frustration not to mention a waste of valuable time! Serviceable unit refitted and unserviceable HSI sent to another repairer on the airport for repair: rightly or wrongly, I am optimistic they will have more success!

Friday's diary from both Ken and John was in techno-speak, but indications were that it was successful techno-speak!

Download latest database from the Bendix/King off the Internet for updating Cessna Caravan 5Y-MAG's #1 KLN90B Global Positioning System. Procedure for doing this found to be out of date; procedure modified.

News from Tanzania was encouraging too. Although Herman was weak, jaundiced and on a drip, he was apparently improving. Lonnie and Aaron in Angola were still being remembered in staff prayers, as was Sammy on his first week of training in England.

Aircraft are only as good as the engineers and mechanics who maintain them, and the MAF engineers and mechanics are among the best!

✈ ✈ ✈ ✈ ✈

Things were busy in the Logistics Department. Tom Otigo is Logistics Manager.

After committing *Monday* to the Lord in the morning devotion, we had a message that the cooking gas had run out in the process of preparing tea. We had to stop other duties to attend to the emergency lest we missed the tea. We had ordered medicine for MAF Dodoma with our supplier.

Surprisingly we had to collect it at 9.00am for 11.30am flight to Dodoma. Amazingly the order was not ready. One of us had to rush there to speed up the order. We thank God because the flight was delayed; otherwise the medicines could have been left because they were ready by noon.

Due to visitors who come from other MAF organisations, we had to release two cars we use in our department, thereby having a shortage of cars. We had to combine our duties together using one car, hence delaying our duties.

We started *Tuesday* with normal duties: cheque payment to NSSF (National Social Security Fund), banking, picking up Telcom bills forms, dropping and picking up mail. After 5.00pm took Herman Lauber to Nairobi Hospital. Picked up a MAF car from the Methodist guesthouse.

I left for Jomo Kenyatta International Airport at 5.49am on *Wednesday* to meet a visitor who had been sent with a medical package for MAF from Heathrow. Dropped visitors to Methodist guesthouse for the ASC meeting, then did deliveries. Took a car from the guesthouse back to Wilson Airport. Picked up and dropped mail as usual. Bought coffee for visitors from UK. Took a mechanic to take Richard Drake's motorcycle for repair. I arranged stores on *Thursday*, delivered a cheque then left to comfort one of our colleagues who had lost his wife. And the week ended with me doing deliveries, collecting a cheque and purchasing vaccines for MAF Dodoma.

✈ ✈ ✈ ✈ ✈

The Personal Assistant to the MAF Kenya Programme Manager, Angela Mwangi, noted the sad beginning to the week.

The week started on a sad note when we received the news that the wife of one of our colleagues had passed away. As the person to release the news to the others I knew it was not going to be an easy thing to do. I had come to work that morning looking forward to the day as I was going to spend some time with Amanda Sotherden from our MAF Ashford office, who was only to be in Kenya for a week. As it was her first visit we had arranged to go to the National Park and the Giraffe Centre. According to our culture when someone we know loses a loved one, visiting the bereaved family is acceptable so, on Wednesday, I had to co-ordinate the visit. The next day we left at 12 noon for Patrick's place and returned to the office about 4pm, emotionally and physically drained.

✈ ✈ ✈ ✈ ✈

That day there were practical problems to be thought about regarding the bereavement. Richard Drake, Finance Manager, had them on his mind.

Many of the national staff visited a colleague whose wife died of pneumonia at the weekend after several days in intensive care. It seems that the hospital bill will be three times the insurance cover and we will need to decide how this is to be funded. The next day we confirmed to our insurers that MAF will guarantee payment of the hospital bill for our staff member's wife. This is necessary for the body to be released and for the funeral to take place.

✈ Saturday

After the sadness of the week, Richard and his wife, who were in Kenya on a short-term assignment, went with a small group of others to Naivasha and the Hell's Gate National Park to see some Rift Valley scenery and, hopefully, some wildlife. They took three Kenyans with them: Mary-Ann, a young teacher from Kawangware; Morris, a community worker who lives in Kibera; and Wanjiku, a house help. They saw hippos, giraffes and much more. Wanjiku had never seen a lake before, let alone all the wild animals. It was quite an experience for her!

✈ ✈ ✈ ✈ ✈

MAF Kenya's other national staff must have been looking forward to the weekend too, as they had had a busy and difficult week. John Waweru, Accounts Clerk, turned into a removal man! Just two days of his diary give a flavour of the variety of things he does.

✦ Wednesday

- ✦ devotion

- ✦ relocating office after completion of repairs

- ✦ fares computer input for August 04

- ✦ issued receipts for money received on behalf of MAF Tanzania—CMS

- ✦ informed bookings on balance owing by De la Salle brothers

- ✦ filing August 04 payment vouchers

- ✦ receipt on behalf of MAF Uganda for a flight on 10.9.04 – Entebbe-Yei (Sudan)

- ✦ issued e-mail client receipt

- ✦ talked to MAF Uganda Ops Dept reporting payment on 10th Sept flight

✈ *Thursday*

- ✈ devotion

- ✈ rang customer asking for payment

- ✈ received a phone from CMA to collect a cheque

- ✈ filed fares ticket in the archives

- ✈ prepared Shell fuel payment analysis schedule – Aug 04 invoices

- ✈ visited a colleague who had lost his wife

- ✈ called a customer for a cheque which would be ready next Wednesday

- ✈ AIM invoices delivered as requested by Finance Manager.

✈ ✈ ✈ ✈ ✈

Mission Aviation Fellowship in Kenya facilitates Information Technology (IT) services beyond its own offices. Paul Waugh, IT Manager, gives three examples of that.

I visited The Bible League (who fly with us and use our IT services) on *Monday* to collect a PC with a problem, and was invited to their daily devotions. Many prayers were offered for projects they were involved in: a leaders' course in Limuru, a bore hole in Northern Kenya, and two containers stuck in Mombasa port. I felt very privileged in being able to share with them. The PC had problems and they were unable to download their e-mails. This was a big thing for them as the Bible League is funded by US churches who require weekly updates on projects. They also need to communicate with pastors around Kenya and elsewhere in the world. After we checked the PC out, it was decided to backup the data and reinstall the software. The Bible League now has a working PC that can download their e-mails.

With 193 mission partners using the MAF Kenya IT services in Nairobi, the IT staff are kept very busy. The e-mail service runs twenty-four hours in order that customers can dial into MAF or collect mail from the Internet. MAF provides antivirus scanning on all e-mails, and there is an average of about 10,000 e-mails trapped with viruses each year. These are deleted and not allowed through to the customers.

The African Committee for the Rehabilitation of Southern Sudan (ACROSS) is a partnership of Christian agencies based in Nairobi but working in South Sudan. MAF Kenya provides IT support twice a week from the Nairobi office. The support covers hardware and software. ACROSS is involved in translating the Bible into the many tribal languages of South Sudan and needs the PCs to be up and running eight hours a day. MAF recently repaired a laptop that was vital for fieldwork in South Sudan.

It is encouraging to know that Mission Aviation Fellowship not only facilitates mission work through its flying programme, but also through sharing its other expertise, especially in the area of information technology.

✦ ✦ ✦ ✦ ✦

The diary kept by Alice Milligan, Ken's wife, was interesting in its variety – from preparing a talk to enjoying the pampering of a pedicure!

✈ *Sunday*

Jenna, my niece, flew home this morning after spending seven weeks in Kenya. She was busy doing voluntary work in two orphanages Monday to Friday but still managed to see a bit of the country. She will be back!! Attended our church, Emmanuel Baptist Church, which is just around the corner! Our church is a little over two years old. It has gone from a congregation of twelve to well over 200. We meet in the school but have now outgrown this and we are looking for a plot of land in this area on which to build a church. There is no church in the immediate area. We hope to be moving shortly to bigger premises but only temporarily.

✈ *Monday*

This is a busy week with children going back to school after the holidays. As I am involved in the sponsorship of some children, I had to see to fees etc. Took Jemema and Joseph back to their school at Kiambu, about an hour's drive from home on busy roads. Jemema has special needs and this is a combined school for her and her brother. They are orphans as their mother recently died from AIDS.

✈ *Tuesday*

Outi and I, as joint guesthouse managers, had a meeting with Margaret, the property manager. There were a few issues that had to be sorted out concerning problems with compound staff etc. It was a very constructive meeting and Margaret had some really good input. It is a blessing to be able to communicate and co-operate with national staff. John, who looks after the guesthouse, was also present.

✈ *Wednesday*

Gave a talk to the East African Women's League about MAF. Showed a 10-minute video and spoke of MAF Kenya and the background of the work. Karen Hillier spoke of her time in Mongolia. The East African Women's League is a non-Christian organisation of which some Christian ladies are members, Karen and myself included.

✈ Thursday

Attended Women @ 10 which is a group of around thirty-five Christian ladies who meet every Thursday and study different Christian books or do Bible study together. It was a good time of fellowship and discussion and has certainly helped me on my walk.

✈ Friday

A little bit of pampering today. Beth, who is a Christian, came and gave me a pedicure—bliss. Beth, who is struggling to put her two children through school, is a trained beautician but doesn't have much work. We have good discussions about church etc.

✈ Saturday

Our church ladies' monthly meeting was held this afternoon. Eleven ladies of different nationalities attended with both our pastors' wives.

✈ ✈ ✈ ✈

Outi Alanne is wife of Aarno, a MAF pilot since 1986. They come from Finland, and they are not the only Finns in that part of the world. Two days taken from Outi's diary make that clear.

A good, busy day! This morning, Tuesday, Alice, Margaret and I had an excellent meeting about the guesthouse and some matters regarding the everyday running of the compound (night guard etc.) It is amazing how we are able to agree about everything. Margaret's input was great! Hopefully the decisions we made will be beneficial for everybody. John, who has worked in the guesthouse for almost fifteen years, joined us in the meeting. His service has been exceptionally faithful.

At 11am Sirpa Rissanen joined Aarno and me and we drove to Karen to attend a Finnish missionary's 60th birthday celebration. There were many Africans from all over East Africa there to honour him and show their gratitude to him and to God. Very touching. Then I rushed home to bake for the evening and tomorrow's Bible study. At 4pm I picked up a big group of teenagers from the International School of Kenya and Braeburn school buses for their Finnish lesson. As one student had his birthday we had some of the cake I made for the evening and tomorrow. It was a challenging lesson for me to teach. Next week I'll have to prepare in even more detail as the students are on four different levels!

Aleks and Aarno had a quick meal of leftovers and then at 8pm we had a MAF prayer meeting at our house. It was the first since March when the meetings were cancelled for security reasons. We shared individual needs, and Aarno told about a friend with terminal cancer. He has been a big burden on Aarno's heart. We prayed for his salvation and for other things too. People stayed until ten having coffee and cake. It is so good to have the meetings going on again! It is precious to pray together, and I also enjoy meeting people and getting to know what is going on in MAF.

Our visit to Kenya has focused on the hangar rather than flights, but the one depends on the other. Remember the statistics at the beginning of the chapter for the two weeks from 4 – 18 September? Ken, John and the others facilitated flights to a total of seventy destinations, operating six planes with nine pilots. Thirty-nine of the flights were to Sudan, one was to Tanzania and thirty were within Kenya.

The report from Kenya's Flight Operations concluded: No incidents or alarming situation reports from the aircrew, and the MAF customers served within the two weeks were all happy with our services.

And that's what matters.

12.

MAF UK

MAF UK is based in Folkestone, on the South Coast of England, not many miles from Ashford and the Headquarters of MAF Europe, of which MAF UK is a part.

The Chief Executive Officer is Keith Jones, himself a former pilot with the Mission, having served in Chad, Kenya and Sudan. Keith's week began by prioritising, always a good thing for a CEO!

✈ Monday
Attended 'First Things', our beginning of the week prayer meeting.

Met PA and prayed together before

catching up on last week: reports to be typed and distributed, action from meeting staff and Chairman in Glasgow, tackle in-tray that has filled from three days out of the office. We then discussed the current week: meetings, papers needed, travel arrangements, staff wanting to see me, letters to sign. That was followed by the ubiquitous mug of coffee and the strategic report and proposals following our meeting in Scotland.

What follows was my 'to do' list.

- ✈ CEO's comment for next *MAF News*. I'm only allowed 250 words; that's never enough! I think, in view of the stresses and strains of recent weeks, I'll write about commitment. Lord, is that of you? If not, show me. If it is, then help me!

- ✈ Following a meeting with my friend and colleague in Operations, I need to write up a report on proposed moves towards integrating the European MAF groups. Meeting the needs of ten national groups and their Operations is not going to be easy.

- ✈ Write a diary of events for a book on 'A Week in the life of MAF'. The things people ask me to do!!! Oh well, better keep the writer happy!

- ✈ Produce a plan of action that, using an electronic chat room and/or a face-to-face forum, will allow debate on specific topics within the organisation to all line managers. This is a bit radical and may ruffle a few feathers!!

- ✈ Sign 100 invitations to the launch of Stuart King's updated book.

Monday's two meetings: The first was with our Direct Marketing Manager. Four specific fundraising initiatives needed detailed attention, one this year and three to sit within the strategic plan. It is critical that we get them right. We spent an hour detailing a course of action that should maximise results. We also spoke about the need for a strategy for raising prayer support, recognising that the success of such activities are difficult to measure, but knowing that without prayer the work would suffer intolerably. The DMM has recently taken on new and additional responsibilities. I wondered how he was coping, and if he looked tired and stressed? He assured me that all is well. We pray.

Next came my bi-weekly update with the Company Secretary. We covered matters of compliance, charity law and company law, MAF Trustees and MAF Members, our Memorandum and Articles of Association, and Board meetings. We finished with prayer at 5.30. As folk left for home, though some stayed on, the office quietened and I went back to the reports again. By 7.30pm one-and-a-half reports were done and I too headed for home.

✈ Tuesday

I arrived at 8.30am and walked into a mini crisis, a situation of conflict between two people. It took almost the entire working day to sort that one out. My evening was spent writing CEO's Comment for *MAF News*. Commitment was the right topic and the Lord gave me the words.

✈ Wednesday

My diary was free. Praise the Lord! I began by signing letters then some residual issues cropped up following yesterday's crisis, but they only took an hour or so. Finished signing letters.

The report on integration was finished by 6.30pm and looked good. Thank you Lord! I read it through again. Is this really where we will be in three years time? How much time, effort and money will this initiative save? How will it go on to benefit those we strive so hard to help? How will it extend God's kingdom on earth? Lord, I leave these issues at your feet.

✦ Thursday

I had an all-day meeting in London with an eminent judge who has asked how he can help support the work of MAF.

✦ Friday

Today saw me at Heathrow, where I met a young airline executive who has offered his skills to MAF as a Trustee. He is prepared to give several days a year to the development of MAF, even to visit our overseas programmes in his own time. Praise the Lord for such people and their marriage partners. Our meeting concluded in prayer, and we both expressed a true sense of excitement over what the future holds for MAF. I drove home grateful to the Lord for a truly wonderful week and for the miniscule part I have played in his great plan for mankind.

✦ ✦ ✦ ✦ ✦

The Folkestone office is a busy place, and the diary report that was submitted has a kind of breathlessness about it!

Supporter relations:

✦ Monday

Attended Monday morning staff prayer meeting. The devotion led by Harriet contrasted our problems with those in the developing world – clean water, national health, food, education – reminding us that much of what we complain about would actually come as welcome relief in some countries. A time of prayer drew attention to the fact that three of the eight members of Supporter Relations staff are on holiday. Help Lord!!

Opened the morning post. The combination of a Monday morning post and two weeks into the current *MAF News* meant that there were countless envelopes, many carrying gifts. Each gift has to be accounted for, listed, checked and banked. All those who send gifts receive a personal individualised letter of thanks. It's a new month but there is still work to be done on August's figures. Income comprising approximately 10,000 separate gifts all had to be checked and reconciled against bank statements.

There were a number of phone calls asking why the prayer diary had not been sent. That's odd, because we don't normally send just the prayer diary! Had the mailing house failed to include the diary with *MAF News*? Research showed that the mailing house had done what was required. In fact, although prayer diaries and *MAF News* had been sent to these people, they had not been received! We concluded that the envelopes were still in transit and that the Post Office also had staff on holiday! Nevertheless, further copies of *MAF News* and prayer diaries were sent, first class, to each enquirer.

✈ *Tuesday to Friday*

We have over one hundred Area Representatives and Local Church Representatives each working hard within their constituencies to promote the work of MAF. Phone calls come through regularly for more literature, more books, more videos, updates—'The church I will be visiting supports a family in Kenya. How are they doing so I can pass this on?' Panic sets in. We're expected to know everything about everyone—immediately. More help, please Lord! 'Could I get back to you on that as I will need to check my facts with the Kenya programme?' 'That's fine, but no later than 11.30 as I'll be leaving the house then. Oh, and while I'm on the phone, let me encourage you with something the Lord did at a meeting last night. ...' Praise the Lord! No really, praise the Lord! Because it is all too easy to get so bogged down in administration that we forget what we are about. Fifteen minutes later I was free to phone Nairobi. Hopefully back to the paperwork this afternoon—but rejoicing!

Each day in the post there are questions, enquiries and offers of help. All need individual attention – no standard replies – and before answering they need to be researched.

Examples:

✈ *'I remember reading a bit about being able to include something in a person's will for MAF, so perhaps you might be able to send details of what to do.'*

✈ *'Some years ago I read a book on the history of MAF. Is that book still available and how much does it cost?'*

✈ *'I appreciated the article "Whatever The Cost" and was encouraged by the example of faith in action.'*

✈ *'My purpose in writing is to ask whether, as Madagascar features in the current magazine, you could send me up to 20 copies if there are still some available. If not, then copies of the previous issues. Please do not send them until 13th September as I'll be away.'*

✈ *'I have recently opened a new bank account – details below – and would like our direct debit arrangement changed to this account. Please write and confirm that you have taken the requested action.'*

✈ *'Please note that the person you have written to is my son not my husband. My son writes cheques on my behalf. I am a widow living on my own. Please amend your records. Thank you.'*

And what about the needs of the staff? How are they coping under immense and relentless pressure? Each head of department has, throughout the week, a number of people issues, every one needing individual and careful attention. All requiring precious time, but each one critically important.

One day we'll introduce a system that prevents unplanned interruptions, yes, and pigs might fly! For 'Have you got a minute?' read 'I hope you're not too busy for the next half hour!' The pile of papers and folders carried by the 'intruder' should have been a warning. 'We are planning an unscheduled mailing later in the year to some of our supporters. How will this affect you?' There are some questions to which there is no answer, other than it will probably bowl me over. But of course I don't say that. Instead, 'Well, praise the Lord! Just how many exactly and when? And what is the likely response? But I'm sure we'll cope.' Help Lord—again!

Friday arrived and Fiona Stanton, Head of Supporter Relations, had two meetings—one to discuss legacies and the other an end of week round up, ensuring nothing had been missed and that the objectives for next week are understood.

Personnel:

✈ Monday

Following Monday morning prayers, the big task was to plan for Enquirers Day – a meeting of all those who have expressed an interest in working with MAF and want to know a little more before any commitments are made. The day has been set for 14 October and, to date, all speakers have confirmed that they are able to attend. We anticipate a good number of people although some are only provisional. They will all require information ahead of time, feeding during the day (any special dietary requirements?) any babes in arms or children – do we need crèche facilities? Worked on the production of the programme and provision of visual aids and associated equipment.

The daily mail always brings a welcome list of enquirers, but this week was special because we advertised in the local and national press for an Assistant Planner and a Media and PR Officer, both to work in Folkestone. It's very odd. A recent advert for a Direct Marketing Executive in the same media saw only one response, where this time we are spoilt for choice.

✦ *Tuesday to Friday*

Phone calls received are often very encouraging, but sometimes unexpectedly different! We have to think on our feet. For example:

✦ 'Hi, my parents were missionaries … and I would like to be a pilot. I can go anytime and I have a Private Pilot's Licence.' … 'Right? Just a thought, and please don't be discouraged, but our pilots are required to hold a Commercial Pilot's Licence…. Sorry, how old did you say… 59? Right? Well, again that raises one other small issue.'

✦ 'Hi, Naomi, we are very keen to hear more about the current vacancies in Dodoma. My husband is an experienced vehicle mechanic and I am a teacher. I used to live in Dodoma when I was a child and, in fact, attended the school in which you need teachers.' … 'That's fantastic. I'll get the details in the post this evening.'

✈ The hardest part of the job is turning away people who have a burning desire to serve the Lord overseas with MAF but, for whatever reason, are unsuitable. The difficulty is compounded when their zeal eclipses all thoughts of unsuitability. 'But God has told me!' You cannot give slick answers. The person is so sincere, wrong maybe, but sincere, and that person needs careful attention.

There is a breathless feel about it, but it is a busy, busy place.

13.

TANZANIA

Across the southern border of Kenya lies Tanzania. Also sharing borders with Tanzania are Uganda, Rwanda, Burundi, the Democratic Republic of Congo, Zambia, just the tip of Malawi, and Mozambique. Of course, the eastern border of Tanzania is the Indian Ocean. It is, however, not the only water that lies on the country's borders, as Lakes Victoria, Tanganyika and Nyasa do too. Tanzania is almost twice the size of Kenya. In 1961 Tanganyika gained independence from Britain, followed by Zanzibar (off the coast at Dar es Salaam) in 1963. Together they became the Republic of Tanzania the following year. Over recent years there has been a dramatic growth in the number of evangelical Christians in the country, and many people have been converted. Mission Aviation Fellowship has considerable input in Tanzania, and it is MAF Europe's second biggest operation. The country's main base is at Dodoma.

Tim and Carol Derbyshire live in Dodoma, a much quieter part of Tanzania than Nairobi. He is a MAF aircraft engineer and Carol teaches English at Msalato Bible College. She is preparing a module on children's ministry for the theological degree programme there. Tim's diary begins with some background information.

The price of the country's staple diet fluctuates wildly. This last season was reasonably good and the price went down from 30,000 shillings for a 100kg bag of maize to 13,000. We decided to buy sixty bags for our house workers and a local orphanage, as we provide four bags of maize a month to the orphanage. It went up last month to 18,500, but has now gone down to 16,500 a bag. So we have sixty bags of maize sitting in a container. The problem is how to stop the weevils eating the grain.

Having gone to the local farmers' co-op and asked for advice, I have bought some fumigation tablets. Now I need to keep the maize sealed in the container with the fumigant for seven days. Then the grain has to be left 90 days before it can be eaten. I have decided to remove three more bags to add to the ones we removed yesterday. Shifting three 100kg bags of maize is thirsty work. The container the maize is stored in has seen better days. We must get a corrugated iron roof put over the top before the rain starts.

✈ Sunday

After a lie in, we decided we would like to cycle to church for a change. This morning we had a family service. Carol and I did a Bible reading each. As Sunday is our rest day, we decided to relax and watch a video this afternoon. In the middle of it we heard a loud crash coming from the hall. The loft hatch had fallen from its frame! It seems that the wood dried out and the batons pulled away. I did a temporary repair and put it on my 'Honey do' list for next Saturday. A bunch of bananas had just ripened on one of our trees. I chopped them up into manageable bunches and went to find some people to give them too. One hundred and four bananas are far too many for the two of us!

✈ Monday

I have decided to start studying again for my Pressurised Airframe Licence. It was a shock to realise that it is a year since I made my last attempt at it. Managed to do one-and-a-half hours of studying before going to work. Our aircraft maintenance schedules need revision. New regulations recommend that each type of aircraft has its own maintenance schedule. Currently we have a 'one size fits all' arrangement for our single-engined piston aircraft. The changeover will take time, as our current maintenance schedules do not conform to the recommended format. How do you eat an elephant? One bite at a time. I spent the morning starting the up-dating process.

Tomorrow I'm going to Nairobi to supervise some Non-destructive Testing that needs to be carried out on our Cessna Caravan. As we do not have the expertise in Dodoma an outside contractor will do the work. I spent the rest of the day preparing for the inspection by reading the manuals to find out which areas are affected, and how much of the aeroplane needs to be dismantled. The work is to be done on 5H-ZBZ, a Cessna Caravan 208. I also need to fix a small oil leak in the engine. As it is not a job I have done before I read the manual and checked that we have the necessary spares to complete the job. While I will be working on the aircraft there is to be an ASC meeting to approve the Flight Operations Manual (FOM), Maintenance Control and Organisation Exposition Manuals (MC&OE). As our maintenance facility is relatively small, we have combined the maintenance control manual and the organisation exposition manual into one. The FOM is a real monster; it is divided up into at least five volumes. The MC&OE describes how planes will be maintained and describes the facility at which they will be maintained. The FOM describes how planes will be flown in the air, handled on the ground, what cargo may be carried and the kind of airstrips that may be used.

After work it was the time in the month when we deliver food to the orphanage. I asked the guards to help me lift four 100kg sacks of maize into the back of our trusty Land Rover. Then Carol and I headed off to the market to buy 40kg of beans, some dried fish (the flies come free), a sack of oranges, 10 litres of oil, a sack of washing powder and 25kg of sugar. As Carol's Swahili is better than mine I man the vehicle while she does the bartering. I don't like bartering. However, it's part and parcel of any transaction here and my wife is an expert. We then drove off to deliver the food. The boys unloaded the vehicle, and one of the younger ones swept out the back with a grass brush. We were asked if we would like to be on the orphanage Board of Management. That took us by surprise, and we asked for a few days to think about it. I think the answer will be yes.

✈ Tuesday

Abandoned studying this morning and checked out the Land Rover, as the car often misbehaves when I'm not around. I gathered all the parts and special tools I'll need to change the oil seal on the engine, then opened a work order and made some more progress on the maintenance schedules.

Herman, an avionics technician from Kenya, has been ill with malaria while on holiday in Tanzania. He was returning to Nairobi with us but, as he was late for the flight, I went to look for him and help him with his luggage. The poor chap looked very frail, but is on the mend. We had a pleasant flight. As the MAF guesthouse was full we are staying in a place next to a big shopping centre. Three of us rushed to do a bit of shopping in the first western-style shops we have seen for a while. We have a MAF car at our disposal, which is great. Herman was met by some friends and no doubt headed for his bed. The Nairobi rush hour is something else after sleepy little Dodoma! I realise it is six months since I drove a saloon car. The roads are not in very good condition, and even at the slowest of speeds I keep scraping the bottom of the car on bumps in the road.

✈ Wednesday

For some reason I woke up at 4am and did not get back to sleep. I must be missing Carol! I had a Spanish omelette for breakfast, very nice. We headed off to the MAF hangar at Wilson Airport, only to discover that the ASC meetings were being held at a different venue. I gave the keys to Andrew and Herman (another Herman – a pilot) and they asked for directions to the place where the conference is being held. That was when we discovered that it was quite close to where we spent the night. Ho hum, Murphy 's Law wins again.

My work was delayed because the MAF Kenya Pilatus PC12 had a warning light come on, and had to land and return to the hangar for investigation. As there is not much room in the hangar, our Tanzanian Caravan 5H-ZBZ needed to stay outside until the problem was fixed. It turned out to be a sticking switch. The switch was exercised and the warning light went off. All was well, and the passengers bound for Southern Sudan got back on their plane.

We then de-fuelled 5H-ZBZ because wing struts had to be removed for the inspection, and we wanted the wings to be as light as possible. As I do not know my way around the Nairobi hangar it all took a little bit longer to find things. Two planes were moved out the way, and 5H-ZBZ was tucked into a corner in the back of the hangar. I had two people to help me: Owen, a Kenyan, and Karen, a UK university student who is studying engineering. Quite a few panels had to be removed, and the headliner in the cabin peeled back around the cargo and passenger doors in order to allow access to the doubler panels that needed inspecting. A lot of the interior trim was also removed. Fibreglass had to be taken out, and vibration-dampening panels glued to the airframe were laboriously scraped off. We spent the rest of the day supporting the wings, undoing the strut-securing bolts and, of course, scraping foam from the anti-vibration panels. On the way back to our guesthouse I indulged in another dose of retail therapy and treated myself to an ice cream cone.

✈ *Thursday*

I was asked if it would be possible for me to attend the ASC meeting concerning the Maintenance Exposition Manual. I said it would depend on how the work on the plane progressed. The Inspector arrived and all went well as no cracks were found. I changed the oil seal on the engine then we started putting the aircraft back in one piece. We made good progress, and by the end of the day all the structural members and engine parts were back together, with only the interior trim and some external fairings still to be fitted. As the Inspector had only one more check to do, and it didn't involve anything being dismantled, I decided I would manage to go to the meeting tomorrow. That night we treated ourselves to an Italian meal. Very nice! The food was hot, nicely presented, arrived reasonably quickly and was what I ordered. Such a combination of events is rare in Dodoma. Not sure how I upset room service in the guesthouse, but there was no towel, soap or toilet paper!

✈ Friday

As I didn't need to be at the meeting until 10am, I popped into the hangar to see how work was progressing. All was going well. I checked with the Stores Department to find the things I needed to take with me to Dodoma. There was quite a list: oil, engine cleaner, propeller governor, compass, some spares and a complete propeller. Andrew and Herman decided that two days of meetings were enough and bowed out of the reading of the Exposition Manual. I told Herman that the plane required an engine run and what cargo was to be loaded. The time spent on finalising the wording of the Manual was very worth while, but not that exciting. Around 5pm Herman and Andrew returned for the part of the discussion that concerned them, then we said goodbye to the other delegates. After dinner we headed for the guesthouse and bed. Happy to report the return of a clean towel, soap and loo paper.

✈ Saturday

After breakfast we headed for the shopping centre and checked the lists our wives had given us. We then spied some flowers. Knowing that taking roses to our wives would earn us some serious Brownie points, we all paused to choose some. While Herman did his pre-flight, I checked that all the panels were back in place then signed off the inspection sheets. We had a propeller to load and it took a bit of time to do that. Although we cleared Customs and Immigration, we were delayed because we couldn't find the official who collects the landing fees. After about thirty minutes we found the right person and paid the fee. It was then a case of 'Home James and don't spare the horses!'

We saw a few wild animals in the park as we climbed to our cruise altitude before settling just above the clouds. The flight, which was nice and smooth, took about two hours. Quite a few people were there to greet us when we landed. The Customs official must have had a boring day as he decided to check all our cargo. As the paperwork was correct, and the serial numbers on the aircraft components matched what was on the import documents, everyone was happy. One of our passengers, a Kenyan trainee pilot, was given a hard time because she had the wrong kind of visa. We explained that we had followed the advice given by the head office in Dar es Salaam. You can't apply for a work permit until you gain a local qualification. Jane was due to sit her Tanzanian pilot's exam two weeks ago, but the authority cancelled it. After some profuse apologies by all concerned they let her stay in the country. We unloaded the plane and delivered the roses. They were a definite hit with the ladies. Carol brought me up to date on how things were while I was away. A roof had been put on the maize container. It is not quite finished, but is ninety per cent complete.

✈ ✈ ✈ ✈ ✈

Jan and Anja Smits, along with their three children, live in Dar es Salaam, where Jan is a pilot. His diary begins with an interesting account of the day before diary week, but it is included anyway.

I left the house at 8.30am and arrived at the airport at 9.25am. Joel, our Passanger and Frieght Handler, was already there. We did the required compressor wash of the engine and the pre-flight inspection, then refuelled. At 10am the passengers arrived, eleven young people from Habitat for Humanity who will spend two weeks in Zanzibar building houses. I was warned that one of them was extremely scared of flying, which was clear from her behaviour. Joel and I loaded the 230kg of bags, and after everybody was boarded I did the briefing and prayed for our flight.

As it was busy at the airport, I had to wait for taxi clearance. During the taxi I went through all my checks, received my departure clearance and we were off. The weather was nice and, eighteen minutes later, we were on the ground in Zanzibar. I asked my scared passenger if it was as bad as she expected, but she only thanked me for bringing her back on the ground alive. I wished the team a very good time and success with their building project. When I arrived at the Marshaller's office to pay the landing fee, they asked if I had been informed of the increase in price. It had more than doubled! If they had sent us the information it hadn't trickled down to me yet. I had to walk back to the aircraft to get some more money. The return flight on my own was uneventful although I needed to fly a circle on my final approach to avoid landing at exactly the same time as an Air Tanzania aircraft taking off crossed my runway. After filling out the paperwork I went home leaving Joel to clean the aircraft and put it to bed. My afternoon was spent correcting the bylaws I am writing for Haven of Peace Academy, the Christian International School here in Dar-es-Salaam, of which I am a Board member.

Anja's additions
This was our last weekend before school started again after a ten-week break. I teach English as a Second Language. Unfortunately we have quite a few vacant positions at present.

This means that, for example, the mathematics teacher will also teach some hours of geography, and the English teacher will teach some Bible and history. A new German teacher is coming, but will be a week late for school. I offered to try to organise the German lessons for a week. After some phoning around, a German mother agreed to help out. After sorting out that issue, the children and I went out. We met with two other mums, each with three kids as well, to chat, shop and have lunch. All three husbands were working this Saturday. Later in the afternoon we returned home to find that Jan was back from his flight to Zanzibar. I cooked dinner and sent some e-mails, then we watched an old Dutch movie that some friends recorded from the television.

Next morning we went to the International Baptist Church as usual. Church is filling up again after many people had been away over the months of July and August. Jan did the congregational prayer and helped to serve Holy Communion. All children and Sunday school teachers came together halfway through the service to start a new season of lessons. Unexpectedly, I discovered I was supposed to take a class of four to six year olds! Fortunately there was a children's Bible with pictures, colouring paper and pencils and some games there that I could use. We had a great time making music and singing our favourite songs accompanied by a variety of local instruments. It was indeed a joyful noise to the Lord.

Jan tells how the working week began

✈ Monday

The alarm was set for 5.45am and everybody was ready to go to school at 7.10am. We took the traditional first schoolday photograph of the children in their uniforms. By 7.15am

I was behind my desk planning what was to be done this week. The only flight planned for me is the weekly shuttle to the South on Thursday. I spent much of my morning answering e-mails, filling in MAF questionnaires, and on the telephone arranging things for this week. As well as that, I worked on the bylaws from Haven of Peace Academy. When Anja came home at 11.15am, we had coffee then she started her preparation for teaching Dutch this afternoon. At two 'o clock we left for school. Anja took Mirjam to Dutch school; the others came home with me. After lunch David and Laura started on their homework then spent their allocated time playing games on the computer before playing in the garden and on the trampoline.

✈ Tuesday

After Anja and the children left for school I revised technical information about the aircraft because I have a base check next Monday. When the guard came with our milk I boiled it for the required ten minutes to make it safe to drink. Hilda (our helper in the house) will put it in the fridge when it is cool. I was in the office by 10am, and completed the form for the renewal of my Airport Entry Pass and had it signed by Ritha (Office Manager). John (Procurement and Partnership Developer) and and I discussed the situation regarding our fuel stocks in the South, and how we plan to replenish them, as they are low at the moment. I sent the information about last week's flights to Dodoma, gave Ritha the money paid to me by passengers, and had money returned for the increased landing fees.

Operations called yesterday to see if I had any ticket books I could send to Kasulu. I brought them this morning and arranged to have them put on a Precision Air flight to Kigoma. John has bought a set of Ordnance Survey maps for the Rufiji Delta, the area we want to target with Youth with a Mission. I spent the rest of my time in the office glueing these together and brooding over them. Leaving the office at 1pm I made it to the school by 2. Today was David and Laura's turn for Dutch, so Anja took them, and Mirjam and her friend came home with me. My afternoon was divided between the girls and adding information to the maps of the Rufiji Delta.

✈ Wednesday

Today started with some revision before I left for the airport around 8.15am as I had to be there before ten to give time to get to the police station to have my fingerprints taken for my new pass. The traffic was not too bad until someone decided to block two lanes of a four-lane road. That cost me an extra thirty minutes travel time. Joel went with me to the police station. When the policeman discovered I speak Swahili he suggested I should get myself a Tanzanian wife. Joel explained that I have a wife and three children, but he said I could always take another one, that the maximum is four! For the fingerprinting they needed the form, my old entry pass and also my passport and residence permit, which I didn't take with me. They decided I could bring them later. Fingerprints were taken from both hands, all fingers separately and as a set. After half an hour we were outside again, me with very black fingers.

Later I went to a meeting with Jeremiah from Youth with a Mission (YWAM) and John. We discussed Jeremiah's meeting with the village elders last week during our visit to one of the bigger centres in the Rufiji Delta. The area is very remote and extremely difficult to reach any other way than by boat. We went by helicopter from Helimission. The three of us discussed the needs and how we would like to develop the project. We also began planning a follow-up visit, and the survey of several other places in the Delta that we would like to target with a medical safari. Then brainstormed about ways of getting a better understanding of the needs of the village and how to help. That was just a small part of another busy day.

✈ *Thursday*

I was at the airport by 6.45am, and found Joel there already and the aircraft prepared. We weighed and loaded the freight that we hadn't been able to carry last week. By 7.15am, the first passengers had arrived. Fifteen minutes later the second group came with another 200kg of freight. It was weighed and loaded so that the centre of gravity was within the limit. As we only had five passengers I took out one seat and all the freight was loaded without a problem. The fuel we have in stock in Songea needs to be used up before it expires. I was therefore able to leave with little excess fuel from Dar and could carry a big load. After loading, the passengers boarded and I explained that we would fly first to Songea, refuel, there then go to Matamanga, where some of the boxes from last week and the doctor were going. Then we would go to Mbesa where my other four passengers would disembark together with all the remaining freight. Having explained that, I gave the pre-flight briefing and prayed.

When I turned on the radio after start-up I heard the Administrator from Mbesa asking Operations if we could take someone from Mbesa to Songea for treatment. I quickly calculated my fuel needs then told Operations that the most economic way to do that would be to take the flight in the other direction. Operations approved. After my take-off clearance we did an immediate runway intersection departure and were in the air just after 8.15am. When we reached cruising altitude I told my passengers of the change of plan. It was well received, as they will all be home earlier than expected.

The weather was good, but there was an almost closed layer of cloud below me. By the time I started my descent I knew that Mbesa was completely covered with cloud, but they estimated it to be medium high, which usually means just on the minimum for descent. Songea had patches of clear sky, and up to ten minutes before Mbesa I could still see holes in the clouds. I planned on flying our self-developed cloud break procedure over Mbesa. But while keeping my lowest safe altitude, five minutes before reaching Mbesa I found a hole in the clouds and descended steeply through it to below cloud level. We landed at 10.20am. As it was a school break, all the children were there to see the aircraft come in, and a lot of local adults came to watch the spectacle too. I off-loaded all the freight then weighed and loaded the baggage, mail and freight going back to Dar. Except for a doctor from the hospital who needed to go to Songea for urgent dental treatment there was one other passenger who was not on my list. As I was flying light it was not a problem to take her. The two booked passengers were also there. I calculated my centre of gravity and take-off weight then noted down the take-off and climb speeds for this weight on my knee-board. In between I tried to drink the coffee and eat the cake that was brought for me, and catch up with several people, as well as make arrangements for the mission station truck to bring the empty fuel drums to Dar in order that we can fill them and send them back.

Forty-five minutes after landing we were airborne again for Matamanga. To avoid having to find a hole in the cloud cover I stayed below cloud level. We landed 20 minutes later. I was accused of trying to sneak in quietly, but I had no fuel to spare for an introductory pass over the mission station! The doctor thanked me for the smooth flight; he had not enjoyed last week's afternoon flight. Afternoon flights are always more turbulent than morning ones. We took off again, climbing up through the clouds into smoother air for our 40-minute flight to Songea. There the cloud cover was more patchy and there was no problem getting down through the clouds. As there was a stiff turbulent crosswind, my landing wasn't as smooth as I would have liked it to be.

The people helping with the refuelling were there but they had forgotten to bring the key to the fuel store! One of them went back to the mission station in town, which meant a 20-minute wait for his return. The local Air Traffic Controller was on holiday and his replacement was from the Tanzanian Civil Aviation Authority from Dar. Knowing the airport was quiet - we were only the second aircraft flying into Songea this week - he had brought his son for company. As he was clearly in need of some distraction, we filled the time by talking about aircraft and flying.

When the man with the key arrived back we prepared to refuel, but one of the padlocks on the store wouldn't open until it was given a thorough clean. I was beginning to fear that we'd need to stay the night in Songea! But the men rolled out two drums of fuel and pumped one into each wingtank. It was hard work, and I was glad of their help. That done, I told my passengers they could board again and we took off for the two-hour flight back to Dar. Joel was waiting for us on landing and, after filling in the aircraft log, I left just after 4pm, not looking forward to another hour in traffic.

✈✈✈✈✈

Back in Dodoma, on the first Sunday of September, Andries Schuttinga and his wife, Jolanda, a doctor, don't have an early morning rush. Jolanda explains why.

We had a sleep in because our church doesn't start until 11am! Today I didn't go, as I'm really tired from all my lectures in Kiswahili last week, though the course I'm doing is interesting. When Andries left for church I went to welcome our neighbours back from their week's holiday in Dar es Salaam. It has been quiet without the three boys next door.

✈ Monday

This morning I went off to my course again. Today, we were being taught about the physical problems that people who live with HIV/AIDS can have. Although the lessons continue for the whole day, I left before lunch because of the children. In the afternoon a worried mom of a two-and-a-half-year-old boy called me. Her son had eaten two metres of bubblegum and she wanted to know if he was in danger! I told her that he'd probably be fine, and that no urgent action was needed. Later I took the girls to a three-year-old American boy's birthday party. A blue Bob the Builder cake, ice cream and lots of other goodies made sure that all the twelve toddlers had a great time.

✈ Wednesday

I left our youngest daughter screaming in the arms of Mama Selina, our house helper , as I rushed off to my course this morning. Today's subject was very heavy: how to take care of terminally ill and dying people. It's a subject that I find very difficult to follow in all its depth because I come from such a different culture. But it was a good opportunity to gain more insight into Tanzanian culture, and that made it very interesting. My afternoon was a lazy one with the children. But what joy when one of my fellow MAF wives popped in with some broccoli! Broccoli! I haven't seen that for at least a year!

✈ *Thursday*

I arranged things so that I could attend the course for the whole of today. The focus was on the responsibilities of home-based care workers and their supervisors. As I will probably become a supervisor I could not miss that lesson. It proved to be a little bit of a disappointment though, as we spent most of the time learning how to fill in a variety of reporting forms. At home this evening I found some comfort in our delicious evening meal: fried fish with … broccoli!

✈ *Friday*

Today we had our fortnightly children's club. This began about a year ago, and has been visited by a lot of Tanzanian children from the neighbourhood. Our aim is to share with them the space and toys we have here on our compound, to get to know them a little bit better and, most important of all, to tell them about the Lord Jesus. We start with singing, praying and Bible teaching, then we do either craft work or a group game before a time of free play that finishes with juice and biscuits. Ruth Hyde (another MAF wife) and I organise the club, along with Lodom and Taxson, two youngsters from our church. Today we welcomed about thirty-five kids. Taxson taught them about 'sharing', Lodom led the singing and Ruth prepared the crafts. The children really enjoy playing with the special parachute, a gift from Ruth's church in England. We've promised them a visit to the MAF hangar next time—they'll enjoy that!

Andries gives his version of the week.

Spent most of *Monday* morning talking to Willem van Rheenen, the Programme Manager of Community-based Health Insurance, an NGO active in community health development. Willem is interested in getting Wireless Internet access both for his office and for himself privately. We have recently started providing Wireless Internet services in Dodoma and its catchment area, due to the lack of a dependable provider. This was an instant hit, and we are serving organisations like the Anglican Church of Tanzania and the Bible Society of Tanzania. Willem, who had worked for six years in a small Ethiopian village, was pleasantly surprised by all the luxuries Dodoma has to offer. That made us see how relative everything is, as most of us see Dodoma as a dusty little town with only the basics available. He was surprised when I told him about all the other things that MAF is able to do for his NGO, things like ordering cars from abroad, doing all legal work, eg work and resident permits, and even banking jobs. People often associate MAF only with flying, although we – at least here in Tanzania – do a great deal more than that.

Tuesday morning was taken up with an Aviation Management Meeting. My colleagues and I talked about the new Tanzanian Aviation requirements. A lot of work has been put into rewriting all our manuals and we are now about to implement them. This is a huge job. Sometimes I wonder whether we, being a small aviation organisation, will ever be on top it. Later in the week I talked with Derek Hyde, Finance Manager, about his department. As we have been reshuffling responsibilities we decided to rewrite job profiles and reaccess the salaries our finance staff receive.

During this week I have also been working on things from Radio Uzima, a Christian Radio station that broadcasts from the MAF premises, where they are located in a container behind our garage. A Tanzanian aircraft engineer, Richard Mbuta, who works for Air Tanzania, started Radio Uzima. He worked for us for a time and friendships developed. Richard received a great deal of help from MAF staff when he decided to start a radio station in Dodoma. A year of test transmissions has just been completed successfully, and he had applied for a three-year permit.

Although the radio authorities were happy with Radio Uzima's progress, they have decided that it must close immediately because a radio station should not broadcast from a container. Radio Uzima can only resume if they find a brick building from which to transmit. MAF can help temporarily by putting them up in one of our houses. But as we have new people coming before long, that can only be a temporary solution. Radio Uzima would really like to stay with us because, Richard says, we are neutral denominationally wise, and have engineers close by for them. I am happy to give them part of my plot to build on. This week I wrote to a Dutch Christian TV and radio station for help. It has a weekly programme that invites people to help fund projects around the world.

I came home at lunchtime on *Friday* to discover a thief, caught red-handed while stealing a bike, tied to a laundry pole. It turned out that our guard/gardener chased him half way through town and finally caught up with him as bystanders were beating him. Tanzanians are very cruel to thieves, and almost every day we read about thieves being lynched and killed. Julius Luhala, our guard/gardener, returned him to our compound and questioned him about two bikes that were stolen a couple of weeks ago. As the thief said he knew the people involved, we turned him over to the police, who are now investigating the case. Our five-year-old daughter was surprised, not only because the thief was not wearing a handkerchief over his mouth, but also because he looked so normal! He did not fit with her idea of a thief or robber!

✈ ✈ ✈ ✈ ✈

Herman and Marjan Sterken, with their two children, also live in Dodoma. Herman is Chief Pilot there. Marjan wrote their family diary for the week.

We had a nice church service on *Sunday,* and guests we have staying with us felt at home. The pastor who preached has flown with MAF in the past. Even on Sundays people come and try to sell things; they seem to come especially when we have guests. I don't like bargaining on Sundays.

Monday is my busy day working for MAF. Today I collected prayer items for *News Share.* Some people see *News Share* as their chance to tell you all that is happening in their lives, others are hard to get talking. We are trying to move house this week—when Herman is busier than ever for MAF. He was flying today. Tomorrow he has an Aviation Management meeting then he flies to Nairobi for meetings that will keep him there till Saturday.

The rest of the week grew busier and busier. We've lived in one house for six years and have too much stuff. One nice thing about living here is that you can ask extra house girls to clean and help prepare for a move. As long as you pay them everybody is happy. I just feel a bit uncomfortable that we have so much stuff and they have so little. They take home anything I want to dispose of.

On *Wednesdays* I help our church with their book keeping. It's not that I'm so good at it, but it is nice to work together with Africans instead of always being 'the missionary'. I hoped to finish the work quickly this week in order that I could get on with the move, but you cannot do things quickly in Africa. You need to take time to talk about other things before coming to the point. Normally I like that, but today I would have liked to move more things.

Thursday is my day for teaching Dutch, but today I also had to flight-follow the whole morning. The Operations Manager was in Nairobi, one pilot had to go on a field trip and another was flying. As the receptionist was on holiday that left the flight-follower/bookings officer on his own. I think he was more pleased with some company than with my help! He is a nice older man, quietly doing as much as he can and never complaining when things are too much. The house is now clean and I'm ready to move. Tomorrow (Friday) I hope to spend all day moving—then I have to find a place to put everything.

Just one more thing—as well as writing the prayer letter, my job for MAF is to help international staff with immigration things and I also help take care of guests.

✈ ✈ ✈ ✈ ✈

Radio communications are of vital importance to the safe operation of MAF's fleet of airplanes. Michael Cole is a radio engineer based in Dodoma, and his wife Kathryn teaches there. But working on radio systems is not all that Michael finds himself doing.

We received an e-mail on *Sunday* that needed dealing with before church, as a friend was talking to his congregation about the need for us to raise more financial support—and showing pictures of our work out here. He needed up-to-date news urgently. We went to the 9.15am service at the cathedral where there were lots of visitors. Afterwards we had coffee with friends and a long chat with a lady from Kondoa, whose husband works for the Summer Institute of Linguistics/Wycliffe (SIL). She doesn't see many European women to chat to. I wrote September's prayer points to be e-mailed to our friends giving them our prayer requests.

Woke up to several e-mails on *Monday*, most in response to our prayer points. This week Michael and others have to go to Kilimatinde Hospital to install a solar panel, charge controller and batteries and supply an HF radio with power. They will stay away at least one night. Today he attended continuation training for the engineers and spent some time studying for his licence exams.

It was Kathryn's first day back at school after a week's holiday.

I expected two new children in the nursery where I work, but only one arrived. On the way home I went to an Asian lady's house; she sews clothes for me. Today I collected a skirt and dress; she charged just £3.50 for making them. I was trying to catch up with e-mails after tea when Wilson, one of the guards, phoned from the hospital, and then came to see us. His wife fell off a bike yesterday and broke her wrist. They spent all day today at the hospital waiting to have it set, only to find they didn't have enough money to pay for the bandages! So she went home to spend another night in a great deal of pain. We were able to give him the money to sort it all out tomorrow.

Michael

Spent all day (*Tuesday*) preparing for my safari into the bush. A frame for the solar panel had to be made in town, and an aerial connection lead was made using new cable but used connectors. Worked late to get everything finished, then loaded the vehicle with Allan Conrad. Too tired to go to the prayer meeting. Had an early night as we aim to be on the road by 7am.

I was on the road by 7.15am (*Wednesday*) with Allan and Markus Riegert, a MAF pilot. Three hours driving found us at Kilimatinde Hospital to meet the people who are levelling two new airstrips. We went through all the protocol of greetings and signing their visitors' book. They had also prepared *chai* for us – Swahili for tea, for the uninitiated – very milky and very sweet! After a suitable time we took to the road again with an extra three people on board. When we inspected the airstrip we found that, although a lot of the groundwork had already been done, a large baobab tree obstructed the approach end of the runway. Markus and Allan requested that the tree be chopped down to give a safer approach.

From there we drove to Mpapa where we off-loaded all the equipment and discussed where the radio aerial was to be sited. Allan asked the man in charge for a team of people to dig holes and collect the sand and stones that we needed to make concrete into which to set the aerial bases. I was left there to do as much of the installation work as possible while Allan and Markus went on to inspect another proposed airstrip. The holes were dug for the posts and the sand arrived—but no stones. Meanwhile, I managed to get the supply cable from solar panel to charge controller under a join in the roof's metal sheeting, and I also screwed the charge controller to the wall and connected the cable to it.

However, I was starting to get worried as it was nearing nightfall and no stones had appeared. Eventually some arrived and the mixing process began. Before long we ran out of stones and had to borrow them from another hole while some boys were sent to collect more. The first post base went in and we waited in the dark for more stones to arrive. The dry mixing was finished, and we were about to start the wet mixing when I noticed Allan and Marcus's headlights in the distance – sigh of relief as we'd already had a puncture and I knew they had no spare tyre! Allan soon took charge and that post base was finished. Our original plan was to sleep in Allan's tent but, as it was too dark to see to put it up, we slept in an unfinished house, after a meal of rice and beans.

Next morning (*Thursday*) Allan and Markus went on to the roof and installed the solar panel and its frame, as well as connecting the cable. I was busy inside making all the necessary connections. Outside the other two, with the help of local men and boys, joined together the lengths of pole to give us two 16 foot masts. All went to plan, and the aerial was erected just as *chai* appeared. Straight after *chai* we fired up the radio and Markus was able to talk to MAF Dodoma. We also spoke with a very surprised MAF Pilot, Andy Blake who was flying right over in the west of the country! After Marcus instructed the people how to use the radio, we said our farewells and headed back to Kilimatinde via yesterday's airstrip. The men had already started to chop down the tree and the last 50m of scrub had been burnt and cleared. That was a lot of work in a short time.

We took the man in charge of the airstrip clearance work back to his village where he proceeded to catch a goat and give it to us as a gift! Having tied its legs together, and secured it into the back of the Land Rover, we left for Kilimatinde Hospital, where we dropped off the men who had gone with us to help. It was still light when we arrived home in Dodoma.

Kathryn

Gave Wilson (the guard) money today to send his son to Dar to see if his wife's younger sister would come back to Dodoma to look after the family while his wife's wrist is in plaster.

Canadian chief pilot Jeff Plett, at right, takes notes as Jon Lewis, far left, interviews two Angolan church representatives as part of an MAF survey of transportation needs in Angola.

Amanda Leek homeschooling in the Arnhem Land (Northern Territories).

Dean Outstation in Arnhem Land (Northern Territories).

A Beaver plane landing in Bangladesh

Emil Kundig (back) standing with Tha and fuel drums in Cambodia

Dan Lawrence (on right) with Student in Three Hills – MAF Canada

Karin Knevel
working with
street kids in Chad

Congo Airstrip

A gunshot
patient in
a plane in
Ecuador

Ken Milligan helping
in a hangar in Kenya

Building a
new airstrip in
Madagascar

Putting
down cement
for a new
airstrip in
Madagascar

Outside a Ger
in Mongolia

Inside a Ger
in Mongolia

Morning
devotions for
the staff in
Mareeba

Unloading plywood off plane in Papua

Chris Hansen and Richard West in Papua New Guinea

Chris and Janice Hansen with Rochells, Jessica and Simeon

Richard and Cherie West with Larissa and Marcus

Twin Otter in flight in Papua New Guinea

Unloading the Caledonian Connenction in South Africa

Zebedius cleaning aircraft in South Africa

A medical plane and ambulance in Tanzania

Village people around the aircraft in Tanzania

Engineers working on the aircraft in the Uganda hangar

Map of Papua New Guinea

Top – Map of Bangladesh
Below – Map of Cambodia

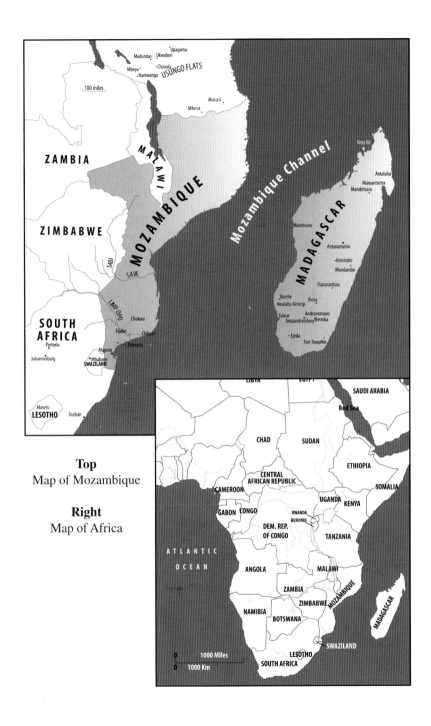

Top
Map of Mozambique

Right
Map of Africa

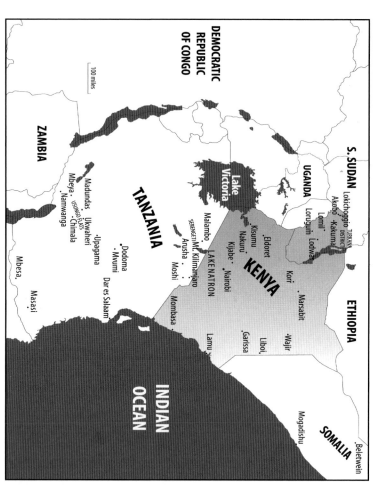

Map of Kenya

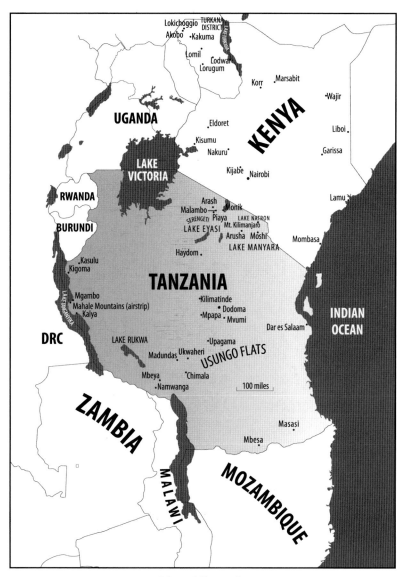

Map of Tanzania

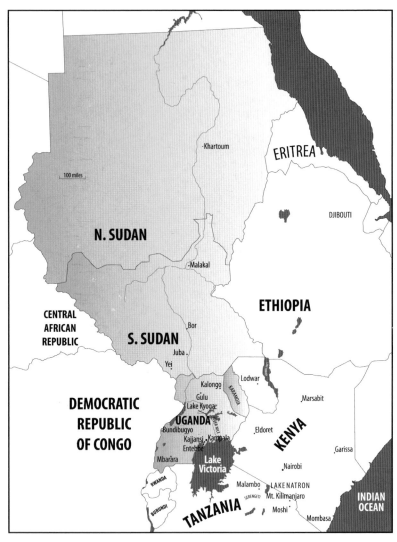

Map of Uganda

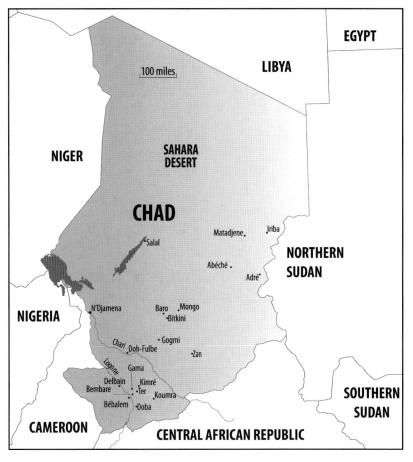

Map of Chad

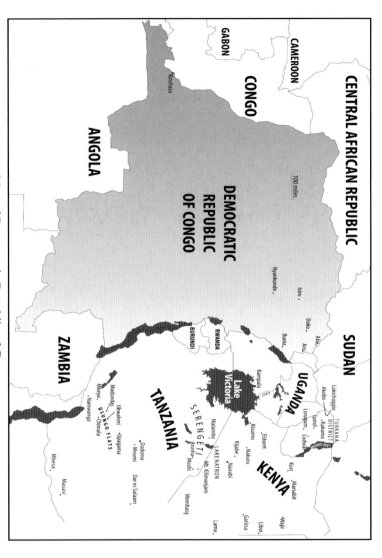

Map of Democratic Republic of Congo

Michael

Everybody was surprised to see me at work as they all thought we were returning today, *Friday*. I continued tidying the rewire of N5329U, the C206 from the MAF Chad programme that I've been working on, not continuously, for almost a year now. Today I started to put light switches and things back in. After work we took Emily, an English university student, to an African home for an African meal. This consisted of ugali (maizemeal), spinach, rice, beans and meat. Kathryn made a coffee sponge cake and we took that and some cold sodas with us. Our hosts were Emanuel, a pastor, and his wife. They have a three-month-old baby son who was dressed in a little woolly hat!

On *Saturday* we both went to the Agape Children's Centre to take some photos of three older boys. When we were in England we were given some money to use towards the education of some individual children. We promised to send photos of the boys who benefited from it, and had arranged for the staff to keep them behind to be photographed.

✈ ✈ ✈ ✈ ✈

Also at the Dodoma base we find the Schlatters and their three children. Hansjoerg is a pilot, and he and Monika lead a busy life.

✈ *Wednesday*

When I finished preparing my flight and the airplane for tomorrow, I decided to take some time with the family to go to the swimming pool. We hadn't been there long when Andries, our Programme Manager, showed up to ask me about a possible medical transfer – also tomorrow – all the way from the west of Tanzania to a bigger hospital near Dodoma. I went over to see if it would be possible to combine the two flights. It looked okay, and I just needed about 200 litres more fuel. As it was already past 5.00pm I could only fuel from 20 litre jerry cans. The patient also needed oxygen, so I checked our kit to make sure there was enough for a two-hour flight. A call came later saying that the medical transfer won't happen, as the patient didn't get a referral to the other hospital. Without that you cannot transfer a patient. Thursday's flight was uneventful.

✈ *Friday*

When I was on my way to town to get a police report for the insurance company about our stolen bicycle, I heard news about another medical transfer from Dodoma to Moshi, to one of the biggest hospitals in Tanzania. This one could not wait till tomorrow. I was ready around noon, but the patient's relative did not arrive till some time after that to pay for the flight. Since the patient had lung problems I flew low, even though that makes for a very bumpy ride. We arrived safely in Moshi and the patient took a taxi to the hospital.

✤ ✤ ✤ ✤ ✤

Annie Lawson, from Scotland, works as an aircraft engineer, but that was not what was occupying her time during diary week. She was on holiday and spent her time in church work.

✈ *Sunday*

On standby but not called out today.

8 – 9.15am. Went to mortuary to pick up a body for a family.

9.30am. Collected the youth choir at church and set off for Ntyuka. As they have no pastor I take it in turns with another pastor to minister there.

10am – 2.30pm. Spoke at the service at Ntyuka, then spent two hours counselling a church elder who responded to the message.

3 - 4pm. Dropped off members of the choir and made a visit.

4.30pm. Met with the church elders to discuss the rather unexpected arrival of a new pastor for one of our village churches.

5pm. Had fellowship at the home of one of our church members in Chang'ombe.

6pm. Home – then my pastor called to tell me to go to one of the church member's homes for something... at 7 - 8pm!

✈ Monday

Up at 6.30am. Did a bit of work on the video equipment in preparation for doing outreach in Iringa.

7am. Did some work on two planes. Both are okay to go although there is no flying booked for them.

8am. Prayers

8.30 –10-ish. Did some training for the engineering team. Joe (Avionics Enginner) and Kees (Chief Enginner) taught for the rest of the day. Made new clean-up rota and a pile of other etceteras. Finished assessing Ben and Erardy's exam papers and prepared a sheet of model answers for them to see where they went wrong!

12.15 – 1.15pm. Arranged for the gardener to feed the hen and the cats every day and for a house-help to clean and get a few things in for me coming back. Made all other necessary arrangements for being away.

4pm. Fixed video equipment and packed the Land Rover then spent the evening preparing for the Iringa trip. We leave first thing tomorrow.

✈ Tuesday

Drove all the way to Iringa and arrived there at about 2pm. Went to the bus station to pick up our preacher who preferred travelling by bus to avoid all the dust! Went a further 35km to Tanangozi where we were welcomed and set up camp in a house.

Spent the evening with the evangelist from the Lutheran church. There was also a long discussion about the necessity for an official paper from the village elder that would allow us to minister under the protection of the law.

✈ Wednesday

Up at 6am for a wash in cold windy shed.

7.30 – 8.30am. Prayer and evaluation with outreach team and local workers—a meeting like this took place every day.

Morning—Henry took the first seminar in the church while Ruth and I taught the prayer and stewarding teams. We also visited the Head Teacher of the school as the meetings are to be held on their football pitch.

2pm. Took equipment to the football field. Ten people made commitments after the big outdoor meeting.

Generator troubles delayed the start of the video till 9pm. All videos this week concern HIV education and the dangers of drunkenness.

11pm-ish. Talked with the team of local church elders about life in general. Most of them had never spoken to a white person.

✈ Thursday

The same routine plus:

9am – 12 noon. Taught a seminar in the church then visited a lady's home. Met a blind chap who prefers beer to Jesus.

1pm. Lunch and counselling, prayed for an impotent chap from the church.

2pm. Took equipment to the football field then started the meeting late to fit in with the school programme. Eleven people made commitments. The sick were prayed for.

2 – 7pm. At base camp we were asked to pray for a lady. Counselling and prayer for thirty minutes; quick meal and then out with the video. Film shown until about 10pm. Friday was much the same.

✦ Saturday

I did a seminar for singles while the Kambengas did the marriage seminar. Then I had lunch at a lady's home and we talked about Christianity. She is keen, and will come to the meeting, but she's frightened about having to stop making beer for a living. I met another lady who is a great drunkard. Both ladies went to the meeting later. We showed the film in two locations in the evening and were home late. That didn't stop us spending an hour talking to the locals again, now that they are used to my white face.

✦✦✦✦✦

Heri Shekinghenda is a Tanzanian engineer, who studied at Moody Bible College in Chicago. He was 'discovered' because he used to be a language trainer in the language school that MAF missionaries attended!

On *Monday* I didn't do a lot on aeroplanes. Instead I worked on getting hangar equipment in good condition. I prepared some new pads for the jacks we use for jacking aeroplanes. I also did some studying for exams that I expect to sit at the end of this month.

I supervised a routine check on 5H-MSM on *Tuesday*. This is an aeroplane we maintain from a customer in Iringa. This check included doing inspections and necessary repairs to comply with the 50-hour inspection schedule. My personal responsibility was to inspect the fuselage, empennage (tail section of the aircraft) and the engine. Supervising included making sure that all the work needing to be done on this check was done and the papers signed accordingly. I also did an engine ground run to make sure that the engine performed as it is required to.

I started working on another 50-hour inspection on *Wednesday*, this time on one of our own aeroplanes from the Kasulu base. A cylinder was removed to replace a worn-out exhaust valve. It was then replaced and I worked on a detailed inspection of the engine. This procedure took more time than a normal inspection. *Thursday* and *Friday* were spent repairing and replacing the engine baffles and continuing with the engine inspection.

✈ ✈ ✈ ✈ ✈

Diary week saw Pilot Andy Blake thinking about further development of MAF's work in the Rufiji Delta Region.

At the beginning of the week I positioned Cessna 206 5H-MSY to Dodoma (for maintenance). There were several snags that needed a bit of TLC. The following day, *Tuesday*, I drove the MAF Land Rover down to Dar es Salaam and stayed the night at Jan and Anja Smit's house. We departed on *Wednesday* morning for Dar Airport to lift three drums of Jet-A into the back and pick up John Mahigu from the MAF Dar office in preparation for our trip to Mchukwi. This is a Free Pentecostal Church in Tanzania airstrip and will be used by MAF as a springboard to further development in the Rufiji Delta Region. On this particular trip I was wearing my Tanzania Civil Aviation Authority (TCAA) hat as an Airstrip Inspector. The idea was to inspect the strip and see if it was ready for granting a renewal of a licence. It didn't take too long to do that then we returned to Dar.

Thursday was spent writing up the report and arranging for it to be sent to TCAA. I also managed to get a number of logistical things done with the help of the Dar office: refilling nine gas bottles for the cooker at home, receiving things from my bank in the UK, and taking delivery of Bibles for Kalemie in Congo. On *Friday* and *Saturday* I was with a friend from Kasulu and his wife; it was nice to catch up with them. I also met with Helimission informally, and was presented with a nice picture of 5H-MSY landing in Mahale! Shopping was the main priority as there are no 'real' shops in or near Kasulu. I even managed to pick up a bicycle for a Dodoma pilot's daughter.

✈ ✈ ✈ ✈ ✈

On the first day on which MAF staff were asked to keep diaries, Allan Conrad, Facilities Manager at Dodoma, went to a church that was new to him.

I went to a church I hadn't visited before, the Africa Inland Church in Dodoma.

There I met with one of the choir leaders who wants to come with me when I go out to some of the villages to have seminars and show the Jesus film. We'll arrange for that to happen. This afternoon I visited a pastor with whom I worked in Sanjaranda from 1991 to 1997. He moved to Dodoma a short time ago.

Allan listed his activities day by day.

✈ Monday

- ✈ Morning prayer in the hangar.
- ✈ Brought freight to the plane.
- ✈ Checked with the departments on the work for today.

✈ Checked a vehicle for the Summer Institute of Linguistics/Wycliffe.

✈ Repaired a seatbelt for the new school bus.

✈ Up-dated the staff pictures.

✈ Made some copies of a CD from our fifty years' jubilee in Sanjaranda for the old Principal who attended and wanted a report of the event.

✈ Tuesday

✈ Morning prayer in the hangar.

✈ Checked house no. 11 for the Sterken family moving in.

✈ Patrick and I exchanged prices on materials for the garage.

✈ Coordinated the trip to Kilimatinde for checking airstrips.

✈ Prepared equipment for HF radio and solar installation.

✈ Packed for overnight in the bush with tent and cooking equipment.

✈ Got the car ready for travel to the bush.

In addition, Michael Cole has previously recorded the remainder of Allan's week.

Derek Hyde is Finance Manager at Dodoma. He and his wife live very busy lives in the service of the Lord and of the people of Tanzania. They have three children. Ruth begins their diary.

When we arrived at church around 9.00am we were pleasantly surprised that the Swahili service (before our

English service) was already coming out. That was good as we had a lot of things to set up for the family service we were taking. I did a drama sketch at the start of the service and led the singing. Derek played his guitar with Marcus Riegert also on guitar and Liza, our recently arrived German teacher, on flute. All the children – our own and others – helped with the action songs.

Afterwards I chatted to an Australian couple who are here for three months, pushing a few doors to see where God leads them. They feel led to Africa and, as they have friends here in Dodoma, they have come out here. The wife, who is a nurse, enjoys small children. I've invited her to come into the nursery sometime next week.

There followed a relaxing afternoon and a game of Risk in the evening. Derek won!

Ruth *(another Ruth, a doctor who was staying with the Hydes)* shared with us the challenges she faces in setting up a medical clinic in Tabora. She's been in Tanzania just over a week and, having travelled by bus to Dodoma, on to Tabora by train and then back here by train, all in the space of ten days, she is ready to set her feet down in one place for a little while. We talked with her about our struggles and the many blessings that God has bestowed on us since our arrival in Dodoma a year ago. Both Derek and I felt encouraged by some things Ruth shared with us, and we had a short time of prayer to round off the evening.

Derek's additions

On Saturday morning, while Ruth was shopping, I watched over Matthew as he did his homework. I also tried to catch up with a few items of work. *Sunday*: it was good to have Marcus joining us in the service, to cover up for my mistakes. The flute sounded great too. The kids were very quiet and attentive during their story. One of the children said that the storyteller should be a teacher, which was no surprise as both her parents and grandparents are/were, though she says she will break the mould! I enjoyed winning *Risk*, even though I thought they were going to gang up on me towards the end, but they left it too late. All in all, we had a very encouraging weekend, especially the chats on Sunday.

Ruth's Monday morning

We did a variety of activities with the children in the nursery, and caught up on the helpers' news. The son of one of them was married last week and that was the main topic of discussion. I've never been to a Tanzanian wedding, and I was invited, but it's not so easy with children in tow, especially as it was in Dar—a six-hour drive away. (Writing that made me realise that it isn't easy trying to immerse yourself in Tanzanian culture, especially when you have the demands of a young family).

Ruth takes up her diary again on Thursday

Awake at 5.30am. Got up and made a cup of tea. Read my Bible and spent some time thinking about whom we live for. It's a real challenge to love God always with all your might and to love others as yourself, always.

- ✦ 7.25am. Children off to school.

- ✦ Left messages for home-helps' work and got things together for nursery.

- ✦ Had a good session at nursery.

- ✦ 12.30pm. Derek returned from office early for lunch today.

✈ Exchanged greetings in Swahili with Mama Pendo and Elizabetti.

✈ The afternoon went fairly quickly. I was on the computer most of it, sorting out presentations and catching up on e-mails.

It was my day off today, *Friday*.

10.00am. Drove into town. I needed to take some batiks and items of clothing for the 'fundi'. I gave her three items to make for me. Then it was on to the old fellow outside Bojanis' material shop for him to hem some things and also to make me some trousers.

Next on the list was 'Two Sisters' – our equivalent of Tesco – to buy a few groceries.

Looked over our furlough presentations and made a few changes to them. At lunchtime Derek showed me how to put a video clip into a PowerPoint presentation. That will be useful.

Children's Club this afternoon. Taxson and Lodom did the teaching and the songs. This was our first afternoon club, before now we met in the morning. Many more children were able to come—praise the Lord!

I had an invitation from Mariam, my nursery help, to go with her and two others from her church to the village of Swaswa to take a service in the church and have lunch together on *Saturday*. She wanted me to see how she acts out the Bible story of Dorcas, which I did some time ago in the infant assembly. Mariam was encouraged by the way I did it and thought it would be a good story to act out to the women and children in the villages. Having picked up Mariam and her friends, we drove to Swaswa, on the other side of Lion Rock, where we were welcomed with hugs and handshakes all round. There was a choir and ladies playing drums and percussion; it was a great sound. Everyone was in good singing voice! The service started around 11.00am. Mariam had asked me if I would share a story in Kiswahili. Thankfully I had one prepared for the children's club and read it.

We played a couple of games with the church members and had some fun together. I felt very relaxed and comfortable, even though my understanding of what was being said was not always great. Mariam helped with some of the translation. It should be good for my learning of the language! Around 2.00pm we stopped for lunch, by which time I was ready to sit down and get some food inside me. We were invited into a home where we shared a large plate of rice, beans and meat in a spicy sauce. It was a really good day and I felt blessed by the experience.

✦✦✦✦✦

Our snapshot of Mission Aviation Fellowship's work in Tanzania concludes with a visit to Andrew and Jean Boyd, who live in Dodoma with their three sons.

On *Sunday*, Jean records, we went to church and stayed for coffee afterwards. In the afternoon we had a visit from our neighbours, then spent the rest of the time with the family. I also caught up on writing some e-mails to friends and supporters. *Monday* saw the children returning to school after the half-term break. I visited a Tanzanian friend who is very unwell then finished the final assignment for the Old Testament Introduction course I'm doing. As the family at home appreciate having photos, I printed out some to send to them, and wrote yet more e-mails to supporters. E-mail is a great way of keeping in touch. On *Tuesday* morning I studied, and read in the afternoon after I'd seen the boys through their homework. Not only the children went to school on *Wednesday* as I spent the morning helping in the classroom. There were no e-mails for a while on *Thursday* because the electricity was off. After spending ten minutes trying to find out why there was no power, I arranged for the generator to be put on. I spent some time in the morning studying, then went to school to help in the classroom again. *Friday* saw me at school for the assembly then it was back to my studies.

It was a week without husband and father for Jean and her boys as Andrew was involved in the meetings in Nairobi. He returned home on Saturday. His meetings have already been well documented. Andrew returned to news of Friday's break-in. Within hours the Boyds had acquired a dog to help with security. It must have been refreshing after his intensive week in Nairobi, for Andrew to relax with Jean, the boys and one new and, no doubt, excitable dog!

14.

THE NETHERLANDS

Several members of MAF's staff who have contributed their diaries to this book come from the Netherlands, among them Pilot Marco Koffeman and his wife, Anneke, who are based in Bangladesh with their two sons. Marco pointed out the importance of the children of those working overseas keeping up with their own language and culture. It is also important that those working far from home are aware of the prayerful and practical support of MAF's home supporters, and often this is channelled to them through their national office. Mission Aviation Fellowship Netherlands' office was busy in the week in which this snapshot was taken. Not only was MAF NL ready for mailing, but a new member of staff joined the team there.

✈ Diary week

We start every morning with a prayer meeting in which we read a short passage from the Bible and focus on two of our international staff, as well as asking the Lord's blessing on our day-to-day work. On *Monday* this week volunteers came in to pack MAF NL, our quarterly magazine. Thanks to their dedicated work we save about €15,000 annually on distribution costs. As some volunteers were still on holiday the group was smaller than usual, but they worked quickly and needed only one day to do what we thought was a two-day job. The afternoon was taken up with a meeting of the business taskforce, made up of six businessmen together with our CEO (Adri van Geffen) and Marketing Manager (Christine Zwanenburg). They considered the best methods of reaching other businessmen for MAF. One of the things discussed was a sponsor-trip to Kenya and Tanzania, another was the possibility of organising a special day for business people.

A new member of staff started work on *Tuesday*, and three mornings this week were spent explaining about MAF and outlining her work in the office. There was a worldwide focus too, as six trusts whose main interest is in Papua were sent proposals for work they might be interested in supporting there and in Papua New Guinea. That evening the CEO called on one of our volunteers who had given a presentation to a church youth group using MAF materials. The presentation was well received and he was given €350 for MAF.

Finance was under discussion on *Wednesday*, specifically the budget for MAF NL's international staff for next year. At the beginning of 2004 we heard from several international staff that their monthly allowance was too low, especially when they had to deal with unexpected expenses. After thorough investigation by the Head of Personnel (Reina Folkerts) it was decided that we would raise the basic amount for 2005 by fifteen percent. Finance was on the agenda till the end of the week, as on *Thursday* the August figures were given to the CEO. It was a good month, and on track to reach the 2004 budget goal. *Friday* brought a letter telling us that we were to receive a legacy of about €70,000, the single highest amount received by MAF NL. We finished the week happy. However, work was not over for everyone as the PR-Coordinator (Evelyne van den Ovear) and two volunteers were present at a MAF display stand on *Saturday*. They were able to tell many people about the Mission, though fewer became donors than was expected.

15.

UGANDA

When Uganda gained its independence from Britain in 1962 it entered into very troubled times. It was not until the late 1980s that the people knew any measure of peace and stability; even now Northern Uganda is troubled by rebel activity. But political unrest is not the only horror that the Ugandan nation has had to face as AIDS went on to cut a swathe through its population. Having lost an unknown number of people during Idi Amin's dictatorship, it went on to lose an unknown number – especially of its young people – through AIDS. However, the Ugandan government tackled the problem head-on and the number of new people being infected by AIDS has slowed down. The church also played a huge role in educating the people.

Formerly known as the Pearl of Africa, Uganda is a much more fertile land than some of those that surround it. The weather in a good year provides three growing seasons, and the main cash crop is coffee. The capital city, Kampala, has a population of upwards of 1.2 million, and the next largest city, Gulu, 110,000. Approximately 87 percent of Ugandans live outside the urban areas, and it is in the most isolated of these areas that MAF works to best effect.

✈ ✈ ✈ ✈ ✈

Christiaan Koetsier, Chief Engineer, describes a week's work in the MAF hangar at Kajjansi, and outlines the aircraft maintenance routine.

✈ Monday

The day in the hangar began, as they all do, with morning devotions and prayer. This week Chad is being prayed for within the whole of MAF. Today I led the worship myself. Our prayers in diary week are to be taken by MAF staff from four different nations. This was the final day of the Cessna 208 Caravan's phase II inspection. When all repairs and checks had been carried out a test run was called for (on the ground) to ensure the engine was functioning to the manufacturer's specifications; it performed without a hitch. The final quality check is a test flight and that was carried out over Lake Victoria for around twenty minutes. Every aspect of chartered flight and safety features were tested to ensure that the aircraft was airworthy. Engine and flight performance data were collected and referenced against known values as a final check of performance. Once again the aircraft performed to textbook standards.

It was also the first day of the Cessna 210 OPS (Operation) 1 check. OPS checks and phase checks were carried out on every aircraft in several stages. The overall aim is to spread the maintenance, and the workload for the engineers, rather than the plane being down for a long period. It also ensures that the aircraft are not out of service for prolonged periods. For the Cessna 206/210 there are four OPS inspections per 200 hours of flying. The first one contains a detailed inspection of the fuselage, cabin and landing gear. It also requires a routine inspection of the engine, propeller, wings and empennage. Each OPS inspection takes about three days, and they are carried out at fifty flying-hour intervals.

With both the Caravan and the 210 in the hangar this leaves only the Cessna 206 operational. Two other MAF aircraft are currently based at Kajjansi airfield. Both belong to MAF US and are used for flights into the Democratic Republic of Congo. They have been here since civil unrest caused them to leave the DRC nearly two years ago. Although they have their own engineering staff, MAF Uganda helps and our facilities are used. This increases the workload and reduces the available space.

We had a phone call today from the Ugandan International School to arrange an educational visit for twenty-one eight-year-olds. This is not uncommon and MAF encourages people taking an interest in what we do. As with any day there is the possibility of something unexpected, and today the unexpected happened. In the afternoon the Cessna 206 returned from its scheduled flight with starting problems. Because both of our other aircraft were in the hangar it was important to remedy the situation quickly.

✦ *Tuesday*

Michael, a Kenyan who has worked for MAF in Uganda for the last year, took our morning prayers today. His responsibility is the parts room and he ensures it is well stocked and that parts are there when required. This is an essential job that requires a full-time staff member.

The OPS 1 check continued on the Cessna 210. Each of the rudder pedals in the cockpit must be removed and the space in which the pedals are positioned is extremely tight. Getting spanners into some of these spaces is tough and very time consuming. While that was being carried out another engineer started the routine inspection of the propeller, wings and engine.

✦ *Wednesday*

Morning devotions were today led by Geoffrey, who is one of MAF's Ugandan national engineers. He is currently working on completing the Cessna 210 OPS 1 maintenance checks. The day's work was focused on finishing that job. The rudder bars were removed allowing the inspection to take place. New rudder bars were obtained and their installation began. The MAF US Cessna 206 aircraft was moved into the hangar today in preparation for new rudder bars being fitted. It also requires an empennage installation and inspection. This will all be carried out towards the end of next week.

✦ *Thursday*

This morning devotions were led by Richard. He is one of the flight dispatchers and, like Geoffrey, is a Ugandan national. Richard also provides assistance with maintenance work and in maintaining the hangar itself. The rudder bars of the Cessna 210 were finally installed and the flight controls checked and adjusted. With this completed the final few checks could be carried out on the aircraft. The internal furnishings were removed from the MAF US aircraft in order that maintenance can be carried out. Starter problems on the Cessna 206 were resolved.

There are several other aircraft operators on Kajjansi airfield. These include private owners and a local flying club. There is also a plane belonging to the Ugandan Wildlife Authority. From time to time MAF is able to lend a helping hand through checking tyre pressure, and so on, for them.

✦ Friday
David led devotions today. He is on a six-month placement with MAF in Uganda as an engineer. This time will allow him to see what life within MAF is really like. It will also enable him to decide if a life serving with MAF is a decision he wishes to take, and also test how adaptable he is to other cultures. The final work was done on the Cessna 210. This included a check of the landing gear to ensure that all was functioning correctly. Due to time restrictions the final test flight was postponed until Monday morning. All other ground checks were carried out and the aircraft performed perfectly. The day ended at 4.30pm, and the engineers left for a well-deserved break

✦ ✦ ✦ ✦ ✦

Erasmus Byaruhanga, Finance Assistant, listed his week's activities day by day. Two days give a good idea of Erasmus's work.

✦ Tuesday 7 September
Preparing for the day.

> ✦ Preparing MTN June payment details. (Paul Brooks, Finance Manager, explains: *MTN is our mobile phone company here in Uganda. Medair have*

their phones through us, along with MAF US. In total there are some forty-four phones to sort out!)

✈ MTN June reconciliation and correcting.

✈ Collecting the previous day's flight manifest.

✈ *Wednesday 8 September*

Preparing for the day.

✈ Checked the posting of vouchers and receipts.

✈ Collecting the previous day's manifest.

✈ Payment of cash on voucher.

✈ Balancing the cash to the cash book.

✈✈✈✈✈

Harriet Aryam, also a Finance Assistant, has different duties to Erasmus.

✈ Call some stubborn customers for payment.

✈ Reconcile a payment to the outstanding invoices and communicate over unpaid balance.

✈ Match accounts (working on August account).

✈ Check through CAA ASC for accuracy.

✈ Call bank to see if all effects are cleared.

✈ Make cheque payments.

✈ Balance reconcile loan balance.

✈ Draw cash from bank.

✈ Help with balancing cash.

Hadija Shirazi, Administrator/Office Manager, listed a day's activities, and a very varied one too.

Every morning I start with a small prayer before we all gather for the official office morning prayers. Then I look at my mail, forward whatever needs to be forwarded, printed or answered.

I list down the assignments of the day for the Logistics Officer. My other duties are: answering phone calls, meeting with people whose problems need solving, dealing with vehicle fuel vouchers, updating the holiday planner, making the monthly timetable for taking prayers, paying the office electricity and phone bills, checking what is prepared for the staff lunch, making sure that the office and compound are kept clean, and a long number of jobs all of which add up to my job.

✈ ✈ ✈ ✈ ✈

Klazina Pap is married to Pilot Gerrit. Klazina gives a full and interesting account of diary week, a real insight into what it is like to be a MAF wife and mother.

✈ Sunday

Sunday morning we went through our usual routine of getting ready for church after breakfast. We finally all climbed in the car, on time for a change, and went to the New City Bible Church. We really like this church. The Ugandan pastor was trained in the US and preaches simple but deep messages. It's a growing Presbyterian church. Some of our friends have also joined us there. We feel that we can really fellowship together as believers.

By 4.30pm we were getting ready for the next service, this time at the International Fellowship we have attended since we first moved to Uganda almost six years ago. Our kids like it because they go to Sunday school. I usually play piano and Gerrit teaches the older boys. We both had today off, and it was a nice change to sit together. Josiah fell asleep on my lap for the entire service. The speaker talked about tribulation. Acts 14:22 says we *will* have tribulation; not that we might go through tribulation. It made me a bit worried about what God has in store for me. On the other hand, it's encouraging to know that trials are not bad but for our good, contrary to what so many try to tell us in the world today. The speaker had a good story of someone who even tried to say that Paul the apostle was a very weak Christian because of all his trials, that had he been thinking more positively these trials wouldn't have come upon him! Very interesting, this western, prosperity-type of thinking, but wrong.

✈ Monday

We were expecting company; since our return to Uganda we have had lots of it. First a medical student asked if he could stay with us for a week. Then last week we had a Kenyan engineer staying. He left on Friday and today a good friend from Bible school is coming with her friend to stay with us for a few days. I've been looking forward to this visit.

Our friends were late, and as we were waiting for them to arrive I started winding myself up. Was the taxi reliable? Were my friends waiting at the airport in vain for it to show up? Explanations were given as soon as they appeared … lost luggage! They had many forms to fill out and our taxi driver had patiently waited for them; he was reliable! After a warm reunion I had to go out, as I am a discussion leader for Bible Study Fellowship, an International Bible study organisation with which I've been involved off and on since 1989, when I first heard of it in Michigan. Since then I have also attended in Canada, Nigeria and now Uganda. I love it because I learn so incredibly much and it helps me to grow spiritually. The structure it gives me is just what I need. It was cute to see the scene I encountered on arriving home. Our guests were sitting outside and our house girl's daughter, Faith, with a little friend who is supposed to look after Faith, were looking up at our friends in an almost holy adoration! It made me stop and think about my attitude toward the people. Power was out again tonight but not for terribly long this time.

✈ Tuesday

I thought I would have a quiet day but things turned out differently. It started with a hard rain and thunderstorm. Thankfully the teacher who teaches our three oldest kids came at 8.15am, just as the first drops started falling. She reminded me that Benjamin still had a project to do that meant me going to the grocery store to check out all the apple products. Sigh! Another run to the store. I hoped it wouldn't be so bad today since it was rainy and people don't like to stand outside waiting for taxis. Riek, my friend, wanted a ride into town to try to withdraw the money that British Airways promised to give her for her lost luggage. So off we went. The ride into town was not bad and we got the information for Benjamin. We also needed whipping cream since Riek was going to try to make ice cream. There was no cream to be found. I decided to skip all smallish, questionable stores and go straight for the gourmet shop, Quality Cuts. Would you believe it? No cream! The owner was able to explain that Jesa's cream machine was out of order. There will be no cream available in Kampala until the end of this week. That reminded me of our first two weeks back in Uganda when there was no butter available. We finally discovered that because of the drought cows weren't producing enough milk. Makes sense, doesn't it? Thankfully the drought is over and butter is available again.

Tonight our MAF team members met together for prayer, as we do every Tuesday. Normally Frances, our house girl, babysits for us, but tonight our friends had the honour. The kids loved it! Gerrit and I climb over the wall to our neighbours. This is not a simple procedure. First we crawl on to our own wall behind the outhouse, then climb into the tree that stands between our walls and ease our way on to their wall. From there Gerrit, my athletic hero, jumps down, but cautious me inches my way to the tree that is about two metres down from where the other tree meets the wall, and I manoeuvre my way down the frangipani tree into their yard. I always breathe a sigh of relief when I have made it again without breaking any of its delicate (or to put it bluntly, plain weak) branches. The reason we take the wall-route is because by road it's a bumpy five-minute ride. There are no paved roads in our neighbourhood, and with these tropical storms the roads don't improve much.

Just before we were about to leave … power out! It came back on within seconds, but at half strength and we sat in a romantic glow. We glanced at our house and it looked suspiciously dark. When we arrived home we were greeted by a cosy candle-lit glow, but there was definitely no glow from the light bulbs. I made yet another call to the electricity company, explaining that everyone around us had at least a glow but we had nothing. The operator didn't seem too interested in my plight and I pressed it on his heart to please do something about it. And he must have done, because within minutes we also had a glow, but not one strong enough to run our fridge and freezer. This was alarming since we were still hoping to make ice cream one of these days, and our ingredients were not getting any colder!

✦ *Wednesday*

Today was our official start to a new Bible Study Fellowship year! But first let me tell you about the night. Gerrit's alarm went off at 3.15am, as he had to catch the 5.30am flight to Kenya. The same taxi driver was asked to pick him up. Gerrit said, as he left the room, that he would start walking up the hill before the taxi arrived, to avoid the noise of him coming into our compound waking the kids. I needed to get up early anyway to prepare for today as I had not read through my first day's procedures and, because of the bad power, I also hadn't been able to practise piano.

There is a children's programme in BSF and Josiah was to be allowed to join in for the first time! I was worried about how that would go, and pressed it on Benjamin's heart that he needed to show some excitement (which he did not feel) for going to BSF because he would then influence Josiah. Well, there was nothing to worry about. We arrived there, they walked into the room, and I never saw or heard from Josiah again until I went to pick the boys up! God is good! All my worries were for nothing. I also enjoyed seeing many old acquaintances again. I didn't realise how attached I had become to many of the ladies and how much love I feel for them. The electric piano I had to use had some loose connections, but better something than nothing. No one complained and we had an accompaniment for most of the songs. The power at home came on again around noon.

A good friend told me tonight that you can make cream by using five ounces of unsalted butter and six-and-a-half ounces of milk. Maybe it's worth a try, I thought. We've GOT to have ice cream! I don't really know how to measure ounces but I do have a gram-scale. It should be the same ratio, I reckoned. As our friends leave on Friday, tomorrow is our last chance for ice cream.

✦ *Thursday*

I have a confession to make. I have a Dutch heritage. I don't want to say I'm Dutch because I don't feel Dutch. I was born in Indonesia and grew up there, went to Holland for my degree, then to the States to work. I did marry a Dutchman and, as we moved to Canada, our children are all Canadian. Now we live in Uganda. Thanks to my heritage I am a stingy Dutchman. My confession is that you can buy ice cream in Kampala but I am too mean to do so. When we first moved here you could buy specialty ice cream at Quality Cuts for about $15.00 for two litres. That was outrageous, and we never bought ice cream. Then a South African store opened, and you wouldn't believe our delight when they sold two litres for $2.50! Gradually their prices went up and, since we came back from furlough, the price is now well over $5.00. Having just been in Canada where you can buy two litres for under $3.00, I refuse to pay almost double that!

We didn't get our ice cream made. I didn't dare try my luck with the butter and milk since I wasn't sure what apparatus my friend uses to make the cream. A 'thingy' she told me, using gestures to make it clear to me. But it wasn't clear at all. Power was out again tonight, but only for two hours. I turned on the generator during that time.

✦ *Friday*

After the prayer meeting I went to the MAF office to pick up dog meat. This is very cheap meat that a young man brings me from the slaughterhouse. My stomach can't really handle the look of it, as it is usually the remains of unborn calves whose mothers were slaughtered. Because the more meat we buy the cheaper it is, I called some friends to see if they were interested as well. So I dragged 35kg home with me. 20kg lasts us two months. Frances, the dear lady, cut it up and packaged it all in small bags for two days at a time. Our dog, Duke, and our cat are having a feast today on all the scraps!

Gerrit came home this evening and I was very happy to see him. He was a few hours later than planned because Kenya Airways had a flat tyre. It's always good to have my husband home again; he is such a big help around the home. We decided to celebrate his homecoming by eating out. The kids loved where we went because they could play there. It's an informal environment and the food is good.

✈ ✈ ✈ ✈ ✈

MAF is, of course, dependent on its Ugandan staff as well as those from overseas.

Godfrey Kitagenda— Operations Manager

I communicated with customers with regards to flight needs and information, and also prepared the news about the work we are doing in Operations for a book on the work of MAF.

I prepared and sent out the monthly statistics.

I prepared, as well as coordinated, applications for renewal of radio licences, Air Operator's Certificate and Pilots' Licences.

I held meetings with customers about flights and also communicated with Kalongo Hospital on security matters.

I chaired the monthly Ops meeting.

Lastly, I communicated regularly with the Ops staff both in the office and at Kajjansi with regards to flight planning and ground operations.

✈ ✈ ✈ ✈ ✈

Fred describes his job as Flight Follower

I am the person working behind the HF radio (High Frequency radio), keeping contact with pilots in the air. Basically I do the same thing every day as I'm doing flight-following. Only the routes of the flights change. I record all calls from pilots with the correct time against each call. These are post take-off calls, position reports and landing calls. And I also collect reports from the stations the pilot is flying to, and inform him before he lands. These reports are: weather, situation on ground or a passenger who is not on his manifest. I want to mention a call I received from Simon Wunderli. He was landing the Caravan on a new airstrip called Pader. He said, 'I'm overhead Pader for landing. But before I land I will be doing one to two low passes.' Since this is a new airstrip he needed to inspect it first before landing. For a normal landing he would just call landing once without doing a low pass.

✈ ✈ ✈ ✈ ✈

Aircraft handlers, Richard Ssengonzi and Maurice Walusimbi, listed their duties during diary week.

- ✈ Passengers and baggage handling.

- ✈ Refuelling aircraft.

- ✈ Applying for flight clearance.

- ✈ Receiving flights.

- ✈ Handling passengers with their baggage.

- ✈ Submission of flight clearance.

- ✈ Hangar help.

✈ ✈ ✈ ✈ ✈

Sarah Tsapwe, Bookings Assistant

I received booking calls and made bookings as requested by the callers. Some bookings are received by e-mail and fax. I confirmed the bookings I made. Every day I make manifests for each of the flights. On Tuesdays and Thursdays I prepare a letter for clearance to the Sudan office for our flights into Sudan.

✈ ✈ ✈ ✈ ✈

There follows the diary from Paul Brooks, Finance Manager, who is married to Edith. Edith is Ugandan. She teaches in the playgroup at Heritage School.

Work on *Monday* started with a time of prayer at 8.20; it always does. My first job should have been downloading e-mails and sorting through as many as possible, but there was a small problem with the network connection. The Information Services Department (ISD) sorted out the problem for me. Much of the day was spent on spreadsheets: a spreadsheet that will download flight details from the MAF Wingman programme to the new accounting software, one for limits on salary advances, another that records the mileage of MAF vehicles, and one for working out the Shell Uganda fuel bill for aircraft. I also sorted out visa questions.

First thing on *Tuesday* I signed cheques and wrote a letter for the bank in order to withdraw cash. While Erasmus went with Richard to the bank I helped at the cash desk. Then it was back to spreadsheets again to enter in the fuel uplifted from Entebbe airport by our planes and MAF US planes for August and to calculate the payment we will need to make this month. Following that, among other things, I started to prepare the bank reconciliations for August. I had a call with a Church Mission Society (CMS) Ireland staff member in Sudan on *Wednesday* to discuss how we could help them get funds into Sudan. It was arranged that we will transfer money from CMS Ireland to the MAF Europe account in the UK, then purchase Ugandan shillings here and send money up in instalments by plane.

Today, *Thursday*, was spent on routine financial matters, for example, checking the bank balance to see if we needed to transfer funds from dollars to shillings to make some payments, and preparing stock sheets for fuel at Kajjansi and up country. I took Edith to Heritage School as usual on *Friday* morning, and spent some time with the Heritage Finance Department. That is part of my role as Board member. Then it was back to MAF and the usual pile of e-mails. Among other things to be done today was making arrangements for money for some children who are being sponsored by ex-MAF Uganda staff. Heritage School was still on my agenda, as I arranged to pay for some books for the school over the Internet. That makes them less expensive as it saves on bank charges.

✈ ✈ ✈ ✈ ✈

Richard Kiyimba, Logistics Manager, wrote a most revealing diary!

It is *Monday* again and all businesses in town wanted to recover from the financial drawback because Sunday was not good business as most people were at home. But with MAF it is different. Being refreshed over the weekend meant I was enthusiastic to get my hands on the wheel and throw the car around in town with the FM stereo booming. I limit the volume because any time after I have left the office my manager might call my mobile and I would not hear it. I had that music hit my soul as I gazed at the long list of activities I had to do today.

At 9am I gathered my work, checked the workshop, updated paperwork, checked and responded to e-mails, all the nitty-gritty things. I left the office at about 11am and returned between 3 and 5pm. That is my daily schedule. I have not mentioned about lunch. In the past I used to fast, but now I have lunch in town. This morning, as the office needed cash, I had to do two trips into town, one to carry cash and the other to do the errands. I cannot combine the trips because of the risk of carrying money after withdrawal. When I am withdrawing money I have to do it with one eye looking at the cashier and another watching around because I do not want to be followed by robbers. The office has taken appropriate precautions and I am not alone in the bank. After withdrawing money, I go to a place in the bank where one of the MAF staff meets me, takes the money from me, and walks out. I leave independently and with no money.

Over the years, as I have been doing MAF's errands, my name has changed in the places I go to. Some people call me MAF. They say, 'Hello MAF, we have your payment.' I try to exhibit the real image of MAF in my presentation. If you came around and found me in the field executing assignments you might think that I was the MAF Country Director because I do my work with all my heart, with all pride, and with the best presentation intellectually and physically.

Today, *Tuesday*, I had to go to the World Food programme. My wife, Flavia (I call her Flash), works with the World Food programme. When I walk in there she sits at the reception and her response is, 'Good morning, sir, how can we help? Please leave your identity card.' She does not take anything for granted because she is dealing with a customer who happens to be her husband. I also went to Immigration to follow up on the visas for MAF and other missionaries. But Immigration is so slow! The work I logged in two months ago is not attended to yet.

When we receive our pay at the end of the month we are not happy to see that we have to pay ten percent of it as taxes to the government. Every month I have to take the compilation of the Pay-as-you-earn taxes to the Uganda Revenue Authority. This is another place where you must go only when you are fit and well fed, as you will have so long to wait. I have looked for a chance to go to the newly-opened supermarket in the town suburb but could not find the time. This morning, *Friday*, the hangar needed a vacuum cleaner, and the type they wanted is only found in this particular supermarket, *Game*. So I had the opportunity to see what else they had in the supermarket while I was there for the vacuum cleaner!

16.

SOUTH AFRICA

The Republic of South Africa covers an area of 1,218,363 sq km, more than twice the size of France. Nine provinces make up the republic, and they vary greatly from each other, the eastern side of South Africa being reasonably well-watered and great parts of the western coast arid desert. MAF's base in South Africa serves not only the republic, but also surrounding countries.

Pilot Mark Liprini thinks back over diary week and about the difference between being a commercial pilot and a MAF missionary.

There are certainly some days when I wonder if flying for a commercial airline wouldn't be less stressful.

Imagine, you just wander up to the aircraft an hour or so before flight, strap yourself in, press the intercom and order one coffee, milk and no sugar please, wind up the engines and off you go. Someone else would have pre-flighted the aircraft, refuelled, worked out the weight and balance, issued the tickets, co-ordinated the various clients, loaded the cargo, tied the cargo down, skinned their knuckles, hassled with Customs, filed the flight plans, paid all the fees, organised the catering, worked out the routes, printed the log sheets, banged their head a few times and collected the paperwork. But that's all to be done by the MAF pilot before taking off! And it all happens again in reverse on the other side of the border ... after you have coaxed a fully laden aircraft into the sky, worked your way around horrid weather, recalculated your fuel a zillion times, struggled to raise flight-following on the HF radio, changed your course a few dozen times for weather, and finally reached your first destination, sweaty, smelly and longing for the toilet and a frosty cold coke ... in that order. Nah! Airline flying would be too tame. How many airline pilots can chat with their passengers, finding out about their projects, discovering what makes a twenty-three-year-old leave home in safe USA or UK to serve people on a continent racked with HIV/AIDS, poverty, war, disease, malaria, potholes and corruption? That's the MAF pilot's privilege.

I flew up to Quelimane in Mozambique to transport a group of World Vision workers back to Nelspruit RSA for some training. These folk are involved in various agricultural and business projects in Mozambique; many were nationals and some were expats. All of them realised that proper agricultural practices and sound business skills are what's really required to improve the lot of many subsistence communities permanently.

At night I flew home to Lanseria and the next day loaded about 150kg of cargo in RSA and headed back to Mozambique, via Nelspruit, loading a further 250kg en route. This cargo was made up of the personal belongings of various missionaries based in Northern Mozambique. I went up there to relocate a fellow MAF missionary pilot (Greg from MAF USA), who is moving on to another field of service. We took the opportunity of the empty aircraft's positioning flight to move his stuff northwards.

Late the next afternoon I touched down at Nampula and began the task of unloading the aircraft, this time with the help of local missionaries. Early the following morning it was time to load up Greg's belongings, piece by piece, after Customs had thoroughly searched everything. Having loaded almost a metric tonne of belongings the aircraft still looked as though it could have taken a tonne more. The Cessna Caravan has an enormous appetite! The flight home was pretty uneventful, but having a fellow pilot share the load certainly helps. One does the paperwork at each stop and the other handles the fuelling, making for very fast turn-around times on the ground. But it also helps to have two heads solve problems and make decisions.

It was an interesting five days: 3750nm (+/- 6950km), 11 airports, 4300L Jet A1, 25 hours flight time, five different beds to sleep in, three currencies to work with, three languages (four if you count American English), and the satisfaction of knowing that once again it had been a real privilege to play a small role in serving the Lord in this corner of Africa. Would I swap this for air-conditioned, pressurised comfort way above the weather? Certainly not!

✦ ✦ ✦ ✦ ✦

Mark mentioned flying the Cessna Caravan. One of the Caravans used in South Africa – it's called the *Caledonian*

Connection – was gifted by MAF supporters in Scotland in 2003. The aircraft's cargo capacity is an obvious advantage, but there were several other reasons why the Caravan was the most suitable plane for the work done by MAF SA, among them that it is capable of long-range performance, it can carry heavy payloads even when flying from high altitude airstrips, and it uses jet fuel that is readily and economically available. It was Scotland's privilege to be involved with facilitating the spread of the gospel in southern Africa, and helping the work of practical Christian compassion there. When the Caledonian Connection went into service in southern Africa it connected MAF in Scotland (Caledonia) with MAF in South Africa and demonstrated the holistic nature of the ministry, where one cares for the other and all aim to work to the glory of God.

✈ ✈ ✈ ✈ ✈

Marry Molomo, who works as a receptionist for MAF, lists her daily duties for our interest. She is a cog in the wheel of the Mission, and all need to move smoothly together for the whole thing to function well.

My day at the office starts out at about 7.45am. I start by clearing the post tray then frank on the correct postage and get it ready for collection. Eddie arrives with a smile at around 9.00am to collect and deliver mail. Answering the switchboard and taking messages, helping to put information packs together for airshows, deputation and conferences are part of my duties. I also help with filling envelopes and mailing the quarterly newsletter and the bi-monthly prayer letter, and I keep track of the stock levels of various items and help with filing.

✈ ✈ ✈ ✈ ✈

The daily prayer time means a great deal to Ruby Braumann.

✈ Monday

I arrived at the office around 8.20 this morning, and that's my usual time. After saying hello to everyone, I switched on the e-mail/banking and accounting computers, and then checked e-mails. Yippee! Alison Heath, Chief Accountant in the Ashford MAF Europe office, may be coming to help me with the change of software early next year. I send her a quick reply, expressing my joy at the thought. 9am is prayer time, for which we all meet in the Boardroom. Through the reading we are reminded that our hope lies in God. We prayed earnestly for a former MAF SA staff member with a health problem.

Garth Moffatt (aircraft maintenance engineer) is visiting at the moment. He's training up in Tanzania and it's good to see him. We spent a bit of time updating his support levels and discussing possibilities for next year. He's so enthusiastic about MAF and the work we do! Moving on, at last I can send off the provisional budget for MAF SA to MAF Europe. Then it was time to do some payments that fell due today, including one for Butch Judge, our Development Manager, who will be attending a Missionary Care Seminar. As two of us have to be available to release the payments, Vera Hardman completes the task for me. The afternoon was spent dealing with the post and sending off a schedule of details for two aircraft.

✈ Tuesday

This morning, my e-mails contained a query about the budget – already! Also my yesterday's e-mail to Zimbabwe was returned and I tried another address. Prayers this morning was challenging. The reading was Malachi 3 on tithing. Are we tithing as MAF SA? We'll have to discuss the finer points of how to do this on Sunday when we meet for our special prayer meeting.

Among other things, the day was taken up with arranging for a visa to be collected and working on the MAF books and petty cash. Could I seriously be just over R1000.00 short? I tried not to panic. I had some lunch and went back to the problem fresh. After checking through everything again, I suddenly realised that I was balancing the actual cash with the balance in the book for the end of August, instead of up-to-date! Please Lord, I need a new memory stick! Everything is in balance and I can breathe freely again.

✦ *Wednesday*

Prayer time this morning, gave us confirmation that what God has said will come to pass. What an encouragement! The data capture is at the stage where I can now do the intercompany accounts for MAF Europe, Canada/Angola, USA and Lesotho. That was my big job today. In the middle of that there was a phone call from one of our donors, saying her debit order is no longer going through her bank account. I promised to look into it and phone her back, and we managed to sort it out between us. As I left for home, I grabbed some of the missionary prayer and support cards. There's a slot at my Disciple Group tonight to find out more about local missionaries; maybe I can make them more aware of the work of MAF.

✦ *Thursday*

During prayer time this morning, we read an extract from the Sermon on the Mount, which is always challenging. Monday's visa situation had been resolved and I arranged for its collection. Then it was back to the data capture and the intercompany accounts. Interspersed with this, three of us organised the roster for duty at the upcoming airshow and spoke to a visitor to the office. The data capture doesn't seem to be progressing, and now the heat is on since I have to have the schedules ready for next Thursday. The intercompany accounts were completed and emailed round the world. I love my contact with the other MAF programmes.

✈ *Friday*

The last day of the working week and there was no MAF e-mail to attend to! Our reading today was from Matthew – 'Do not worry'. That's always very appropriate. While at prayer the post arrived and there was a strange invoice in it. It was from one of the companies at the airport—for a prop sock fan for ZS-OPS (not even one of our aircraft). I phoned them but couldn't get through to the relevant department. So I phoned the pilots. Yes, they had ordered something, but it was definitely not called a prop sock fan! Then I realised why they had used ZS-OPS—from the OPerationS order number!

The gate buzzer rang and a very smart vehicle drew up in the parking space below us. It was our auditors bringing back our financials from the year 2003. Vera and I had tea with them in the Boardroom while we discussed business and sorted out the various documents they need for their records. When we were finished I took them on the 'grand tour' of the hangar; they were clearly impressed. The afternoon brought some headway on the data capture, at last. I'm almost ready to transfer the final figures to the MAF Europe schedules. And so another busy week has come to an end.

✦ ✦ ✦ ✦ ✦

Sandy Wilson, Chief Pilot, MAF SA, was on a flight to Kuito, Angola, during diary week. His account begins on Friday 3rd September.

I was up at 4.30am in order to be ready for a 6.30am departure. The team were from OMS International, (formerly Oriental Missionary Society), consisting of the South Africa Director, the Chairman of the OMS SA Board, two directors and an assistant from the OMS office in the US, and finally two friends of OMS in SA. We cleared Customs and Immigration and were airborne by 7.30am, somewhat later than planned, but things were okay as we gained one hour in travelling to Angola. Our routing took us to Maun in Botswana, then over Rundu in Namibia and on to Lubango, Angola. The three-hour flight to Maun was smooth and uneventful. Re-fuelling and the necessary paperwork did not take too long and we were airborne again in just over an hour.

The next leg again was smooth until we got into Angola in the late afternoon heat. We arrived in Lubango after four hours and fifteen minutes flight. Being processed into Angola was no problem. Our friends from MAF Canada in Angola helped us with the Portuguese language and asked for the Immigration Officer to be available the next day for our early flight to Kuito. I enquired why we needed Immigration for a domestic flight and was told this is standard procedure in Angola, something different to get used to! We were well looked after by the MAF family, and that is always very much appreciated, especially after a long day flying.

✈ Saturday

Got up at 4.45am, not used to the early mornings yet; we're not designed to be getting up before the sun! The Immigration Officer was there for us and we were airborne by 7.30am. Today's flight was about one hour fifty minutes to Kuito, a town almost in the middle of Angola. On arrival we once again had a visit from Immigration. But it was more of a courtesy check, no names taken, just 'hello'; the pastors with whom we're staying know him well. One of the first things you notice on arrival in Kuito is that part of the airport buildings have been shot and bombed and there is a bombed-out tank just outside. All the main buildings in the town have bullet and bomb holes in them. Although some are falling, or half fallen down, people still live in them. We were told that things are much better than they were. That made me wonder what the place looked like a year ago.

It was time for a late breakfast when we reached the pastor's house, or was it early lunch? Either way, we were presented with a nice meal and it was time to meet the pastors we will be working with in the next couple of days. We were told that we will be split in pairs for Sunday and that we are all expected to preach at different churches for at least twenty minutes. Nothing like a bit of warning!

This afternoon we had a two-hour drive planned, to a village where some village church planters had been working over the past year. The drive ended up being just over four hours on very bumpy, difficult roads. At times it would have been quicker to get out of the van and walk. The problem about doing that was that we went through areas that had red and white bricks/stones by the edge of the road, indicating minefields. So it was not a good idea to walk! Sometimes we wondered if we were going the right way, partly because the drive took so much longer than we thought, but mainly because the driver and pastors kept asking for directions from local villagers.

When we eventually arrived, we were welcomed into the village by a hundred or so people singing and dancing and forming an aisle for us to walk through down the hill. That was quite a moving experience. It was great to see the joy on people's faces when you think back to the years of terror and hiding they have had to live through. It's our prayer that this peace will last. There were twenty-three villages represented at the gathering of around 500 adults, plus lots of children, some of whom had walked for three days to be there. The plan was to do some singing, followed by teaching/preaching and then show the *Jesus* film. We ended up not showing the film because a few essential things had been left behind. Leaving the village as the sun was setting, we were all very happy four-and-a-half hours later when our drive back in the dark was over.

⊀ Sunday

This morning the eight of us split into twos to preach in four different churches. I went with Dawie Crous, Chairman of the OMS International Board in South Africa. We ended up preaching at two churches as they were both expecting us. As a pilot, it is not that common that I am asked to preach, but it does happen, and I must say I rather enjoyed the challenge and the opportunity. The first church was Assemblies of God with about 350 people attending, although we had to leave before everyone had arrived. At the second there were about 250 people in attendance.

After lunch we all went to a graduation ceremony for eighty pastors who had spent the past eight years completing a three-year degree. Their studies took so long because they had worked at them throughout the war. The pastors were from all church backgrounds in Kuito and the surrounding area. It was a great opportunity to honour these pastors and to share the gospel with the 1,000 or so people in the service. One of those attending was the Governor of the Kuito province.

✈ *Monday*

Today there was a meeting of about forty-five village church planters from in and around Kuito. They received some teaching and were given new Bibles. One of the amazing things about this gathering was that during the war sixty per cent had fought for the MPLA (government) and forty per cent for UNITA, and here they were studying and working together in peace and friendship. Let's pray that through people like them real peace and healing can come to Angola.

While this meeting was going on a group of us were shown around an orphanage run by the church in Kuito. The word orphanage makes us think of a place where children live, but in Angola the children are not allowed to stay in such places. The preference is for them to live with their extended families or with people in the local area. So an orphanage is more of a day care centre where the children are fed, go to school and receive health care. There were about sixty children at the centre, which is a very clean well-run place. However, we were told that there are many others who need a place, but there is no space for them. After that we went to a school run by the church. It seems that providing a reasonable education is one of the real problems facing Angola, and because of that the schools are overcrowded. Often there are adults still attending school trying to finish their education. That means that many classes are held on the veranda, as there is no space inside. Later in the afternoon we flew back to Lubango and spent the night with the MAF folk there.

✈ *Tuesday*

By 7.40am we were in the air on our way back to South Africa. One of the problems heading back is that we lose an hour due to the time change. And when the flight plus stop is about nine hours, there is no room for too many delays if we want to land before sunset. The flight was smooth and uneventful and we arrived about forty-five minutes before sunset. We were glad to be back home, but our minds were full of thoughts on what had been a very interesting trip, and about the need for help and prayer for the country and people of Angola.

✈ ✈ ✈ ✈ ✈

Vera Hardman, Administrator, had a real problem at the beginning of the week.

On *Sunday* my son's car was stolen while he was at band practice and a meeting. What a blow, and a huge logistical nightmare that was. There is no suitable means of public transport available especially for the long distances we have to travel to get around in Johannesburg.

During diary week I was busy preparing the necessary documents for a shipment of borehole water-drilling equipment that was donated to Here's Life Tanzania Mission. A pilot in MAF Tanzania, who knows the people at the Mission, offered to help with the logistics of getting this equipment from SA to Tanzania. He contacted me and that is how I became involved with this shipment. This drilling equipment is going to be such a blessing, a real lifesaver, to Here's Life Tanzania Mission and the community in which it is serving.

Other than attending to the daily telephone calls and assisting with queries etc, this week, I helped Butch Judge, our Development Manager, with information in order that he could put together a comprehensive proposal for a volunteer who is planning to come over from the UK to assist our programme for three months next year. This entailed getting accommodation, transport and meals arranged, and working out the cost thereof as well as putting various jobs/functions in place for him.

Final arrangements were made via e-mail this week for the pilot/missionary Knevel family who were arriving from Chad. Jeroen Knevel needs to do his conversion on the Caravan aircraft and also get a SA CAA licence validation. As we are lending our Chief Pilot, Sandy Wilson, and family, with an aircraft to the MAF Chad programme for six months, this conversion, training and validation process needs to be done.

I am presently teaching Lynnie Judge, Butch's wife, who is volunteering her services in the office on a daily basis. She will be in charge of hospitality and catering; she will also look after the Logistics Department. Lynnie helps with donor database capturing and donor communications via letter or phone calls, and she also takes care of a bi-monthly prayer letter that goes out to our prayer supporters. I handle the printing and mailing thereof. Part of Lynnie's portfolio is the care ministry of MAF SA staff and families. One of my other responsibilities is to make sure our donors are looked after and recognised, an extremely important function in our type of ministry where we rely totally on donor support, both prayer and financial! I also look after the needs of our MAF SA missionary families who have been seconded to programmes in other parts of the world, making sure that their prayer letters are printed and mailed out regularly.

Final preparations were made this week for the Waterkloof Airshow. MAF SA plans each year to be present at a minimum of four airshows. Waterkloof SA Aerospace & Defence Force is the largest airshow in the country. Over 250,000 people attend the event that takes place over five days. We promote our ministry, chat to people and other pilots, hand out brochures, newsletters and little giveaways, sell promotional items for fundraising, receive donations and also expand our mailing list. It's a lot of hard work setting up the gazebo and display each day, but we do have fun too!

These are just some of the functions I perform for MAF, and I can only do them with the wonderful support of the others in the office. I am so blessed and privileged to be working in this wonderful environment. It is such a great mix: my passion for flying, not as pilot but as passenger, and being full-time in God's ministry! Wow, I just love it!

✦ ✦ ✦ ✦ ✦

Work also needs to be done outside the Johannesburg office. That's where Zebedius Mathiba Makgoba comes in. He is the hangar helper and grounds keeper. Zebedius shares his work for the week.

- ✈ *Monday.* Because of the weekend the hangar is very much dirty, so I have to clean the hangar.

- ✈ *Tuesday.* I cleaned the aircraft inside and outside.

- ✈ *Wednesday.* I mopped the hangar with water and soap.

- ✈ *Thursday.* I worked in the garden.

- ✈ *Friday.* I made sure that everything was in its position.

Every day I go to the chapel before we start to work. The work I do that I did not mention is that sometimes I drive to get things, clean the cars and tow the aircraft outside.

✦ ✦ ✦ ✦ ✦

John Mulinge, Operations Assistant and Flight Scheduler, wrote his diary beginning on Monday 13th, but it still gives an insight to his contribution to MAF SA.

As my work title suggests, I support the pilots and Programme Manager in running the aircraft operations. I joined MAF SA as a volunteer in November of last year and have been here ever since. The atmosphere is great. I love flying, hold a Private Pilot's Licence, and aim soon to have my Commercial Pilot's Licence, which I can hopefully use to fly with MAF.

Monday was a good day. One of our pilots left for the States for an interview. Our remaining pilot is preparing to go, with an aircraft, to Chad to help out in the MAF Chad programme. I had to arrange for his flight permits in all the countries through which he will travel. If Africa were like the EU it would be easy, but this is not the case. I had to figure out the different regulations for the different countries to which we fly. Some countries are quite organised like SA and Zimbabwe, but others are not.

Our chief pilot, Sandy Wilson, had his medical today. One of my jobs is to keep a check on the currency of the Pilots' Licences and medical certificates. This is easy to do in a small flight department like ours, with the help of a good computer programme. We had a surprise charter from Fugro, which does survey work all over Africa. As they needed to get some equipment to the border between Namibia and Angola, they called and asked if we could do the flight for them. We agreed to do it tomorrow. I managed to get the flight permits for Botswana and Namibia on the same day.

Pilots are lucky, today in Jo'burg, tomorrow in the bundus! My part in all this was to prepare his paperwork and confirm his flight details with the charter company.

17.

CHAD

The country of Chad is a little larger than the Republic of South Africa, though it only has about a fifth of the population. While in South Africa over fifty per cent of the population live in urban areas, in Chad the proportion is more like twenty per cent. The land varies enormously, from thick bush in the south, through dry grassland in the centre to desert in the north. Chad is bounded by Libya, Sudan, Central African Republic, Cameroon, Nigeria and Niger. It is totally landlocked, being over 1,000km from the nearest sea.

Chad, which gained independence from France in 1960, has a subsistence economy and is without the benefit of many natural resources. However it has recently begun developing huge oil deposits in the south east of the country and a pipeline is taking exports to Douala in Cameroon for refining. Severe droughts have plagued the land, as has political unrest and civil wars. But Chad is not without its beauties, as Jeroen Knevel is quick to note.

✈ ✈ ✈ ✈ ✈

Jeroen Knevel, Programme Manager, started diary week on a motorbike trip to the bush! Jeroen is from the Netherlands.

What a wonderful time we had. Two colleagues went with me into the bush on our motorbikes. We were just away overnight – two days of holiday from MAF and compound life. We shared some good talks, had a laugh and enjoyed Chad's nature. Among other things, we saw monkeys, wild horses and crane birds.

The beginning of the week: What a day! I seem to have been running up and down all day. The building of the hangar is slow and I had to be firm with the contractor concerning some construction and financial issues. Hopefully things will improve from now on. Fortunately the house we're renting is going okay. With just a few more upgrades it will be ready for the new MAF family to move into. This afternoon I studied for the Caravan training and South African Licence.

A day or two later: We heard that there is no Avgas available. Fortunately we have a proper stock level and that should enable us to continue for a couple of weeks. Flying is going well though studying is difficult. There are so many bits and pieces demanding attention.

At the beginning of the following week, Jeroen noted: In the morning I went with my wife, Karin, to the street children. She loves the work and it's good to see how she's accepted. I was impressed to hear the critical questions they asked after the Bible story. Later in the day I was at the hangar again. It's looking positive! The floor sections are being poured and they are good quality.

It has been some time since we had rain, and today we can see huge storm clouds coming in. The smell after the pouring rain—I love it!

PART THREE

MAF CANADA

ANGOLA

✈

AND OTHER MAF REGIONS

18.

ANGOLA

Angola lies on the Atlantic coast of Africa. The capital city, Luanda, which is on the coast, has an unofficial estimated population of five million people. Continual war over the last forty years has chased people from the countryside into towns and cities, and the urban population may now be as high as fifty per cent. Angola is a mineral and oil rich land, but much of its wealth has been used to fund civil war. Today the population is so poor that without international aid many Angolians would not survive.

MAF staff in Angola provide an interesting overview of their situation.

Our MAF Angola programme has been in operation since 1989 and is run by MAF Canada. The Cessna C-208 Caravan flown is Canadian registered. Its call sign is C-GWOH. The aircraft is called Wings of Hope, which incorporates the last three letters of its call sign.

The programme's main base is in Lubango in south-western Angola. Three full-term Canadian missionary families and one short-term family staff the programme. Along with local Angolan staff they handle the day-to-day responsibilities of running the programme. The Programme Manager is Gary Toews, who serves there with his wife, Doreen. Gary is a pilot/engineer. Pilot Brent Mudde looks after the computer technology. Pilot Lonnie Wasik and his wife, Chris, are part of the team. Lonnie is also Base Engineer. And they are joined by short-term pilot Fred Keier and his wife, Kimberley. MAF Angola's local staff in Lubango consists of four office personnel (Rui, Bela, Chaviuca and Jose), one aircraft maintenance apprentice (Basilio) and a group of guards employed to be on duty in the evenings at the MAF office and the airport hangar.

Up until the escalation of the Angolan civil war in 1999, MAF had a base of operations in the capital city of Luanda. Today MAF employs three local staff (Cesar, Anastacio and Henrique) in Luanda to assist with administration and help with the upkeep of the MAF compound. MAF Angola also operates an administration office in Windhoek, Namibia, since we hold a Namibian Operators Certificate. This allows us to make flights to Windhoek for medical evacuations, aircraft maintenance and for the movement of personnel and freight. Two part-time staff (Leonie and John) work in the Windhoek office.

MAF Angola has a contract to fly for the World Food programme, an arm of the United Nations, until the end of 2004. We also do charter flights for the local Angolan church, missionaries and other non-government organisations working in Angola. We offer one subsidised flight each month for church or mission groups. We call these subsidised flights World Changers Flights.

Chris Wasik kept the team's diary for the week.

✈ Sunday

The MAF families attend local church services in Lubango. In the afternoon Gary and Fred had a 2.00pm departure for a flight to Kalukembe. Kalukembe has a mission hospital and nursing school; it formerly operated a leprosy clinic. The leprosy clinic has now been closed and the patients integrated back into the local community. The plane flew out eleven 20-litre cans of paint for the hospital and then brought back five passengers, a Swiss couple, their son – a pastor – and two Angolans. The Swiss couple had worked in Kalikembe from 1953 to 1957. They enjoyed a few days visiting the mission's work and observing the changes that had taken place since they worked there.

✈ Monday

Today's flights were to Menongue and Mavinga for World Food programme. These towns are east of Lubango. Gary and Fred departed at 8.00am for Menongue. They had to wait there for the arrival of WFP's Head of Security, who was travelling from Luanda on the local commercial airline. When he arrived they flew on to Mavinga, where he held a two-hour meeting with local WFP security officers. Since Gary and Fred had two hours on the ground they took a tour of Mavinga. During that time they had an opportunity to speak with a de-miner from Halo Trust about the de-mining operations in the area and the process involved in moving mines for detonation rather than exploding them at the sites where they are found.

Gary and Fred toured the local Médecins sans Frontières (MSF) Hospital and were impressed with the feeding programme the hospital is sponsoring for patients. This is not typical of care received in local Angolan hospitals. They observed the WFP feeding programme and noticed that their food supplies are getting low. A point of interest was the local telephone booth, situated in an old sea container with a satellite dish on the outside, from which local calls as well as international telephone calls can be made! Two hours later they departed with a full load of passengers, including the WFP security man and two passengers from the Angolan Congregational Church (IECA). The Irish government is sponsoring a Seed/Tool Project through the IECA church for around 6000 people living 12km from Mavinga. They flew back to Menongue for a refuelling stop, then on to Lubango.

✦ Tuesday

The two of them headed off again at 6.00am to the airport with the OMS team. The team had an early morning departure in the MAF SA Caravan back to Johannesburg. Gary and Fred had an 8.00am departure for the World Food programme flights to Caconda and Chipindo. They flew two WFP personnel, who were able to do some maintenance at Caconda for an hour while the plane went on to Chipindo with other passengers. On returning to Caconda the maintenance workers were picked up and the plane headed to Lubango.

Routinely Chaviuca flight follows all scheduled MAF flights from Lubango on the HF radio and Anastacio does the same in Luanda. Chaviuca and Anastacio are available to the pilots in order that they can give position reports, as well as take-off and landing information. Depending on the plane's location, or the weather, one or other will receive the flight information more clearly. This is an important safety feature of our operations, one that allows the aircraft to be tracked during its entire flight. Basilio has been working on his own out at the MAF hangar this week doing odd jobs, as Lonnie, our Base Engineer, has malaria. Today he cleaned out cobwebs in the hangar and looked for fire hazards in preparation for the Lubango Fire Department check of facilities and fire extinguishers tomorrow.

Doreen handles the accounting for the Windhoek office. She enters the information that Leonie submits each month, as well as compiling accounting information from Lubango and Luanda, then balances the MAF Angola accounts and sends the information to our head office in Guelph, Ontario, on a monthly basis.

Fred and Kimberley Heier only arrived in Angola ten days ago. They will be here for the next three months to assist in the programme, and to give the full-time missionary staff an opportunity to take some of their vacation time. One piece of their luggage was missing when they arrived. This was a concern for them as many necessary items were in it. Thankfully, their luggage was found and arrived safely today. This evening saw the safe return of Brent from his six-day vacation. He had been trekking with other expatriate families through Southern Angola to the mouth of the Cunene River on the Atlantic Ocean.

⊁ Wednesday

Today was a day off for Gary and Fred after working nine duty days in a row. Most of the MAF missionary staff spent the day writing letters to family, friends and supporters to be sent with another missionary who will be flying off to Canada on Thursday. Using such willing letter carriers is a reliable way of sending mail back to North America.

✦ Thursday

Gary spent most of the day in the office catching up with paperwork. He worked on filling out a new form required by UTCAH (Technical Unit for the Corridation of the Humanitarian Assistance), the government organisation that overseas all NGOs in Angola. Fred was able to study and do ground school re-currency training to fly in Angola. In the afternoon Gary and Doreen took our two new arrivals on an orientation trip to the local market. Jose accompanied them to keep an eye on the vehicle while they were wandering around. A large and varied selection of items is available at the market. People would be surprised at what you can buy in Angola, they'd probably also be surprised at the price! Brent was back in the computer repair business, not to mention repairing a washing machine! Rui and Jose spent the afternoon purchasing diesel fuel in town and then hauling it in barrels to fill the MAF generator tanks. The MAF generator supplies steady and reliable power to all the homes on the missionary compound.

✦ Friday

Gary was in the office again, working on missionary staff and programme reports for the upcoming October MAF Canada Board meeting. He also prepared Fred's ground school exam. In Luanda, Cesar tried successfully to get Doreen's passport out of the Angolan Immigration Office that approves exit and work visas. This means that she can travel out of Angola with Gary for their upcoming vacation. He also tried to locate a new government organisation that will approve all letters of invitation for visitors to Angola. Luanda is a city of five million people and the traffic jams are awful. Cesar spends at least one to two hours travelling approximately 15km each way depending on the office he is visiting, and then from one to three hours waiting at the office to be served. Brent spent the day in Rio de Huila, a little village south of Lubango. He was helping Dr Karen Henriksen with some plumbing difficulties. He also did some tests on her mobile phone to try to get her better coverage.

Friday night is often 'Movie Night' on the missionary compound where the MAF families live. This gives expatriate missionaries a chance to have a relaxing evening together. Brent hosted tonight's well-attended Movie Night.

19.

MAF CANADA

Mission Aviation Fellowship of Canada has two offices in Canada and one flight programme located in the southwest African nation of Angola. MAF Canada has overseen the Angola programme since 1989. A unique aspect of MAF Canada is that it actively recruits Canadian personnel – pilots, aircraft maintenance engineers, avionics technicians and schoolteachers – to serve in countries where MAF Europe, MAF Australia and MAF US have flight programmes. At present, Canadians serve in: Angola, Botswana, Brazil, Canada, Central Asia, Chad, Indonesia, Kenya, Lesotho, Papua New Guinea and South Africa.

MAF Canada provided a broad sweep of the work it does and how it does it.

At the head office in Guelph, Ontario, we hold orientation classes for Canadians heading into overseas service, and we are also busy with fundraising, producing a quarterly newsletter, sending out missionary prayer letters and cards, and arranging travel and insurance. In addition, we also oversee the strategic, financial and operational aspects of our Angola programme. We gather together daily to pray for our missionaries as well as other missions working all around the world.

MAF Canada's Western Canada recruiting office is in Three Hills, Alberta. Prairie Bible College has a mission aviation programme at Three Hills, where two Canadian MAF pilots, Richard Ebel and Dan Lawrance, live with their families and provide leadership to the programme and flight training for the students. Richard and his wife, Susan, previously served as MAF missionaries in northern Australia. Dan used to be an MAF pilot in Brazil.

Twelve members of staff work under Ron Epp, Executive Director and CEO in Guelph. The day before the MAF snapshot week began, most of the staff and their spouses drove out to a Mennonite community north of Guelph, to attend the wedding of our receipting manager, Shannon Bowman, to Kenny Martin. A beautiful late summer's day, a solid message on marriage and a generous sampling of Mennonite humour and hospitality blessed them. On the Monday that followed both MAF offices were closed for Canada's annual Labour Day holiday.

Every weekday morning from 10.30 – 11am the Guelph staff meets for devotions and prayers for MAF staff families around the world, and for any other needs made known to us by supporters, acquaintances or other ministries. Staff members take turns leading the daily devotional time. On *Tuesday*, after a working day in the office, Ron Epp met with visiting Brazil missionary, Neil Bittle, and two others. Neil, a long-serving Canadian MAF pilot/engineer, was in Canada to arrange the shipment of an aircraft engine from Canada to Brazil for use in the aviation training school at Anapolis, where he serves as a senior instructor. The school is a ministry of MAF's Brazil affiliate known as Asas de Socorro (Wings of Help).

The group discussed the progress of MAF Canada's newly graduated Angolan aviation students, now serving as missionaries with Asas de Socorro. Neil has overseen the training of these young men in Brazil since they arrived from Angola in February 2000. Two of them, Misayely Abias and Norberto Isaac, have earned private and commercial pilot licences and completed basic training in aircraft maintenance. The third, Romao Meto, who hopes to become an aircraft maintenance engineer, has completed basic training and started apprenticing in a maintenance shop licensed for turbine aircraft. In September 2002, Misayely married an Argentinian aeronautical engineer who serves as a volunteer missionary at Anapolis. They are expecting their first baby. In December 2002, Norberto married his Angolan fiancée who came to join him in Brazil. They now have a daughter, Naomi. This year, Romao became engaged to a Brazilian church's assistant pastor who was already preparing for missionary service in Africa. When Misayely and Norberto have added sufficiently to their flight hours, and Romao has his full aircraft maintenance credentials, the three families plan to serve in Africa as missionaries.

Greg Constable (Human Resources) attended a budget meeting and updated his people-tracker calendar. Dick Craig (Major Funding) worked on his report for the MAF

Canada Board meetings in October. He met with Art Mitchell (Ministry Partnership) regarding volunteer area representatives and their involvement in major gifts, and also discussed details with Lea Uotila (Human Resources Assistant) of his trip to Angola this November, as well as making several phone calls to prospective donors about the new capital campaign to raise funds for another aircraft for Angola, outlining the urgent need and the challenge.

Judy Hearn (Finance) reconciled financial accounts with MAF US and had meetings with office staff, while Lee-Ann Kaczorowski (Receptionist/Executive Assistant) answered phones, and sorted through the day's regular mail and e-mails. As one e-mail concerned a request for a flight in Chad, Lee-Ann provided contact information for the MAF programme there. She updated her records of the August 27 golf tournament that raised $2,800 in pledges for a new MAF scholarship fund. Lea Uotila helped Neil by making several calls to the Brazilian consulate regarding documentation needed for the shipment of the aircraft engine. For other missionaries, she checked into problems with lost luggage, immigration matters and visas.

In Three Hills, today, *Tuesday*, was the first day of classes for the mission aviation students. Richard was occupied with orientation activities for new students, while Dan Lawrance completed the new Preparatory Ground Instruction curriculum. Richard responded to new interest in MAF by e-mail or phone, and made preparations for an upcoming MAF meeting to be held in Three Hills. The following day, *Wednesday*, Dan worked with new students while Richard helped sort out course conflicts. Richard and his wife, Susan, checked out facilities for a staff/student retreat planned for later in the year. For the MAF recruitment office, he mailed out information packages, and made preparations for a mission trip to Papua New Guinea. *Thursday* saw Dan doing some teaching while his colleague worked on the process required for licensing the aviation programme as an approved vocational programme. Jeff Plett (Chief Pilot) plans to be in Three Hills later this month to do check flights with MAF candidate pilots. Dan was busy instructing students on *Friday*. Richard had a meeting with the President of Prairie Bible Institute, on a partnership proposal. He also contacted people inviting them to attend an MAF gathering, and began preparing for a fall recruiting trip and missions conferences.

The working week in Guelph had some interesting things to note.

Dick Craig received and reviewed his final flight schedule for Angola in November when he will meet Canadian staff serving in Angola, South Africa and Botswana. Judy Hearn spent an afternoon with Neil Bittle discussing the Angolan Training Project in Brazil. Judy and her husband, Ken, previously served the Lord as MAF missionaries in Angola. Lea looked into insurance matters regarding the poor availability of health care in Chad. She also inquired whether verbal prescriptions by phone/radio would be acceptable for insurance reimbursement, if Canadian staff serving in remote areas of Papua New Guinea cannot see a doctor for diagnosis and treatment. Judy prepared a support summary to be used for the Angolan families in Brazil as they are evaluated and begin preparations to become MAF missionaries. Claudia Van Riesen (Communications) got an update on the Angolan missionaries and discussed possible Brazil stories for future issues of the *Life Link* newsletter. This eight-page quarterly highlights Canadian missionaries serving with MAF worldwide.

At lunch on *Thursday*, Lea and Greg Constable presented our volunteer translator, Ludgero Nascimento, with a certificate of appreciation for his work on MAF Canada's visa applications for Angola. Ludgero was thrilled, and said he'd never received anything like it before! MAF Canada's visa application for the Heier family (serving short term in Angola) has been a long and difficult one. Without Ludgero we would never have had the completed translations required for the application. We had searched for a couple of weeks for a Portuguese notary since our regular contact was on holiday, and were running out of time when Ludgero heard that there was such a notary in a large office building in Kitchener (a city near Guelph) … but he didn't have the lawyer's name. Ludgero went to the building, praying as he went in, and found the lawyer in the first office he entered! The lawyer was able to help us.

PART FOUR

MAF US

SOUTH AND CENTRAL AMERICA

✈

SOUTH-EAST AND CENTRAL ASIA

✈

AFRICA

20.

DEMOCRATIC REPUBLIC OF CONGO

The Democratic Republic of Congo is right at the heart of Africa. One of the continent's largest countries, it is nearly twice the size of South Africa, and has an estimated population of about sixty million people, a quarter of whom live in the country's towns and cities. For sixty years the Democratic Republic of Congo was a Belgian colony, but freedom from Belgium in the 1960s marked the beginning of a period of violence that could only be described as a bloodbath. The country is still effectively cut into a number of regions, each with its own army, and all – most of the time – in an uneasy peace. But it takes very little, even today, for violence to erupt there. The Congo infrastructure has borne the brunt of the troubles and transportation is in meltdown.

✈ ✈ ✈ ✈ ✈

Sam and Margaret Norman are both MAF pilots. She hails from Norway and her husband is Swedish. Margaret explains the airport and aircraft situation in the DRC.

At the time of writing we are between airports. N'dolo is the smaller city airport. MAF used to have a hangar there, but in 1996 the airport closed due to an accident. A Russian transport plane did not get in the air on take off, and continued into a market, killing a lot of people. The airport was closed until July 2004. MAF and many others have been praying for the opening for those eight years. N'dolo is a lot closer and more convenient for us than the international airport of N'djili. Here in Kinshasa we have one Caravan, one Cessna 207 and five 206s (two of them grounded for long time maintenance waiting to be sold).

✈ ✈ ✈ ✈ ✈

Pilot Garth Pederson did a great deal of flying during the week in which he was asked to keep a diary of his activities. He and his wife and children are based in Kinshasa.

Garth describes a trip out of Kinshasa.

✈ Monday

I met with my travelling companions at the office on Monday morning at 6.15am and drove to Ndolo, the general aviation airport in Kinshasa, to load the Caravan and get ready for the trip. Sam Norman, our Swedish pilot, was assigned to accompany me and help out. As the details of where we would be staying overnight each night were sketchy, I had purchased twelve 1.5 litre water bottles for the trip and we both had some food with us. The purpose of the trip was to deliver school books for the fifth and sixth grade students in the Equateur province of Congo. The Belgian government, in cooperation with the Congolese government, provided these books, and the plan was to transport them to all the fifth and sixth grade students in the whole country. A 2001 census was used as the basis for determining the number of students, and the books were produced for maths, French and science. The arrangement was that books were to be pre-positioned at three of the large airstrips in Equateur, and we would fly them on to some smaller airstrips.

Sam and I loaded the first 900kg of books along with our passenger, a Congolese representative of GTM, the company responsible for the transport of all the books throughout the country. I'll call him Dany. We took off about 8.00am and flew just over an hour north along the Congo River to Lukalela. There we landed and unloaded the books. An official with the Catholic Church had been notified of our coming and was supposed to be there to receive them. After waiting for thirty minutes, I began to be impatient and someone was dispatched by bicycle to find the man. As we heard that it could take hours to drive the 20km from the mission station to the airstrip, after waiting an hour we found some immigration officials who, along with the police, were prepared to sign for the books.

From there we took off to overfly Ntondo, a Baptist mission station another half hour north, to see if the airstrip was usable. We did a low pass but found that it was overgrown and that the trees were too close on both sides for the Caravan to use the strip. So we continued on to Mbandaka to refuel. On landing I went for the fuel truck, Sam paid our taxes, and Dany got on the cell phone to report to his boss in Kinshasa about the delivery in Lukolela and the parcels dropped in Mbandaka. I added 350 litres and paid just over $3 a gallon for the jet fuel.

Our next stop, Boende, was about 150 nautical miles east. Sam took the chance to sit in the left seat and get some instruction and experience flying the Caravan as he hadn't flown it before, and I'm now qualified as a Caravan instructor pilot. As there were too many books to do the next destination in one flight, I unloaded all the passenger seats except two to take more weight and left Sam behind too. GTM wanted a second person on the flight, so that factored into the equation. I took off for Ikela, 156 miles to the east, and started to pick up storms on radar. Diverting to the south around some of them, I then picked my way through. Unfortunately, because we had no radio contact with Ikela, I had no way of knowing what the weather was like there. I was soon in continuous rain and couldn't see any ground references. Although I had never been there before I had some GPS and map coordinates for Ikela and had the map, but when I arrived at where the GPS said the airstrip was supposed to be, all I saw were trees and one trail! The ceiling was fairly good, but the forward visibility was only one to two miles in rain. So after making a couple of big circles I decided to head back to Boende. The GPS moving map showed that I was over the river, near to where the airstrip was supposed to be, but I never saw the river, the village or the strip. A lot of the terrain and airstrip locations in the GPS database are not correct. That is why we always write down the coordinates when we land somewhere new and put them in our airstrip directory.

I had rain all the way back and was grateful to have an instrument approach procedure for Boende. As I flew the approach to the minimum altitude I was still in the clouds, but broke out on time to see the last third of the airstrip and was able to keep ground contact, circled and landed. We normally plan to land with a two hour reserve of fuel, but I had used up 15 minutes of that with diversions and circling, and it was within an hour of sunset. I was glad to be on the ground! At Boende I met a French pilot with Aviation Sans Frontières who had more accurate coordinates for Ikela, which I noted down. After the French pilots were delivered to where they were staying, Sam, Dany and I were given a ride in what may have been the only running vehicle in Boende. It was a totally abused Toyota Landcruiser that had to be pushed to start, and the seats weren't locked down to the floor! We went to a Catholic mission where there was a room with two dry beds. Except for a caretaker, the place seemed to be abandoned. Although there was no electricity, running water, food, blankets or pillows, we were glad to have a dry place to spend the night. Breaking into my food bags, I ate a can of tuna, some potato chips and a granola bar. We had our bottled water and light from a kerosene lantern and our flashlights. Stringing up our mosquito nets we went to sleep about 8pm.

✦ Tuesday

Although four barrels of jet fuel had been pre-positioned for us, I needed more on Tuesday, as I had not been able to land at Ikela with the first load of books. I talked to the French ASF pilot and he agreed to lend us two barrels, with the promise that they would be replaced the next day, and made arrangements for Filair to drop the replacement barrels on their regular flight the next day. We have a custom pump set-up that we bring along sometimes that uses the aircraft battery to power a 24-volt pump to pump fuel from a barrel to refuel the Caravan. The fuel goes through a filter and then up a hose to the fuel tank opening on the top of the wing. That usually attracts interest as most people in the bush are used to rotary hand pumps. Because the weather was better the second day, I was able to find Ikela. It ended up being about seven miles from where our first position had placed it. Sam came on the second trip to Ikela, and we also landed at Bokungu. After another trip back and forth to Bokungu we had delivered almost 9,500 pounds of books. We refuelled at the end of the day and loaded books to be ready to leave early the next morning. Then it was back to our same accommodation and dinner of tuna and crackers.

✈ Wednesday

We flew to Djolu and then on to Bumba. We were originally supposed to go to Lisala, but the military had been causing problems there so Bumba was used instead. After landing, the military commander approached me and wanted to know why they hadn't been informed of our arrival. As he was wearing a beret with UN insignias and pins I asked him if he was with the UN. He said, 'No, it was a gift.' I called his commander and explained that we were delivering school books on a humanitarian flight in cooperation with the Belgian and Congolese governments. I told him where we were going and the schedule and asked permission to continue, but I didn't give him my name, as I believed he was the same man who detained me for about seven hours a year ago. After my speech he told me to give the phone back to the local man; they talked a while and I was relieved to find out that everything was fine. The local man had a passenger he wanted me to take to the next destination and I had to work a way out of that. We made a big production of leaving the seats behind and I explained that even the second pilot had to remain because of the weight. Eventually we got around having to take the extra passenger. The fuel that was supposed to be waiting for us wasn't there, and we waited four hours until a Russian built cargo plane arrived with our fuel barrels.

I was then able to do two flights to Yakoma, delivering over 6000 pounds of books. An official there wanted me to pay a $100 landing fee, but I was able to negotiate down to $20. Then, after returning to Bumba, we fuelled up and went into town where we stayed at a Catholic convent. It was a bit nicer than our previous place; it even had a shower (cold) and a sink with running water. We were invited to dinner with the five nuns there and talked to the one in charge, who was from Peru. They asked Sam to say a prayer before the meal and me to say one afterwards. We had spaghetti noodles with pork and some rice. They also had a generator that provided electricity from 6 to 8pm.

✦ *Thursday*

In the morning it was time once again to negotiate taxes at the airport before flying just over an hour west to Gemena. We had enough fuel to do the first two trips from Gemena to Loko, but then had to refuel. MAF has its own fuel reserves there since we used to do regular flights to Gemena. Unfortunately the 'man with the key' had gone, which meant breaking the lock off of the container where our fuel was stored! There was a bit of confusion over Avgas and Jet fuel too, which added to the delay. Finally I was able to do the last flight of the day to Goyongo, a very picturesque mission station fifty-eight miles north of Gemena. Goyongo has a theological seminary started by the Evangelical Free Church and Covenant Church. The airstrip is one-way for the Caravan because of its slope and tall trees at one end. There are hills all around which makes it a very interesting place to land.

That evening we stayed with Pastor Selenga, the President of the Evangelical Free Church in Congo. As he had studied at Goyongo, I asked him how long it took to drive from Gemena to Goyongo. He said about twelve to fourteen hours with a four-wheel drive vehicle. It was twenty-five minutes in the Caravan. We had a traditional Congolese meal and were joined by four other visiting Congolese officials. Pastor Selenga, his wife and five kids, live in a former missionary's house. The house was pillaged and stripped during the war, but they are in the process of repairing it.

✈ *Friday*

Today we just had one more book delivery to do before heading home. We flew ninety-seven miles to Zongo, right on the border across the river from Bangui, capital of Central African Republic. We took with us three students en route to FATEB, the Evangelical Theology seminary at Bangui. Zongo was the seventh new airstrip for me on this trip, and we were the first MAF airplane to land there. After gathering all the data we could for our airstrip directory, we flew on to Mbandaka for fuel and home to Kinshasa. Totals for the five days: 25.4 flight hours, 27 landings, over 3,500 nautical miles, and 13,989kg (30,776lbs) of freight.

✈ ✈ ✈ ✈ ✈

Ruth Heller, the Programme Manager's wife, noted what she did each day. Some were things most wives do, other certainly were not!

As the water tanks were empty, I bucketed water from barrels into the tanks. The rest of *Monday* was taken up with housekeeping, sharing in the school car pool and attending the ladies' Bible study. The next day I worked in the office reconciling accounts before picking up the kids from school.

There was still no water. *Wednesday's* accounting was done at home and intermingled with housework. Our water came on during the night and the tanks filled up! Today was a baking day as there is a sale being held at the school.

Ruth works in MAF Congo's Accounts Department, though she can do some of her work from home.

✈ ✈ ✈ ✈ ✈

Makasy Kimvangu, Airport Chaplain, has seen a great change in the last six months.

After years of waiting, we give thanks to God for giving us an office at the airport. It was inaugurated on 18 March 2004. Now we have a meeting during the lunch hour with others who work at N'djili, the international airport in Kinshasa. The first day there were six people present. Later between eight and sixteen people showed up every day. We meet for prayer, and we pray specifically for the activities that are going on at the airport. In addition to the prayer meetings, I usually visit the different services at the airports and distribute tracts and Bibles. Sometimes I even have the privilege of leading people to Jesus Christ.

Once God gave us the opportunity to travel to Luozi in Bas Congo. We shared about Jesus Christ with some of the agents there and distributed tracts. Then we continued our flight to Kimpese, also in the Bas Congo, and did the same there. We have testimonies of people who were not going to church before, and others who were having problems in their lives. After reading the tracts and praying, God met them and they are now serving him. I pray that God will continue to use me in his service.

✈ ✈ ✈ ✈ ✈

Avutu Simeon, in the IT Department, begins his day by making sure the servers are working well and verifying that the anti-virus programme is updated. Internet gremlins are no respecter of MAF bases!

On *Monday* I was in touch with the legal representative of the Methodist Church who wanted to use our e-mail services at his office. I went there and found that we would need a full wireless antenna kit with a 1-Watt amplifier and a triple length of cable due to the distance. We do, however, have difficulty with legality. The Congolese government has not yet authorised MAF to provide Internet services. After a meeting with the legal representative, I passed the case on to the director for a decision. Next day I continued a job I was doing, that was copying folders from a laptop to a new desktop PC. Our goal was to empty the laptop of all financial documents. Later in the week I had to buy IT equipment for the Baptist Union. In order to find everything they needed we had to visit several stores.

✈ ✈ ✈ ✈ ✈

Leta Kupa works in Finances, and does a bit of juggling between currencies.

Today, *Tuesday*, one of the things I did was exchange dollars to francs for the business cash box and cash transfer to Vanga base. In the Democratic Republic of Congo most financial transactions are handled in US dollars. So we use dollars in cash, I guess, more than they are used in the States since they use other means such as cheques, money orders, credit cards and so on. One of the reasons for that is the depreciation of the local currency, the franc. For example, today the rate is 405Fcs/1$ US. If we need 100$ US notes we have to carry two hundred and two 200 franc notes to get it. The biggest note we have in the country is 200 francs.

That means it is easier to carry dollars cash than to carry francs. It is also possible to keep dollar notes without them losing their value.

Leta goes on to give some background information regarding church life in the Democratic Republic of Congo.

In Africa we live in community, while in Europe life is individual. Solidarity is very common to Africans. In DRC Protestants have a structure that is almost as rigid as the one we see in our government. The different denominations are tied up as a body of Christ in a structure that can oversee what is going on in each denomination and assist with advice and help for the improvement and progress of the Lord's work. This is called Église du Christ au Congo. The President is Bishop Pierre Marini Bodho, who is also President of Parliament. On 4 September Bishop Pierre Marini Bodho lost his oldest daughter in Germany. To bear the burden and express our emotion with him in an African culture we, in the MAF team, along with all other such organisations, made a little contribution in cash to help provide some food and drink for those who visit the family during and after the funeral. MAF is very much part of our church community in the Democratic Republic of Congo.

21.

ECUADOR

We travel from a community right in the centre of Africa across the Atlantic Ocean, over Brazil and Peru to Ecuador, on the Pacific coast of Latin America. Ecuador is, like the Democratic Republic of Congo, a land of contrasts. It is made up of a fertile coastal plain along the Pacific, the high Andean Sierra in the centre of the country, and the Amazon jungle on the east. A large proportion of the people – over 60 per cent – live in towns and cities, but those who do not are sometimes very remote indeed.

Ecuador has a special place in the hearts of all who have an interest in the work of Mission Aviation Fellowship, for it was there in 1956 that MAF pilot Nate Saint, along with four other godly young men, was martyred for his faith. The Auca Indians (who are now known as the Waorani) killed the men who tried to take them the good news that eternal life can be found in Jesus Christ. Since then many of the Waorani people have come to know the Lord, and in 2000, MAF had the privilege of transporting building materials to be used in the erection of a Bible college in the heart of what was Auca territory. The work that Nate Saint and others pioneered goes on today, but it is still not easy.

✈ ✈ ✈ ✈ ✈

Dave McCleery tells a little of life there with MAF.

One of our pilots, Dale Shaylor, was involved in a traffic accident on the evening of August 29th. He came upon a broken down truck on a curve and was unable to stop before hitting debris in the road that the bus driver had placed there as a warning—a typical procedure here. When he hit the debris, including a large post, his vehicle skidded sideways into an oncoming car. Thankfully, there were no injuries. As traffic accidents are illegal here, Dale spent the next nine nights in jail until the judge was satisfied with the investigation and all the paperwork was processed. During the process we were reminded of the high level of corruption within the government and police department. It is amazing that such a thing can happen to an innocent person. Dale was finally released from jail last night, 7 September.

That was not the only good news as Curtis (one of our aircraft mechanics) and Rachel Kelley were blessed with the birth of their first child, Connor Patrick, yesterday morning, the Minister of Health signed our Air Ambulance contract renewal, and we found out that our US mechanics will not have to take multiple exams in Spanish to renew or receive new licences. A spectacular day for the Ecuador staff!

We fly over 2,000 patients each year in our six airplanes here in Ecuador under a contract with the government's Ministry of Health. They reimburse eighty per cent of our flight costs to fly these patients. Up until a few years ago, the majority of the patients were treated at the local evangelical mission hospital. There they received treatment of their souls as well as their sickness or injury. Recently the Ministry of Health has been putting on pressure to ensure that these jungle patients are treated at public hospitals since it is a public health programme. Now only the most gravely ill are sent to the mission hospital. We have just begun a new Chaplancy programme within MAF and our hope is to link local evangelical Christians with these patients in a compassion and evangelism ministry. Manuel, who has worked with us for the past 10 years and Pastors a church 'on the side', will coordinate this programme. Local Christians will visit the jungle patients and attempt to help them with their needs as well as share the love of Christ with them. Beyond this direct contact during their hospital stay, Manuel will work with jungle churches to help in follow-up and discipleship. The potential Kingdom gain for this ministry is incredible, and we are excited to see how the Lord leads.

The pastor of a jungle church called in to see me this afternoon. He is seeking help from evangelical missionaries or pastors for his church in a small jungle community called San Jose. He reports severe persecution from the Roman Catholics in the area, and is currently on his way to the capital to ask the Ministry of Government to appoint a commission to investigate the problems. It is sad to see this kind of thing happening, although it seems to be a fairly isolated case of problems between evangelicals and Catholics. In recent years the Catholic Church has been more open to evangelical efforts in the jungle and has even been encouraging Catholics to read the Bible themselves. I arranged for the pastor to be flown to Makuma next week to meet with the Shuar Evangelical Church Association to see how they can help him. I believe a major purpose of MAF is to bring Christians who are working in different areas together in order that we can all be stronger by sharing the different gifts we have in Christ.

✦ ✦ ✦ ✦ ✦

David Hoffman describes a day in the IT Department, but was it normal or not?

Today was a varied day on the IT front but, for the most part, a normal one. Let me digress for a moment and say that there are two kinds of normal days. The first kind of normal day is where there is a variety of IT tasks to accomplish: maintenance, user support, research, troubleshooting, documentation and future planning. The other kind of normal day involves trying to solve a computer hardware or software problem. The solution is not obvious, and the problem can take hours to solve. A worst-case scenario is to have two or more of these types of problem to solve on the same day. What can really get me down, and make me obsessed, is having a couple of these problems remaining unsolved for two or more days.

Today I was able to re-do the cables for the UPS batteries. We have a bank of 12-volt batteries that run the two servers when the power is out. The batteries are in their second life, having first been used at a radio repeater site. We were down to five batteries and last week one went bad. Even with five batteries I wasn't able to be sure that the system would keep the servers running even for a couple of hours. Today's task was to take out the oldest of the four surviving batteries, add five new ones, and bring the total to eight. Along the way I re-did the cables, as the battery terminals of the newer batteries are different. The next step will be to figure out a way of knowing how long the batteries will power the computers in a long power outage.

This whole episode highlights how the roles of MAF staff work here. Normally the avionics technician takes care of the Uninterruptible Power Supply, which provides power to computers when the main electricity goes off so nothing gets lost. I don't know much about the system, and rely on him in that area. As he is currently on a six-month furlough, it's all up to me. I was able to get some information and coaching by e-mail and then completed the job on my own. The end result is that I now know more about the system. When someone is on furlough it's up to the rest to take on the extra load.

After school was out today I walked across the street to the Nate Saint School. The teacher of grades 1 – 3 needed some help with the classroom computer in order that she can use instructional CDs. When that was done we worked to install software for a new printer/scanner/fax. Finally, I showed her how to connect her digital camera to her computer to download photos. The computer and digital camera are important tools for writing news letters that keep ministry partners informed about what is happening on the mission field.

✈✈✈✈✈

Back to Dave McCleery for another encouragement.

✈ *Friday 10 September*

Yesterday, on a normal ops flight to drop off a patient going home, transport a national pastor's family and pick up some education inspectors, I was able to fit in the opening of a new airstrip. There are just over 200 airstrips in the main area where we fly in the southeastern jungles of Ecuador. This new one, called Pitiur (it required some tongue gymnastics for me to say it correctly), lies about seventy miles southeast of Shell.

The people of Pituir were excited to see our red and white Cessna arrive for the first time at their new strip. They had spent over a year preparing it with only machetes, axes, shovels and a couple of wheelbarrows to do the job. Bearing that in mind it was amazing to see the result. The airstrip measured 500 by 20 metres, it was nice and flat and the arrival and departure ends were well cleared. I took the needed measurements, installed the markers that help us to judge takeoffs and landings, installed a wind indicator and looked for hazards, such as soft spots from where tree trunks were removed. It all checked out great! Now the people have access to emergency flights when they are sick, and also potential visits from missionaries and national pastors.

The beginning of MAF's work in Ecuador was marked with sadness, but in the early years of the twenty-first century there is much happening in that land to rejoice the hearts of God's people.

22.
PAPUA

Having left the programme MAF US operates in Ecuador we travel west, right across the Pacific Ocean, above the Solomon Islands, then high over the mountains of Papua New Guinea to reach our final destination, the western end of the island of New Guinea, the land of Papua. The mountains there range even higher than in PNG, reaching a magnificent 5030 metres. Rain forests cover most of the land, and there are some vast swamped areas too. MAF USA operates in Papua, while MAF Australia operates in PNG.

MAF USA says:

As recently as 1997, Stone Age tribes living in Papua had remained undiscovered, untouched, and unreached. Today, there are other primitive tribes still living in the hidden crevices of the island. They have yet to hear of Jesus Christ, and they live in fear of spirits and the outside world. Basic services, such as schools and health clinics, are unavailable in these remote locations. As a result, countless Papuans suffer in spiritual darkness, unsuccessfully battling chronic malaria, rampant skin fungi, malnutrition, and intestinal worms. The need in Papua is so great that our pilot/missionaries report they are able to accommodate less than half of the flight requests they receive. There are very few viable alternatives to Mission Aviation Fellowship air services throughout most of Papua.

Since 1952, MAF missionary pilots have brought hope and support to this rugged and forbidding place. Today, MAF planes and communications networks multiply the effectiveness of Christian agencies ministering in Papua. Mission Aviation Fellowship services sustain evangelism, church nurture, medical assistance, community development, education, crisis relief, and national training. The value of the MAF ministry is without question.

✈✈✈✈✈

Lest anyone think that a land with areas as remote as some parts of Papua are beyond reach, Roy Kidjo reminds us otherwise. Roy serves the Lord in Papua with his wife Lientje.

Recently Brent Palmer, Nyoman Iriandi and I, as MAF Sentani IT technicians, went to install a VSAT system in the village of Pass Valley. This system will allow missionaries and community development workers to connect to the Internet via satellite. They can, therefore, have instant e-mail access. Pass Valley is a small village about fifty minutes south of Sentani by airplane and located in the mountains at about 6000 ft elevation. The NRC training centre is located there as well as Oikonomos, a community development foundation. After two days of hard work, and with the help of many villagers, we completed the installation. We then tested the system and were able to listen to a direct audio streaming from a Christian radio station in the US. That was exciting! It is amazing that we can be connected with the rest of the world through the Internet in this very remote jungle in Papua. The technology is present to make it possible to listen to the preaching of the Gospel and to receive God's Word even in the most remote places on earth. This means that there is actually nowhere on earth that is not accessible. What is needed to complete this mission is people willing to go, people willing to pray, and people willing to give for God's Kingdom.

✈ ✈ ✈ ✈

Clarence Togeretz, a pilot/mechanic, is on loan to MAF in Papua from MAF Canada. Based in Nabire, both his flying and mechanical skills are called into service.

Several days ago I flew to Enarotali on my way home from Timika, and thought I was going to have a fast turn-around, as there usually aren't any passengers. However, after shutting down the engine, I learned that there was a patient on her way to the airplane for a flight to Nabire. She would be 'only five minutes'. Well, I wasn't sure about that, as only five minutes usually turns into thirty-five or fifty-five. However, in five minutes she really was at the airplane, and we lifted her unconscious body on to the floor of the aircraft where I could tie her down properly. She was having major complications during the delivery of her baby and we really needed to get her to hospital soon. Once in the aircraft, she started to come around slightly and caused quite a stir in her confusion. All the way to Nabire she kept the two attendants busy as she squirmed and groaned and cried in her effort to get out of the safety belts that held her in place. However, she made it safely to the city, where she could have proper medical care.

Another day I flew roofing material for a church building to an interior airstrip called Beoga. On the way home I made an extra stop to pick up five more medical patients. Thankfully these planned a little further ahead and requested to be picked up before their conditions turned into emergencies. One lady was pregnant and due to deliver in two days. After that, I flew some more church roofing material to a different village.

My wife was teaching in the school, as she has been doing for the last two weeks while our regular teacher takes a once-in-a-lifetime trip to a jungle village with some former missionaries.

This morning I took off only to have an audible warning and flashing light illuminate while climbing through 400 feet. My annunciator panel told me that the alternator had failed, and a verifying check of the ammeter showed me that my battery was discharging. So I turned back to base. Fortunately we had a second 206 parked on the ramp as its pilot is on vacation. After a forty-five minute delay, because we had to unload one aircraft then fuel, preflight, and reload the second one, I was on my way again. Guess what the load was? Well, rice was one thing, and more aluminium roofing for yet another church in yet another village. Later in the day I managed to find my way out through some heavy rain and bad weather to Mulia, where I picked up our teacher and a spare alternator for the broken airplane. I hoped to fix the first aircraft at the end of my day, but I arrived home too late and tired to do anything about it.

✈ ✈ ✈ ✈ ✈

Fellow MAF pilot, Harry Berghuis, who is on loan from Holland, took careful note of his activities. He is based in Wamena.

Climb check complete! It was time to sit back, relax and enjoy the view. A fellow pilot always thought that the first flight of the day was the most enjoyable. Today's certainly was. The weather was perfect, high overcast and underneath everything was clear, at least where I was going, and much better than in the other direction. Having made my calls, I started my descent to Mamit, a station opened by Regions Beyond Missionary Union in the 1960s. I was carrying a variety of passengers. When I landed I could hardly see a cloud below, but as soon as I got out the airplane, the approach end from which I had just come completely closed up with fog. It can happen as quickly as that! But as I knew that it wouldn't be long before it opened up again, I got my load ready for Mulia. As well as a number of passengers, there was produce from their gardens and several pigs. No doubt they hoped to sell the lot in Mulia where they can get a good price.

In Mulia there was a muddle because, although they said there were nine passengers – a full load for the Caravan – to Beoga, there were only five. As a result I changed plans and decided to go straight back to Wamena. But by the time I had the tickets and the money together for Wamena, the five for Beoga had found friends to go with them, enough to fill the remaining seats! Normally we do not have time to switch back and forward with our schedule, but it was possible that day. The passengers, all Papuans, would have been very disappointed if I had cancelled the Beoga run. As soon as I told them that we would be going to Beoga, and asked them to get ready, the most amazing chaos erupted, with people shouting back and forward, money flying left and right and baggage put on and off the scale. Having calculated how much I needed for the tickets, I discovered there was more than that on the table. I was just happy that there was enough because usually there is not. Patiently I urged the passengers to start boarding the airplane because I was also scheduled to go to an airstrip where wind is a factor. I made it to Beoga and the wind-affected airstrip in time, and was able to complete the rest of my schedule without further abnormalities.

Another day I departed at 6.20am for Mamit as I had local passengers to take back there, though I'm not sure why they were in Wamena. On the way back I had five passengers and the rest of the cargo was peanuts to be sold in Wamena. The second trip went to Kobakma with people from Oikonomos, a community development foundation. They were going to have a ceremony to 'officially' open up the kiosk that they have there. This kiosk is a project they are trying out. At it you can buy stuff like soap, cooking oil, etc., with local produce, like peanuts. Oikonomos takes the local produce to Wamena where it is sold. Store goods are bought with the proceeds, and these are taken back to be sold at the kiosk in Kobakma. This kiosk has been open for a while, but today was the official opening. I was invited but had to do another flight to Wunin first. It was a quick turn-around, which is unique in Kobakma, because of the wind curfew.

By the time I returned to Kobakma I had missed the official opening of the kiosk, but still had time to enjoy lunch with the people. Of course, there were lots of pigs slaughtered and cooked in the famous local fashion with hot stones in a hole in the ground covered up with grass to keep the heat in. When I came back to Wamena in the afternoon, I needed to prepare the local staff's half-month salary as the girl who does our finances is off ill.

And yet another day:

Coming home after a base meeting, I saw smoke coming from near the fuel *gudang* (shed) at the MAF hangar in Wamena. I walked across the street to investigate. When I got there, I saw that one of the guards from an Indonesian airline had started a fire for trash very near to MAF's fuel *gudang*. I told the guard that there was fuel near there and asked him to put the fire out to avoid an accident. 'Oh no, it's ok, I have it under control,' he replied casually. I was shocked, as only a few days before, a whole block of the town burned down because a man looking for something in the dark lit a match near some drums of fuel. I told the man about this, asking him if he hadn't heard about the fire, and didn't he realise that fire near fuel was very, very dangerous. The man replied that it was okay; he would control it, that it was really safe since he was watching it and would put it out if it got too near the fuel *gudang*. Finally, when I realised that he wasn't going to put it out, I took a hose and, with an MAF guard's help, put the fire out. I just thank God that I was able to do that before anything bad happened.

✦ ✦ ✦ ✦ ✦

Harry's wife, Willie, had an unsettling experience as she did the school run. It's a reminder of how violent some societies can be.

Friday was a rainy morning, so instead of going on our bikes I piled the kids into the car to go to school. As I was about to turn into the road to the new base, all of a sudden there was a bunch of police. When they gestured that I should go on, I turned into that street. But there were policemen all over the place and crowds of people. Everywhere people had come out of their houses and were looking around. It was obvious that something had happened, but I couldn't figure out what. When I arrived at school I heard the story from one of the other moms. There had been a drunken man on the street and the police came to arrest him. But drunk as he was, he didn't want to cooperate. At that, a policeman pulled his gun and shot the man. He died instantly.

Willie heard some remarkable news when her helpers arrived at work.

One morning, my *pembantus* (helpers) showed up to work very excited. They said, 'Have you heard the news? Have you heard?' I asked them what had happened. They told me that a woman had given birth to a piglet, and that it was all over the newspaper and everyone was talking about it. In Indonesia pigs are good, and giving birth to one would not have been a bad thing. I asked how they could believe such nonsense. They told me that an elder in the church had explained it to them. He said that either the lady had slept with a pig, or she had slept with a man who was a pig in the day and a man at night. I rebuked them, and told them that such a thing was not possible, that they should not believe such nonsense, and that I thought they knew better. One of my pembantus told me that, as she knew the Lord Jesus was coming soon, she thought such strange things could happen. Again, I told them very strongly that such a thing could not have happened and that they should not believe it.

A Bible study is part of Willie's routine with her pembantus, *and it is sometimes very encouraging.*

Only one other woman, a widow, showed up besides my *pembantus* for our Bible study, in which I wanted to focus on God's love. I spoke of how much God loves us, how we are created in his image, how he looked at *everything* he had created and said it was 'very good', and how special we are to him. Then I read Isaiah 49:16 to them, which says, 'Behold,

I have carved you on the palms of My hands; your walls are always before Me' (LITV). I suggested they should think of a young man in love and how he will carve the initials of his girl on trees and benches. God is just as much in love with us as that, I explained. I could see that they needed to realise God's great love for them. The widow was really soaking it all in. That day they needed to hear nothing more than the message of God's great love.

When I asked them for prayer requests, I was struck again by how much the message was just right for them. The man who works in my yard asked for prayer because a while ago, during an election campaign, a government official took his pig and hasn't paid him back, though he promised to do so. Whenever he sees the man, he asks about his money, but the official acts busy or doesn't take any notice. On top of all that, when he took his girl to school to register, he was turned away for no reason at all. I saw how much these people are treated like junk a lot of the time, and how desperately they need to realise that God loves them and values them immensely, even if others do not.

Many missionaries attend indigenous churches, and Willie records a rather unusual sermon she heard.

The preacher told the story of when God created Adam and Eve. He reminded the congregation that when God created Eve, he took a rib from Adam and filled in the space with meat. God created only one wife and took only one rib. Therefore, the preacher asserted, if a man wants more wives, more ribs would have to be removed and filled in with meat. If too many ribs were removed the man would not be able to breathe. There would be nothing around his lungs to support them and they would collapse inwards. The preacher pretended to be out of breath. He took quick shallow breaths to show the congregation how men would be unable to breathe with so many wives. He said that if polygamy were God's plan, men would be unable to breathe, and again pretended to be out of breath. Yes, it's a little unorthodox, but a good example of a different culture's perspective on the issue of polygamy, and in some ways, very true!

✈ ✈ ✈ ✈ ✈

MAF missionaries are privileged to live among the people of Papua, and they both teach and learn together. Alyssa Harris, wife of Maintanance Specialist Matthew Harris, discovered a strange tradition from a lady she met.

Day by day many people pass though our gate. Kids come to play, helpers come to work and folks come selling fresh produce. Many are in need of the extra income generated by selling fruits and vegetables. After buying two pineapples and chatting with one dear lady, I took her hands and thanked her for coming. Her left hand felt different; she was missing two fingers. Since we have an established relationship, I didn't feel badly asking what had happened. She explained, 'Before Jesus came to our village, it was the practice to cut off fingers from the family members of someone who died. When I was a little girl that happened to me.' This strange ritual accentuated loss and mourning in her tribe. I am sure that little girl must have been terrified, not to mention confused at the loss of a loved one. It was interesting to me that Ibu Tariamban began to express what happened with, 'Before Jesus came.' When we face such daily encounters we know why God has us here. We are privileged to hear of villages changed and lives reconciled to Jesus through his bond of peace.

Alyssa looks back on God's wonderful work.

Ibu Termina's great uncle died last week. Ibu is our helper. That uncle is being remembered by hundreds of people as one of a group of twenty men from the village of Tagime who travelled into the enemy territory of Pyramid. Why would a man risk travelling into an area where he might be killed? Why face the hardship of a long trek, and swim across the treacherous Baliem River to reach Pyramid? Presumably he wanted to know if the rumours were true. Had the people of Pyramid changed because of the words of the white man who had come from a far-off place? Were the people no longer fierce, head hunting warriors?

When Punguni's group reached Pyramid they found that the rumours were true. The people were different! What was this message he was hearing in the Dani language? God had sent these white men to teach them of the great God's love for them. Upon hearing the 'Injil'– or Gospel of Jesus – he accepted the message with an open heart. When he returned to Tagime, there was still some opposition to the Gospel. But over the course of time an airstrip, church, seminary, hospital and Christian school for children have been established in Tagime.

Fifty years later, only two of the original group of twenty men are still alive. Bapak Punguni (who also went to seminary to become a pastor) was being remembered as one of the Dani forefathers of the faith. Praise God for the work of the Holy Spirit, drawing many Dani sons and daughters to him through these bold men.

✈ ✈ ✈ ✈ ✈

Brent Palmer, who is a pilot, flies out of Wamena. He describes a medical evacuation from a village which, unlike Tagime, had no medical facilities at all.

This particular day started out like any other. My schedule included several flights out of Wamena to interior villages here in the mountains of Papua, formerly Irian Jaya, Indonesia. During my first flight a village called in to our Wamena office with a medical emergency. When I arrived back in Wamena after completing my first flight, I was informed of it. This meant that my next scheduled flight had to be cancelled in order that I could go to the interior and pick up the patient. After refuelling and loading up the cargo we had stored in our warehouse for my next stop, I headed over the mountains to Nipsan. My patient was a child about nine years old. No one was really sure what was wrong with him because there are no medically trained people in the villages. The boy was very sick and needed to get to hospital. His father accompanied him in the plane, holding him on his knee. We had an uneventful flight back to Wamena, and I was careful to not fly too high as this can sometimes aggravate medical problems. I chose the low altitude route back home, only climbing to 8,000 feet above sea level, rather than the high route at 11,000 feet that I had used to get there. The rest of the day's flights went as scheduled.

The next day I was scheduled to do Information Technology work. I usually split my time about half and half between flying and managing MAF's IT Department here in Papua. Early in the morning I had a call from the office. I was needed to make a medical emergency flight since the other pilots were flying the larger Cessna Caravan airplanes that could not get into the small airstrip where the patient was. I changed into my pilot uniform and headed to the hangar across town. This emergency was in Mapenduma, another mountain airstrip located about a 30-minute flight west of Wamena. I preflighted the plane and took off. On arrival in Mapenduma, I noticed everyone was sombre. As it turned out this patient was also a child, about the same age as the one the day before. Only it was very clear what his problem was. This child had been playing with a stick and somehow poked the stick into one of his eyes. He was all bandaged up and very lethargic. His father accompanied him on the flight. In fact, the father and son were the only passengers wanting to leave. I loaded them up and we flew back to Wamena.

Due to pilots being away on furlough, I have been the only one flying the smaller Cessna 206 aircraft out of Wamena for the past few months. Because of this, I seem to be doing more medical emergency flights than usual, four or five a week lately. I see a lot of hurting people, desperate for help. Some have fallen out of trees, or off steep hillsides or mountains; others have malaria so badly they can hardly walk. Many are pregnancy related and others are ill with unknown complaints. Each time I bring a patient back to Wamena to get medical help, I pray that the Lord will heal and show his mercy in time of need. And I thank him that I am able to do my part in helping.

✈ ✈ ✈ ✈ ✈

Brent's wife, Melanie, shares some of the frustrations of life in Papua.

We continue to have long periods of time without electricity, and that's taking its toll on our appliances, food, patience level, etc. The local store owners who have freezers or refrigerators are really upset. Some took it upon themselves to 'trash' the electric company's office, which *always* has electricity. Just yesterday, one of our friends went to the office to find out why their house had no electricity even though it was on the same block as the office. She was waiting for someone to speak to, when in marched half-a-dozen local folk carrying their crock pots and rice cookers. They plugged in and told the electric company people that they'd be doing their cooking at the office if things weren't straightened out. Why didn't I think of that? I just might trot over to perk my coffee one of these days.

Coffee was on Melanie's mind on another day, but much more serious things came first.

A fire consumed an entire block of homes and shops a mere kilometre from our housing complex. Brent came home before the kids even left for school the next morning, due to bad weather, and reported what he saw at the site of the fire. Nothing. There was absolutely nothing except for grey, smouldering ash piles. Later in the day we were told that twenty-seven families lost everything they owned, including their homes and shops. I couldn't believe it. Twenty-seven families wondering what to do now. Probably rebuilding will be their decision. In the meantime, they have no clothes except what they were wearing when they fled in the night. They have no food or shelter except what friends or relatives can give them. As a community we expats are going to do what we can to ease their situation. Our little fellowship takes an offering each week in order that we can be ready to meet these kinds of needs as they arise. It still doesn't seem like enough, you know. These folks were our neighbours and we hope, someday, they will be again.

I finally got around to going to the coffee warehouse to pick up my supply of fresh roasted coffee beans this week. It's been at least nine months since I was last there. When I walked in, the fellow who works there popped up from his desk and clapped his hands together as he said, 'You're back! Did you just arrive?' I felt a bit awkward when I said that we'd been back for three months, but had been very busy. He was surprised but not offended. As I felt I owed him some time, I sat down and we had a nice long chat about America and our time there. He seemed pleased that I wasn't in any hurry to leave his office. It was that fact that reminded me of one reason why I love living here most of the time. 'There's really no hurry, because there's always tomorrow,' could be the motto of Wamena.

On *Thursday* the expat ladies, kids and teachers got together at the site of the burned-out shops and homes to meet the former residents. While a few of us collected personal information on each fire victim, the kids and teachers handed out some bags, each containing a blanket, soap, juice, a towel, and other miscellaneous things. It went well and we're now in a position to find the people again and help in other ways. The local churches are expected to pitch in and actually take over relief efforts, which is another way of establishing relationships as they demonstrate the heart of our Saviour.

✈ ✈ ✈ ✈ ✈

The Assistant Programme Manager in Sentani is Jonathan Raney. He takes up his story in the early hours of a morning.

I rose in the dark hours of the morning to catch a local domestic carrier along with two other MAF staff to our interior base of Wamena for two days of meetings with staff, employees and users. On getting to the airport, we found that our tickets had not been delivered as promised, and we were stuck waiting in the smoke-filled check-in area to see if they'd show up before our departure. After waiting for some time without any sign of tickets, and being concerned we'd miss the flight if we kept on waiting, we went ahead and purchased new tickets and proceeded to the waiting room. It wasn't long before our lungs were met with extra resistance as we stepped into the aircraft and were forced to breathe the heavy humid morning air filled with rice dust and its odour. Looking at our feet, the aisle carpet was scattered with rice as full rice sacks were buckled in the aft number of rows of passenger seats with only a flimsy tarpaulin covering them to camouflage their existence. The cargo door to the front of the aircraft popped open letting us see pallets and pallets of rice tied under cargo ropes waiting for their journey to this highland town which is one hundred per cent supported by air transportation for supplies from the outside world. After a non-eventful flight, the way they're supposed to be, Wamena met us with cool refreshing early morning air and our day's meetings began.

Next day I was again up before light to go with our MAF Caravan as we delivered a CMA missionary to an outpost station, along with other church leaders and supplies. The outstation needed some maintenance in order to keep the water system functioning. This gave the national church leadership time to meet with church leaders in the area. I was blessed with a tour of the rustic mission housing facilities and by the warmth of the people, and then it was off back to Wamena with a full load of passengers and a pod full of pigs. Routine administration kept me busy thereafter.

I was off and going the following morning with Harry Berghuis, taking a full load to Ninia, where we picked up nine passengers to take back to Wamena, one of these being a young boy who had fallen out of a tree and landed on his wrist, causing a bad compound fracture. Though the wound was wrapped, it had been bleeding through the wrap and it was obvious this roughly ten-year-old boy was in a lot of pain. We taxied down the steep sloped runway and took off for Wamena so the boy could get medical care at the government hospital.

From there we were off to Mulia and Ilaga. In Ilaga, while Harry was loading the airplane, collecting tickets, and gently saying sorry to the eighteen other passengers who were waiting for a flight out, I took a short walk to Gary Willems' grave. This was the site of a very unfortunate MAF Twin Otter accident on 25th May 1987. As I stood in front of his grave, surrounded by curious onlookers, I thanked the Lord for the great sacrifice that was made to bring the Gospel to this very remote area of Papua. At the same time, I prayed for the dear people who surrounded me, that the Lord would continue to touch them and bring them to himself, and that Gary's life given seventeen years ago would still make an eternal impact in this place. My thoughts moved to my father, who was killed in an airplane accident serving the Lord in missions back in 1968. Is the Lord still using his death to reach the people of Palawan in the Philippines? Indeed, it is a privilege to serve our Lord even when the cost is great.

✈ ✈ ✈ ✈ ✈

Pilot Mike Brooks had been in the US on furlough prior to the snapshot week, and his return to work gives an interesting insight into the stringent measures that are taken to ensure the competence of pilots and the safety of flights. Mike is based in Sentani.

Having returned from a three-month furlough in the States, it was time to get my proficiency check and re-currency in the Cessna 208 Caravan prior to resuming normal flight duties in Papua. This checkout process would include a full day of re-familiarisation flying with the chief pilot, Rick Willms, and a full flight evaluation regime, including a Proficiency Flight Review and an Instrument Proficiency Check. What follows is a recap of the flying that took place:

✦ Day one

I arrived at the airplane at 5.15am to begin the preflight. It was relatively dark, but the sun was starting to rise. My body is still adjusting to the time change. I noted that our particular Caravan (PK-MPF) needed a Return to Service flight before we could depart to our first destination. This RTS flight is required each time an aircraft comes out of a maintenance inspection. Rick said the RTS flight would accomplish two goals; it would complete the maintenance requirement for the aircraft and also give me an opportunity to get used to flying the Caravan again. Great idea! This was especially beneficial because during the flight I was able to practise take-off and landing techniques on a nice long and wide concrete runway in Sentani. These are crucial at short (600 metres average), narrow, unprepared airstrips in the interior.

After the RTS fight we returned to the MAF parking area where the load crew prepared the aircraft for our first flight to Oksibil. Oksibil is south of Sentani, near the PNG border. It is situated on the south side of the major mountain range in Papua, about a one-hour flight for the Caravan. The load crew filled our plane to 1,200 pounds of Jet-A fuel and configured it for our nine Indonesian passengers. After hearing a favourable weather report via HF radio, we asked the men to load up the passengers for departure. On some mornings, and during certain times of the year, the weather in Oksibil can change fast. We were on the later side of the window of best weather, but we would give it a try nonetheless.

By the time we arrived over the Oksibil area clouds had already begun to form in the valley as well as on the high ridges surrounding it, but the approach and landing area were still clear. As it is necessary to make a 'short-field' landing at Oksibil, the practice during the RTS flight came in handy. While we were on the ground the valley basin continued to fill with cloud. Rick and I worked together to make our ground time as short as possible in order not to have to spend the rest of the day, and possibly overnight, at Oksibil. There was one glitch during our time on the ground as a passenger's bag was mistakenly left in Sentani. That is almost as bad as forgetting a missionary's mail. While Rick was apologising for the mistake, and getting the passenger's name and information, I prepared the airplane for engine start in order that we could 'beat feet' and depart out of the Oksibil valley before the weather grew any worse.

After take-off we manoeuvred around the valley to stay clear of clouds then began our climb to 13,500 feet. This altitude gave us 2,000 feet above the highest mountain peak and allowed us to fly in the clouds as we headed north. After arriving back in Sentani, the load crew prepared for our second flight of the day to Mulia. Mulia is southwest of Sentani in the mountain range of Papua. On this flight we carried 1,150kg of cargo, including construction materials for various projects taking place in the village of Mulia.

Shortly after take-off Rick put me 'under the hood'. That meant I donned a plastic visual restriction brow on my head to restrict my view of outside the aircraft. I could only see the aircraft instrumentation. This allows the pilot to simulate flying IMC (Instrument Meteorological Conditions) with no visual ground references or references to the earth's horizon. It is great practice! One hour and fifteen minutes into the flight, as we approached Mulia airstrip, Rick told me to take the hood off, and I saw that there was cloud and the chance of rain brewing in the Mulia valley. So we planned to make a normal approach and landing, and decided to work together to make our time on the ground as short as possible in order not to not get stuck in Mulia due to weather.

On our departure out of Mulia, we again had to climb to 13,500 feet to be legal to fly IFR and fly safely 2,000 feet above the highest mountains in that area. We were on our way to Wamena, one of our MAF bases located in the Baliem Valley, and one of MAF's busiest ones in terms of flight activity per day. We had to pick up Harry Weibe, a short-term teacher at the mission school in Wamena. Harry is from MAF Canada and he has come out to teach for a couple of years. He has to travel to Sentani today, and then on to Vanimo in Papua New Guinea tomorrow, to get his passport, visa and immigration paperwork completed at the Indonesian Consulate in Vanimo.

Having picked up Harry and departed Wamena in short order we then headed to Sentani. As Rick decided that I had not had enough 'punishment' for one day, he put me under the hood again for our one-hour flight. Actually, as I enjoy flying instruments, it was fun despite the long day. We arrived in Sentani around 3pm. The weather there was not that good. Rick asked me to take the hood off in order that I could see the weather situation up ahead. Rain had reduced visibility right over the Sentani airport. It had totally obscured the approach path to Runway 30, but Runway 12 was open, though with rain as well. A Merpati Airlines Boeing 737 had just tried to make the instrument approach to Runway 30 and had to go around because he could not see the runway on a short final approach. We opted to land visually on Runway 12 since we have the capability with our smaller, lighter Cessna Caravan. This was not a safe option for the Merpati 737 because of the size and speed of the airplane and the significantly reduced visibility. After we landed and were taxiing to MAF's parking ramp, we heard the Merpati 737 ask for clearance from the control tower for a visual approach to Runway 12. Rick and I agreed that wasn't such a good idea. Just a few minutes later we heard the Merpati captain advise the Sentani control tower that he was returning to his point of departure due to the poor weather conditions. We thought that was the right decision.

After parking at the MAF ramp and shutting down the engine, Rick had to rush off to an operations management meeting. Since it was still pouring with rain, I decided to stay in the airplane and complete my post-flight paperwork. That was an 11-hour duty day with 6.2 hours of flying. A long day. But the return process was still not complete.

⊀ Day two

When I showed up at the airplane at 5.15am for check-ride day, I saw that, for maintenance reasons, I had to switch to another Cessna Caravan. Shame! I like the Garmin 430 GPS flight system in the Caravan I flew yesterday and was hoping to fly it for my check-ride. Well, such is life! Our destination was Oksibil again. This time we carried almost 1,200kg of cement and other construction materials for various projects in the village of Oksibil. The weather there was not good – rain and fog.

Rick decided that we would go up and fly anyway and perform the required check-ride flight manoeuvres, and simulated instrument flight and approaches, in the local Sentani area while we waited for the Oksibil weather to improve. We took off at around 6.00am and performed various simulated emergency procedures in the local traffic pattern. Afterwards we flew about twenty miles east of Sentani to over the Papua provincial capital of Jayapura, right on the Pacific Ocean. I enjoy local flights over this area because of the amazing view. But Rick didn't have me fly there to enjoy the sights, but rather to make me sweat, and challenge my airmanship and aircraft systems memorisation with more simulated emergency procedures and instrument manoeuvres, all while 'under the hood', as part of the check-ride.

We then requested clearance for an instrument approach VOR-DME to Runway 30 at Sentani airport. As there was a lot of aircraft traffic departing and arriving, we spent some time orbiting in the instrument holding pattern while waiting for clearance to fly the approach and land. Two hours and fifteen minutes later we finally landed, parked the airplane and shut down the engine having completed one major phase of the check-ride. I was happy about that! Just then we heard that Oksibil's weather was getting worse, so our flight scheduler decided to cancel the flight there and fly to Mulia instead. That meant our load crew had to unload 1,200kg of cement and other cargo and upload the 1,200kg of cargo for Mulia instead. That was hard work, but it happens from time to time.

While waiting for the airplane to be refuelled and cargo to be uploaded, Rick debriefed/critiqued me on the phase of the check-ride just accomplished. He started off by saying, 'If I didn't know any better, I would not believe that you haven't flown this airplane in over three months by the way you handled it and performed the procedures.' I was flattered, but was able to reciprocate that this was due to the superb training that he, as Chief Pilot, and other MAF Papua instructor pilots, give all of us who fly in this programme. It was a good critique. I still had the route-check portion to do before it was over. That route-check would be to Mulia, and we departed for Mulia with our cargo. The weather was good along the way and on arrival. During the flight Rick continued to quiz me on aircraft systems abnormalities and emergency procedures. We descended and landed safely.

Just as we were completing the off-loading of the cargo and preparing to depart, a government official came to us and asked if we would be able to carry a medical emergency patient to Sentani. It turned out that this patient was an Indonesian military soldier who was seriously wounded by gunfire somewhere in the interior near the Mulia area. The patient was at the village medical facility, located about thirty to forty-five minutes from the airstrip. Rick and I agreed that this was a legitimate medical emergency and that we would wait for the patient and medical escort personnel to arrive. While we waited, we stood under the shadow of the left Caravan wing and Rick finished quizzing me on aircraft systems and gave me a final critique. The check-ride was officially over!

From then on Rick and I worked as a two-pilot crew to handle the medical emergency flight to a safe and successful outcome. When the patient arrived at the airplane, he looked as though he was in a lot of pain. The medical personnel helped as we took him out of the ambulance and lifted the stretcher into the aircraft. Rick strapped him down and secured the stretcher to the aircraft floor, and we found a suitable place to hang the IV bag. Meanwhile, I took care of the ticketing process and prepared the aircraft for engine start and departure. A female Indonesian doctor and a military officer accompanied the patient to Sentani. Rick acted as co-pilot as I flew the Caravan back. We are here in Papua to serve in any way we can, all in the name of the Lord Jesus Christ. It is a blessing that we MAF Papua pilots, and maintenance technicians are well trained to serve.

✈ Day Three

Believe it or not, I tried to get that 1,200kg of cement and construction materials into Oksibil this morning, and departed Sentani based on a good weather report. However, while en route the weather deteriorated significantly and I had to fly back to Sentani, after having flown right over Oksibil! The load crew unloaded the 1,200kg and uploaded it on another Caravan as the pilot planned to try later in the morning should the Oksibil weather improve. The flight scheduler changed my plans to take a load of passengers and a little bit of cargo to Mulia. Thirty minutes later, Doug Allrich started his engine, based on a good Oksibil weather report, and taxied out for takeoff. While taxiing he had a radio call that the weather was again deteriorating so he taxied the Caravan back to MAF. The load crew unloaded the 1,200kg of cargo and prepared his airplane for another destination in the interior! The cement was placed in the warehouse to try again yet another day.

✈ ✈ ✈ ✈ ✈

The diary week brought back memories to Eve Brooks, wife of Mike. Eve is a Speech/Language Pathologist at Hillcrest International School in Sentani.

On 6 September, 2004, a little boy walked into my speech classroom for a follow-up speech evaluation. 'Hi, Miss Eve. Guess what? I'm having a birthday in a few days. I'm going to be six.' It was hard to believe that just three years ago I would not have understood the few sentences that J said. In 2001, after hearing J speak, the missionary doctor in Papua suggested to his mom that she bring him to my class to be tested. J, who was very friendly, polite and talkative, had just turned three years old. The only problem was that, other than his parents, no one could understand him. Having had ten years experience as a certified speech pathologist, I knew if I could understand the context of J's conversation, I could communicate with him. 'J, how old are you?' J's response was to try to say his name. Then I asked him, 'What is your name?' His response was, 'Fee' (three). After asking him a series of questions, I realised that not only was J's speech delayed, but his language development was too, and he had difficulty understanding questions. Because his mom mostly understood him, she had to be convinced that he did indeed have a speech and language delay. Unfortunately, my caseload was full. So I gave her suggestions to improve J's communication skills. In 2002 I re-evaluated him and found marked improvements in his language and comprehension of questions but not in his speech.

The boy's missionary parents desired to move to the interior of Papua but were unable to do so due to the severity of their son's communication disorder. By then he was considered a high priority and I began providing speech and language therapy for him. J worked hard in speech class and at home to improve his communication skills. In May 2004, after two years of therapy, J's parents were released to the interior. The purpose of this follow-up visit in September was to check for continued improvement. It was determined that J's speech was normal for an almost six-year-old boy. I told his mom that because his speech was corrected at a young age, J would not remember his early problems.

✈ ✈ ✈ ✈ ✈

Another teacher at Hillcrest is Alyssa Taylor, who shares a brief glance into one day at school.

I spent my day teaching eleven fifth graders. My day started with Bible class where we began our week focusing on integrity. We looked at the life of a Bible character and a modern day Christian who both demonstrated integrity in their lives. The day continued with teaching reading, writing, grammar and spelling. After a fifteen minute recess break, the school day went on with a lesson in fractions. Then the students made a timeline on the classroom wall to which they will add important dates throughout the school year. After lunch it was back to the classroom for science then computer class. When I sent the students off to music, I corrected papers and finished preparing for tomorrow's lessons.

✈ ✈ ✈ ✈ ✈

Harry Wiebe (of MAF Canada) teaches grades 1–5 at a small school in Wamena that is a satellite from the main school in Sentani. Harry is retired after teaching in a one-room school in a Hutterite community in Canada.

Being a missionary means you need a visa from the country you work in. I entered Papua (was Irian Jaya), with a two months visa. Now that required to be corrected. To get my visa I needed to leave the country and come in again. The Director of Education, who has been involved in this before, made plans for me to go to Vanimo (in Papua New Guinea) on Monday. He forgot that Monday was a national holiday. The Director changed his mind and made plans to have me go on Tuesday. There was, however, a kink in the gears, as the official at the Consulate was not informed of the change. When I arrived at the Consulate on Tuesday he was a little angry and, as a result, made me wait… and wait… and wait. But I did get my visa eventually.

While I waited I exchanged some money and did a little shopping then sat by the ocean and enjoyed the cool breeze. I saw a local man cut off some palm fronds that he was going to use for shelter from the sun for an upcoming celebration. I also saw him scramble down the tree. Interesting.

The logistics of the journey were complex. As Wamena has no roads leading out or in, I had to fly to Sentani and spend the night there. The following day I flew on to Vanimo, got my visa and flew back to Sentani. I spent the night there then flew to Wamena the next morning. Such is missionary life in Papua.

✈ ✈ ✈ ✈ ✈

Emily Flegal's parents teach at Hillcrest International School. Emily wrote a report of a memorable occasion that should have happened during the book's time window. However, Emily's report deserves to be read.

MAF held a dedication ceremony for one of its 'new' planes. This plane has made a long journey to get to Papua. It served six years ago in Africa for MAF, in what is now known as the Democratic Republic of Congo. That country has seen three civil wars, one in 1991, one in 1996 and one in 1998, which is still going on now. The political situation was one factor in taking the plane out of the area, but it was in need of repair as well. So it was shipped to Redlands, California. There the plane received 'heavy structural repair', said Matt Harris, MAF mechanic. The repairs included tearing up the floor, de-skinning the wings, changing the gear brackets, changing and rebuilding the tail services, inspecting the engine cradle, changing the seat tracks and also changing the seats themselves, among other things. These modifications will make the plane easier and safer to fly, thanks to all the mechanics who helped!

When the repairs were finished the decision was made to use the plane in Papua. Bill Leahy flew it across the Pacific Ocean to get it to Papua. Bill runs his own international aircraft delivery business, and has been involved in all of MAF's deliveries in the past five years. The longest leg of this trip was from Oakland, CA, to Honolulu, and lasted 17 hours 40 minutes. While in Hawaii, Bill Leahy realised that his paperwork, including his passport, logbooks, and some money, had been stolen from the back of his car. A flight that normally takes eight days took twelve due to this delay. He said that other than the problems in Hawaii, everything else went well, thankfully, and he arrived in Sentani safe and sound.

The ceremony began at 4 o'clock on Monday afternoon. About seventy people were there, nearly half of them Indonesian MAF employees. There were also several children who came to experience the exciting time. Wally Wiley began by asking everyone to gather around the plane. Then he gave a short speech, in Indonesian, about it. He told some of the history of the plane and talked about the many people who helped repair it. Kevin Lynne, who had worked on it in Redlands, talked about the condition that it was in when he first saw it ('garbage'). Wally continued by explaining that the plane is a symbol of what MAF does, but God doesn't need people or airplanes. We are blessed to serve him; it is a privilege. Not only should we thank God for the tool that he has given us, but also for the opportunity we have to serve him here in Papua.

After that everyone held hands and stood in a circle around the plane and offered up their prayers for it and for the work that it will help to accomplish. Once everyone was finished praying, Paul Dukes climbed on top of the hangar to take a picture of everyone in the circle. As soon as he was safely down, Coca-Cola was distributed and the plane was opened up in order that curious spectators could look inside. Everyone agreed that it was a good way to dedicate the plane to God's work in Papua. It will be based in Sentani, at least for now, and no further plans for its future have been revealed. Its first flight is scheduled for October 5, 2004. Wolfgang Baumruck will fly it to Okhika to bring materials for a National Church in that area. Then he'll fly to Pagai taking passengers and supplies to a national church. We hope and pray that this plane will be a real blessing to the programme here in Papua.

✈ ✈ ✈ ✈ ✈

Short-term teachers at Hillcrest International School, Tim and Carol Flegal, noted some of their activities. They are Emily's parents. Tim first.

I am working at the international school where most of the missionary and aviation workers send their kids. My job is to provide computer support, teach computer classes, and I am the teacher-advocate for the freshman class. We had homeroom this morning, which included a short devotion, prayer requests and prayer. I spent the next hour working on a new computer system to provide Internet filtering, then prepared for my classes in the afternoon, and helped folks with computer problems. Late morning I substituted for the science teacher who had gone to do a team-building seminar for the MAF pilots. After lunch I had two computer classes in which we were finishing a study on word processing. Mid-afternoon I worked with my oldest daughter (a high school graduate), who provides grading and class support for me, before going home to help my younger daughter with her homework. Later, when I received word from the clinic that I have malaria, I borrowed a car and went to the local pharmacy to get medication to treat it.

Then Carol.

I teach second grade, but sometimes they teach me. We have a morning ritual of gathering on the carpet at the front of the room for our 'Morning Meeting'. Not only is this time used for teaching maths and language concepts by using the calendar and my daily written morning message, it is also a time to pray together, sharing needs and praises. This week my morning message had included the word 'paradise' in relation to how I viewed this beautiful country in which we live. I wanted to convey to my students how amazed I am to wake up to a view of green jungle, blue skies and the sparkle of Lake Sentani right outside my window. 'Just another day in paradise!' I wrote. We had a nice discussion about how each of them viewed paradise, and the pictures they had in their heads when they heard that word. It was the usual white sandy beaches with palm trees swaying in a breeze, the ocean clear and blue. For some it was Pizza Hut!

We finished our discussion, concluded calendar time and moved into prayer. At first the prayers of these seven-year-olds were much the same as they were every day. There were prayers for sick family members, prayers for various bumps, bruises and other 'boo-boos'. But then things began to change. One boy thanked God for sending Jesus to die on the cross so that our sins would be forgiven. Then another boy joined him in thanking God, not only for sending Jesus to die for us, but thanking him that we don't have to die on a cross. I perked up and listened more intently. Finally, another boy began to pray, saying, 'Dear God, thank you that Jesus didn't stay here. Thank you that he has gone to prepare a place for us where we won't be sick anymore, and where there won't be any more crying or bad things. We will all be together there with you forever, and that is paradise.'

That is paradise! I was humbled, blessed, moved to tears and brought to joy by the reminder that as beautiful as it is here, this is not paradise! This is not my home. I have something much better to look forward to. And God used a seven-year-old to remind me.

✈ ✈ ✈ ✈ ✈

When anyone asks Tim and Carol Flegal what they do, their answer is not hard to find. They are short-term teachers in Hillcrest International School. Barb Dukes, whose husband Paul is Manager of Maintenance in Sentani, doesn't find it quite so simple.

I have always wished I had a title. Nothing so pretentious as 'Duchess' or anything. (Which would be quite strange with the last name of 'Dukes' anyway.) I want a title so that I can answer the question 'What do you do?' with an easy 'I'm a nurse!' or 'I'm a teacher!' But alas, no such deal. What do I do? Well, this last week I worked on some writing projects for our Programme Manager, Wally Wiley. I'm a 'sort-of-secretary'. See, I can't even say I'm a secretary! I'm not allowed to work in the office because it would make it look as though I was taking a job away from a national person. However, I'm not. I only compose letters or papers in English, something a national can't do. I digress...

This last week I rooted around in a very hot closet upstairs in our warehouse to find household goods for some folks who are here short term. We call that job 'Accommodations.' It's not terribly glamorous. And I did mean that the closet was hot. I was working in there one day when it was 40 degrees C! The other day I answered many questions via e-mail; they were from a family that is heading our way and in the process of packing their crate. When they get here I am often involved with new people's orientation to life in Papua. This is especially challenging when short-termers come unable to speak the Indonesian language. The local folks here sure don't know English!

We have an HF radio in our house that allows me to speak with ladies from each of the MAF bases on the island.

Every morning at 6.30 we have a fifteen-minute slot for a base check-in. For some of these ladies that is the only 15 minutes in their entire day when they have another English-speaking woman to talk to. It's an important time to check in and see how they're doing. A couple of days ago I told them all about some improvements that were made at our guesthouse, guests who were there, and what could be found in the store here in Sentani. Pretty mundane stuff, but it is the stuff that keeps ladies feeling that they are part of the whole.

On *Monday* afternoon I went to our Indonesian church where I'm helping a couple of Indonesian young people to learn to use the computer. I'm not a whiz, but I know enough to get them on their way. Unemployment is very high in Papua, therefore any skills they have are important in helping them find jobs. The other day I chatted with a young lady who has a degree in agriculture, and she can't find a job. She helps her dad in his garden, selling bananas and vegetables door to door. That's tough.

I spent time this morning talking with a friend who was going through a minor crisis. As she cried and told me her situation, I prayed and asked God to help me say the right things. Another friend called about an hour later with a dilemma she wanted my help to sort out. As I'm not in her mission, she figured that I could be impartial. Relationships are a big part of my life here.

Hospitality! Having folks over for meals is a fun part of what I do, provided I've been to the market and have food to prepare! Almost every week I invite people over. We sit on the porch and chat in the cooler evening air. Last night my husband and I enjoyed the fellowship of a single pilot, Kevin Lynne, who is in Sentani right now, as well as a Wamena pilot who was overnighting. We had some good laughs.

Kevin counts on getting his weekly dose of vegetables when he comes to our house for supper.

My role has changed a lot. Just two months ago we said good-bye to our last child to graduate from high school and leave the house. Now it's just Paul and me. Good thing we like each other! I'm still at the stage of missing mothering, but I'm thankful for the gift of e-mail that means I can keep in touch with my three kids. So what do I do? I can't give a word for that, but I can tell you who I am! I am a child of God who seeks to obey my Father. It doesn't get any better than that!

✈ ✈ ✈ ✈ ✈

Pilot/mechanic Mike Brown flies out of Wamena. He gives an interesting account of some of the more unusual things that a MAF pilot might find himself doing.

Besides flying a plane, there are other responsibilities that a pilot has when he flies in a place like Indonesia. My diary will tell you about some of them. In Indonesia there are lots of pigs, and pilots don't like it when one wanders on to the runway. In fact, they have a rule that if a pig walks on the airstrip while the plane is landing, it either has to be killed by the time the plane takes off or be given to MAF. On this particular day, the pig hadn't been killed in time, and I said that the village needed to hand it over. They handed over a pig, but not the pig. The pig on the airstrip was big and black; the pig they gave me was small and white. However, I didn't press the matter, loaded the pig up and flew home. The pig was all tied up, of course, as they can be quite dangerous. A stick went from its snout to its tail, its legs were tied together, and its mouth was tied shut. It could still squeal pretty loudly!

I returned to Wamena, unloaded the pig and left it in the *gudang*, where all the cargo is kept. After lunch I drove back to the base because I needed to take the pig to a friend of mine, Todd Adams, to raise it. When I told my wife I'd be right back as I was just going to take a pig to Todd, she asked 'Where are you going to put it?' 'On the top rack,' I replied. 'You're going to *drive* with it on top of the *car*!' she gasped. 'Well, I'm not putting it *in* there!' I said, laughing.

Back at the base I went into the *gudang* where the pig was lying, all tied up, where I left it. It didn't make a sound until picked it up by the legs. Then it began to squeal and squeal; even with its little mouth tied shut it made a racket. We swung it up on top of the car and I climbed in and began to drive. There were many children on the crowded street. Imagine their surprise when they looked on top of a big, yellow jeep and saw a pig! Many of them stared and pointed, saying to their friends, '*Babi!*' which means pig in Indonesian. A short drive took me to Todd's house where I dropped off the pig with his wife, Deb. One of the Adams' helpers carried the pig to the backyard where it will have a happy new home, at least for the time being.

I was told that the next day I was to take the Cessna 206 to Gilika to pick up a sick evangelist and take him to Anggruk. I knew that meant that I would have to be in Angrruk by 10am because of the winds and, since it wasn't a long flight, I thought I could sleep in a little and not get up at five as usual. The next morning there was a medical emergency in Kono. A woman had delivered a baby, but the placenta hadn't delivered. I decided to take my friend Todd, a CMA missionary, which turned out to be a really good idea. We flew to Kono and arrived there at 8.15am, barely in time to make it out again before the winds picked up. In fifteen minutes we were in Gilika, where the sick evangelist was. I had never seen someone with eyes so yellow. He was a very ill man and had to lie down in the plane. His family came along with him. Leaving Gilika, we were in Anggruk at 9.30am, with half an hour to spare.

After we dropped the woman and the sick evangelist and his family, we took off and were flying back home when we had a call. There was a man in Aphalapsili who hadn't had anything to eat or drink for three days, and they wanted me to take him to Wamena. So I flew to Aphalapsili and picked up the man and his two friends, all policemen. Everything seemed to be going fine until we reached an altitude of 10,000 feet, when the sick man started trying to crawl out the plane! He was kicking my seat and crawling up between the pilot and co-pilot's chairs. Todd grabbed the man's foot and arm and held him while I kept a firm grip on his jacket and managed to fly the plane at the same time. One of the policemen was also holding on to him, while the other had to hold the door shut to prevent the sick man from opening it. All the way home we had to hold on to the man while he kicked and struggled to get out of the plane. When we finally landed, one of his friends told us that they suspected that he was under the influence of black magic. That would have been nice to know before we were 10,000 feet in the air, but the Lord kept us safe.

On Saturday morning I was scheduled to fly people in the Caravan to a church conference in a village called Holowon. But since the weather was bad that flight was cancelled. However, there was a medical emergency in Senggo that another pilot was supposed to take care of in the Cessna 206, but he was off that day. As I didn't have to do the church conference, I went to take care of the medical emergency. The problem was that a pregnant lady's baby had died inside her. Only its hand had emerged from the mother so she needed to go to hospital in Merauke to have the dead baby removed. It just so happened that in Senggo there was also a lady who had given birth to a severely deformed baby with two skulls and a cleft palate. This baby needed to go to Jakarta by way of Merauke.

I picked up the two mothers and the baby and began flying to Merauke. On the way there, I was called about another medical emergency. A man in Kimam had been shot in the back with an arrow, and internal organ damage was suspected. So I stopped in Kimam and picked him up. At that point there were two people lying strapped to the floor, plus seven other passengers! Lucky for them that Brent Palmer was off that day, because so many people wouldn't have fitted in the Cessna 206. I called for two ambulances to meet us at the airstrip in Merauke. When we finally arrived, I helped the man with the arrow in his back out first, then looked at the floor of the plane and saw that it was covered in blood. For a minute I stood there, confused, then realised that the woman had given birth to her dead child. She was hiding the baby under her dress. No one heard her cry or noticed that she had delivered a child. She had done it all by herself. Both the man who had been shot and the woman with the dead baby got to the hospital. The deformed baby was sent off to Jakarta. After all the excitement of the day, I hardly had time to get home before the airstrip closed.

✦ ✦ ✦ ✦ ✦

Sometimes people think of missionaries as a race apart, people whose experiences are totally different from their own. Christy Brown, wife of Mike, illustrates that there is much in common between family homes wherever they are, though perhaps the number of dogs varies!

This morning I turned on my radio for our ladies MAF radio scheduled time at 6.30am. Mike had already been flying for at least an hour. I was able to spend a few minutes talking to the MAF ladies at the other bases, and then it was off to get the children up – Collin (7), Joshua (5) and Megan (3) – and prepare for school. Collin and I rode our bikes to school just around the block. I was able to spend a few minutes talking with the other moms. This is a valuable time to catch up with them and find out what is going on in their lives.

At home I began to prepare for teaching kindergarten. By 8.30am my helpers had arrived and I gave them instructions for the day's work. One helper's job is to watch Megan while I teach Joshua and another little girl. I organise some activities to help keep them occupied. Today they ran to the corner market and bought some vegetables for us and for our eight dogs; more about them later. My other helper was kept busy with housework.

9:00am. School started: we began with a Bible story followed by Bible verse memorisation, then on to phonics. That's a very important part of the day.

10:15am. We all took a break and had snack time. Megan joined us and the children had a few minutes to play together. Several fruit and vegetable sellers came to my door this morning with oranges, pineapples, bananas and leaf lettuce (a treat). After break we continued with school, doing maths, science, and reading.

11:30am. School was over and Jordan, Joshua's classmate, was picked up.

Then came the dilemma of what to do about six puppies with a skin problem. Our dog had puppies four weeks ago. They have now all contracted some kind of skin disease that I am trying to eradicate without pet store medicines. This is a lengthy process, and trying to keep all six puppies organised and out of trouble while bathing each one is a difficult task, not to mention trying to keep Megan out of the way as well. The kids had fun playing with all the puppies. Then it was into the kitchen to figure out what to feed these little guys as their mom is not nursing them as much as before. I thought I was done with the infant stage—until six puppies arrived. Having helped me bathe and feed and play with the puppies, Megan was ready for her nap. That gave me time to spend in God's Word and praying, as Joshua was out playing with one of our neighbouring kids.

At 2.30pm it was time to pick up Collin from school. All had gone well and he had no homework except spelling and reading. We talked for a few minutes, had a snack and off he went to play with his friends. Then I tried to organise my thoughts about dinner. It was to be simple tonight – spaghetti (from scratch), with homemade bread and green beans. I said goodbye to my helpers and thanked them for the day's work. They really are a very valuable part of life here in Papua. I couldn't be here without them.

Mike arrived back about the same time Collin came home from school. We talked about his day: where he went, whom he flew and some of the stresses he had encountered. Mike took time to relax by playing soccer with some Indonesians and expat men. The rest of the day was consumed with dinner preparations, baths, reading, spelling and Bible story. Then it was off to bed for the kids, after which Mike and I had another chance to sit and talk, and read e-mails.

That is a day in my life, though there are many variations, as I never know what the Lord will bring to me. I pray I will keep an open heart and mind and be a light for him wherever I am, whatever I am doing. Right now my job is to be in our home, taking care of our kids and teaching them.

✈ ✈ ✈ ✈ ✈

Having not flown for some time, Pilot Phil Nelson had some serious thinking to do. Phil is based in Merauke.

I hadn't flown for over six weeks, as there was an extensive inspection on my Cessna 206 on amphibious floats, and I was excited to get back in the air once again. My schedule was to shuttle some retired missionaries between a couple of villages they'd worked in, from Manggelum to Boma. As I first took off I noticed something was not quite right; the plane seemed heavy. When I arrived in Boma I discovered water in the floats – a good amount of it – and pumped out both floats, emptying many gallons of water. I had no idea what the cause was, but I knew I wanted to finish the flights I'd started. I felt it was important, as my passengers were on a rare visit to these villages. After pumping the floats out I had to move speedily, getting off the water as quickly as possible. I'd given my video camera to Justin (Justin Koens, another MAF pilot in Papua, son-in-law of the missionaries) and he was able to take some good shots of the take-off, then the landing when I returned.

Safety is a huge issue. What was the right thing to do considering that the plane was slightly overweight? Should I have cancelled the flights? That would have meant a significant delay for the missionaries as they contacted HeliMission to arrange alternative transport. Manggelum has no airstrip, which is why I land on floats there; the helicopter could land in a field. Knowing the importance of the flights, and wanting so badly to meet their needs, was I compromising? These are issues we grapple with from time to time. I finally came to the conclusion that I could, indeed, be safe. I was not letting my desire to help these people cloud my judgment. We pumped like crazy at each stop and took off quickly. All went well. It turned out that there was some undetected damage from a procedure that was done during the inspection. I was able to fly to Sentani and make the repairs, and am back on line again.

✈✈✈✈✈

Aircraft only fly safely if they are well maintained. Ann Boss, who is on loan to MAF USA in Papua from MAF Netherlands, is meticulous in his care, as this little two-day snapshot shows.

Thursday September 9, I finished the installation of a brand new engine on PK-MPW. I made the final adjustments today on the fuel flow, mixture, rpm and went on with the balancing of the propeller. We installed the previous propeller because there was still 400 hours on it. But, during the balancing process, I found the prop exceeding the balance limitations. This made me shut the engine down and install a new propeller. The next day, after balancing the new propeller, I rode along on the return to service flight that went really well. No major problems; praise the Lord!

✈✈✈✈✈

Ella, Anne (Johannes) Bos's wife, no longer needs to wonder what she does with her days.

There are days that I wonder what I'm doing with myself! I have no job outside the house and our children are in school, the boys for the whole day and our daughter till noon. But still the days fly by and there isn't much time for myself. Yesterday I realised how many unexpected things happen in a day. As I thought I had a day to myself, I planned to make bread, do some housework, and prepare for the women's Bible study next week. As soon I had done the dishes and had the bread in the oven, the phone rang. It was my husband telling me that people were waiting at the airport and I had to pick them up. So I left my bread in the oven and drove out to the airport. After I picked the family up, and found that their room at the guesthouse wasn't ready, I invited them over to our place.

The family left before lunch, and my husband and daughter came home for their meal. Till 2.30pm I was busy cleaning the house, then I drove to the school with the guitar in order that our oldest could have his guitar lessons. While I was there I talked with our daughter's teacher because of our upcoming move. There will be no kindergarten for her where we are going. Around 4pm we came home together with husband/daddy and had a cup of coffee. When I was heading to the kitchen the power went out—and we were planning on eating fries with chicken nuggets in front of the television! We waited for ninety minutes then decided to have tortillas at the table instead.

I could not count on both hands the times that local children came to our door asking to pick the berries we have in our backyard. They really strip the whole bush down, taking even the unripe berries. Right now the bush doesn't have a single berry on it, but they don't understand when I try to explain that to them! It is kind of nice when a little girl comes to the door and I see her wearing slacks from our daughter and a shirt from our son. I cleaned out our kids' closets and thought they could do without some of the things in them. So I asked our guard if he knew some kids who could use them. And ... the result was right at our door.

✈ ✈ ✈ ✈ ✈

While Anne and Ella Bos are in Papua in order to keep MAF's fleet maintained, Rick Willms and Wolfgang Baumruck are there to fly. Both Rick and Wolfgang are also mechanics. Rick rarely works on aircraft maintance as he is chief pilot, but Wolfgang is often found in the hanger. They have some challenges to face, among them a runway with a 14 per cent slope and a cliff partway along the side of it!

Yesterday I went with Wolfgang to the Eastern Highlands to get Wolf current at some of the strips out there. The first place we went to was Okhika. I did a first landing there on 21 September 1999, followed by the official first landing with the government inspectors on 1 August 2000. It's quite a nice strip, 540m long and 28m wide, with 14 per cent slope, situated at 4,650 feet. It has possibilities for upgrade to Caravan if they can work on removing a cliff that sits off the side near the top end of the strip.

After doing the required five takeoffs and landings with Wolfgang, we walked down the strip with the strip agents and local men. We discussed various things that need to be done to the strip to keep it in good shape, as well as what they would require to do to upgrade to Caravan. Smoothing the rollable surface was one issue, working on the cliff near the top end to give more wing clearance was another. They had already started work on the cliff area. I explained that getting the surface smooth and hard was the higher priority job, suggesting that when they finish that we would send in a Caravan to do a test landing. The wing clearance at the cliff is already within MAF standards; it just wants a little more margin there if we can get it. My comments were met with a round of applause and big grins. They promised they would finish the surface work in two weeks!

After Okhika, Wolf and I continued on to Mipol and Yapil. We did the required number of landings at each, and walked the strips with the agents and interested local males. Yapil has also been trying to upgrade their strip to Caravan. Their main problem is soft areas on the runway caused by long, thick grass growing where black earth was used in the construction of the strip. I instructed them to scalp the grass and sod from those areas and to crown the strip better in order that the moisture will run off more efficiently. They were excited by the possibility of being able to bring a Caravan into their area.

At Okhika the local people gave us some cabbage as their expression of thanks. At Yapil we were given tomatoes, some eggs and more cabbage. Flight service is very important to these people. We had a number of requests from the men asking us to please provide more flights in the future. MAF's ability to supply service to this area in the last few years has been minimal. Thankfully, with a few more pilots in Sentani, we have the potential to do better now.

✈ ✈ ✈ ✈ ✈

Kevin Lynne, a pilot/mechanic, took blow-by-blow notes on his week. Having spent Saturday at a retreat for middle-school boys and their fathers, he woke to a beautiful Sunday morning. Kevin's own father, also a MAF pilot, was killed in Papua New Guinea many years ago.

✈ Sunday

Beautiful morning. Got to know an Asia Pacific Christian Mission translator and hear about his work in Kobakma and call to missions.

Shared my testimony and a challenge to the boys and fathers about the importance of looking to the Source of 'Quality Manhood'. Followed that with snorkelling and roughhousing until it started raining, rain that continued until we got back to the docks approximately two-and-a-half hours later.

Sound asleep by 8.10 that evening and not a move until 6.00 on Monday morning for work.

✈ Monday

National Holiday—only the expat mechanics and pilots working today.

I finished closing up PK-MAR from last week's Wednesday to Friday inspection. Did the runup and post-runup checks.

Received checkout on procedures to prepare for tomorrow's cross-border flight to Papua New Guinea—flight clearances, visas and exit/re-entry permits in hand, as well as flight plan filed and route briefed for all pilots. Went home with a folder full of information to read up and 'get smart' on for Tuesday's early flight.

Supporter e-mails answered and prayer letter started, then one long phone call with a supporter before bed.

✦ Tuesday

- ✦ 0530. Preflight.

- ✦ 0620. Take off.

- ✦ 0700. Arrival Vanimo.

- ✦ 0730 (0830 local). Cleared Customs and headed for Immigration.

- ✦ 0800 (0900 local). Turned in paperwork and visa requests (13 passports total).

- ✦ 0830 (0930 local). Changed US$ at bank to PNG Kina and proceeded to shop in small general stores to kill time.

- ✦ 1000 (1100 local). Checked at Consulate – were assured that by 1400 we'd have the visas.

- ✦ 1100 (1200 local). Lunch across the street from Consulate turned into a 1.5-hour extravaganza (I think we overloaded their kitchen/waiting staff). Consulate was empty and appeared deserted at 1400 when we checked again.

- ✦ 1510 (1610 local). Blazing sun, sweating, waiting, finally a sign of life inside the Consulate and a man peeked his head out to assure us it would be 'just ten minutes more'.

✈ 1600 (1700 local). Our ten minutes were up and all visas were granted. Unfortunately the Immigration men have long since gone home, so...

✈ 1615 (1715 local). Airborne for Sentani—I'm still getting checked out, but Doug lets me fly the Caravan across the border and land it back home at 1645. Long day, but dinner at the Dukes' perks my blood sugar up and I'm able to answer a few e-mails before falling asleep about 2100.

✈ *Wednesday*

Assisted with PK-MPV inspection. Right-hand magneto needed to be replaced. Parts room is out of RH mags, so I would do a 500-hour inspection to get a magneto ready to be used.

Mag 500hr takes the rest of the day – should be done tomorrow.

1715. Phone call inviting me to a teacher family's house for dinner. Good to have dinner and social time with some new friends. Their 11th grade daughter asked questions about my call to missions and where God was working around us.

I encouraged the teacher/dad in his job as a mentor and teacher of mission kids (MKs)—turned out he'd been a MK himself. He went to Dalat and knew some of my friends when he was at Wheaton! It's a small world when you were a MK, even smaller when you go out as a missionary yourself.

✈ *Thursday*

Magneto 500hr inspection ate up the morning. Several parts were out of tolerance and needed replacement. Revised estimate of completion is sometime tomorrow.

Lunch with Phil Nelson, heard about Merauke flying and discussed philosophy of where to station newly arrived pilots (still waiting to hear where I'll be assigned). Caught up with Justin Koens for half an hour after lunch and heard about Nabire work and flying.

✈ Friday

Technical meeting all day. Lunch with the pilots and mechanics. Dinner at the volleyball game at Hillcrest International School, also a good social time with various missionaries from the community.

✈ ✈ ✈ ✈ ✈

The Programme Manager in Papua is Wally Wiley, who serves the Lord there with his wife, Joan. A forthcoming presidential election gave him some unusual opportunities.

Prior to the presidential elections, two of the candidates came to Papua to have meetings with church leaders. Men were brought from churches from the entire archipelago to hear the candidates' positions on supporting the church in Indonesia. I was invited to attend the three-day-long meetings as a member of a church leadership committee. The first day the vice-presidential candidate, Yusuf Kala, was invited. He is Susilo Bambang Yudhoyono's running mate. As of this writing the elections are over and it appears these men are now the new president and vice-president. The second day Megawati Sukarnoputri spoke. She was the then president, and just about to step down.

That day I talked to so many people; it was incredible. I had lunch with the Governor of Papua and was able to bring up the issue of getting fuel, especially Avgas. He asked that the various aviation operators in Papua write letters about the problems they're having. He was heading to Jakarta and wanted to have these letters in hand to address the issues at the top level. All of our fuels, kerosene and Avgas included, are shipped to Papua. The supplies have been dwindling so low that our ministry with the Cessna 206 is threatened.

I was also able to discuss the issue of better education for Papuan children. It has long been a passion of mine to see that Papuan children get a top-level education that will allow them to be in high positions. But my concern is not only that they maximise their intelligence but, more importantly, that they are taught integrity. The Pelita Harapan Schools in Jakarta work on that principle. However, for Papuans the idea of being able to enter a school like that in Jakarta is impossible. I have, therefore, been working with the leadership of the Pelita Harapan Schools to bring such an education to Papua.

For some time I have been trying to get land in Sentani on which to build the school, but met resistance at a 'county' level. While at these meetings, I was with a former Governor of Papua who also has a deep passion for educating Papuans. He gave me good advice. While I was talking to him, the resistant official came and sat down. As he was involved with the conversation, he was almost forced to agree how important the issue was, and get on board! I was rejoicing inside since the former Governor did not know that this man had been blocking progress. However, God used this divine appointment to pull the resistant official into not only agreeing, but also really desiring, to help see it happen!

This week I went to Timika to meet with officials from a mining company. The company wants us to help them get several airstrips open in order that they can use the cheaper and easier airplane rather than a helicopter to move people to and from those villages. They know that we have a history of working with villagers to get airstrips built to specifications that meet government standards. As we discussed the airplane situation, I explained that we were going to take one of our four Cessna Caravans off wheels and put on amphibious floats for ministry at Merauke, the southern tip of Papua. The men asked how we would be placing our other three Caravans, and realised that there would only be three aircraft rotating between four main locations. At that point one of the men suggested that we put in a proposal that the mining company purchase a Cessna Caravan on amphibious floats for the Merauke project, thus freeing up our current four Caravans in order that one could stay permanently in Timika.

Over several years I have prayed that God would provide us with a proposal writer. I know that there are resources available that we have missed out on all these years because we were ignorant of the process of submitting proposals for funding. One day last week I had a new MAF family in my office, just checking up on how they were doing. The wife, Carole, is a 2nd grade teacher at Hillcrest International School. Her husband, Tim, works with IT at the school and teaches a couple of computer classes. As we were chatting, it came up that he'd written proposals in his previous job. I sat up and paid attention! Then I told him that I was praying for someone who could write a proposal to a mining company in Papua for them to consider buying us a Cessna Caravan on amphibious floats. Here Tim was – the answer to my prayers! Within two days he'd put together a beautiful proposal, complete with pictures, stories, history and many things we would never have thought of. I look at these as 'God meetings'. First the idea was proposed to me from out of the blue to request a new aircraft, and then God provided the proposal writer to work on the paper that could possibly fill that need. I cannot tell you enough how much it blessed me that God provided the right man at the right time.

Every Tuesday I meet with the Sentani Management Team. This last week we spent time discussing a master plan for the Sentani base. Our hangar, warehouse and offices have been cobbled together through the years. Recently a safety audit demanded that our wood shop be entirely removed from the main structure, as it is a fire hazard. This has made us think 'bigger picture'. A most generous Christian architect from the Netherlands provided the plans for our Wamena and Merauke hangars and offices. Now he is willing to put together a master plan for the fifty-year-old Sentani base. We have been so blessed by the Christian community around the world. It is exciting for our team to look at how to make the base a more efficient and safe place to work.

Other meetings have been of a very unusual nature. There is a military base located next to our school. The name Hillcrest International School comes from the fact that it lies on the crest of a hill, and there is a military base, complete with shooting range, below it. The range has been there for years, but recently has become a problem for the school because of stray bullets. In years past the range was shorter and they used handguns. Now it is longer and they fire rifles. This has resulted in frequent stray bullets on the campus. The problem came to a head when one 5th grader got a bullet in his back. Praise the Lord, it entered only two inches and was in a location that didn't threaten anything vital. Meetings with military officials have been going on for several months now as we work on the problem. This last week a stray bullet landed near the school's office doors. Whoops – bad place to land! We now have the shooting stopped temporarily (for the first time) until we can help them work on the range to make it safer. Again, God provided us with the right man at the right time, as the husband of the kindergarten teacher, a military shooting instructor, brings his background and knowledge to resolving the problem. Thank you Lord!

Every other week I host a prayer meeting for mission leaders in Sentani. This has been an incredible time of sharing burdens and encouraging each other in the area of leading a group of people. So many times we are able to help out in practical ways as well as in prayer. The unity we experience here is no accident; it is something we strive towards. We know Satan would like nothing better than to split the missions apart, but we refuse to surrender! Greater is he that is in us, than he that is in the world.

✦ ✦ ✦ ✦ ✦

Wally's wife, Joan, teaches English, but it was outdoor education that was on her mind when she wrote the beginning of her diary.

Today I asked Emily Flegal to substitute for my classes and flew about one-and-a-half hours by Cessna to Biri in the lowland swamp area of the north coast. Tammy Wisley, wife of our Bible teacher, and I went to survey for a place to hold outdoor education next January. Every year we take our high school – about sixty people including students and chaperones – on a missions/outdoor education trip. We spent the morning hiking around investigating the river (with a view to clothes washing and bathing), the church (to hold kids clubs and to show the *Jesus* film), the local people's houses (to sleep our students), and the local missionary's home (as a place for our students to cook and wash dishes).

We also brainstormed ministry opportunities and work/community development projects such as pure water catchments systems and tree planting. Dan Dority, the missionary from Biri, was very gracious and offered to host our group for two weeks. He has expertise in the areas of language, anthropology, geology and entomology. Besides all that, he is a gifted speaker and really communicates God's Word. What a blessing! Now I will have to pray about whether we should make this our next destination. For the past ten years the Lord has blessed Hillcrest International High School with an annual trip that has transformed the lives of both students and members of staff.

In 2001 we went on outdoor education to a place in the highlands called Okbap. From Okbap we divided into groups and hiked into small villages. My group went into the village of Maksum to do children's Bible clubs, interact with the people, and work on the airstrip that they were trying to build. At that time I met the pastor. Nine months ago he had to move his family out to the coast because his wife has tuberculosis. There is a free cure, but the clinic has to administer all medications because of the fear of having an antibiotic course started and not completed. That was the beginning of a great deal of family illness and accidents due to the different living conditions. The first time the pastor came by was last April. He was desperate because his four-year-old son got up one night and went back to bed with a candle between his knees, thus setting his pants on fire. He did not have any money to have the boy treated. We got him to Michelle, an expatriate nurse, immediately, and she treated the boy.

After that his daughter's baby took malaria, his older and younger sons both had scabies and his younger boy caught impetigo. He and several of his children took pink eye, and the same son who was burned stepped on a broken bottle while he was bathing and sliced his foot almost in half. Each time the pastor came for help I called Michelle or another nurse for advice then obtained the medicines they needed.

The pastor came back another day and I gave him medicine for pink eye again. He then told me that his daughter was coughing so hard that she grew dizzy, and that he can't get any cough medicine that helps. That made me worry that there could be more tuberculosis in the family. I called a doctor who recommended chest X-rays and blood work for the daughter.

A few days later Joan's suspicions were confirmed.

Today I found out that the Maksum pastor's eight-year-old daughter does have tuberculosis. Now we will have the rest of the family tested because it is very likely others also have the disease. I am thankful that it has been discovered while there is still hope of recovery. It is good to catch hold of the fact that nothing is accidental with God.

During diary week, Joan and Wally took farewell of their son who had been home for his summer holiday. The couple also have a daughter who is away from home.

It has been a great blessing having Jared home for the summer. He came for six weeks with a team of five from Seattle Pacific University, and we travelled from the coast to the interior and back again. They were untiring in their quest for ministry, and in their love for one another and for the local people. After the team left, he still had a few weeks before school started, so we had him home with us again.

✈ ✈ ✈ ✈ ✈

Marlene Loucks and her husband, Brad, (who teaches at Hillcrest) are short-termers with MAF. Their daughter was very much in their minds in the middle of diary week.

We have only been in Sentani for a month. This is always a special day in our family because it is our oldest daughter's birthday. This one was particularly special because Erin is turning eighteen. Erin is still very much a little girl though as she is developmentally disabled, and thoughts of independence are far from her mind. We wondered what this day would be like being so far from home. Erin loves her birthday; she especially enjoys celebrating with her cousin, Hannah, who lives in Colorado and shares the same birth date. We planned a party and invited some of the other MAF teachers and their families and Kevin Lynne, a MAF pilot/mechanic, who arrived in Sentani about the same time we did. Everyone came, shared, and loved our little girl. You know you are with a great group of people when they all agree to wear funky Indonesian party hats! Kevin came to fly, Carol, Tim and Ann Marie came to teach, but they all ministered in a special way to an MK on her special day. Erin had one of her most memorable birthdays ever because these dear MAF people have such servant hearts.

Those whom the Lord has called to serve him with MAF in Papua have made sacrifices; some have been mentioned in their diaries. They have left homes and families but, as Erin discovered on her special birthday, the Lord's people are real family because they are sons and daughters of their Father in heaven. All would agree that anything given up in service of Jesus is nothing to what he gave up for his people when he gave his life on the cross at Calvary for their salvation.

23.

MAF Worldwide

We have circled the world with Mission Aviation Fellowship, looking at snapshots taken over the course of a week, give or take an occasional memory. MAF has approximately 1,000 members of staff working in thirty-nine countries using 134 aircraft, numerous radio and communications networks and logistics expertise in support of thousands of remote communities, and the Christian and other agencies that serve them. Our tour has visited over twenty of the countries in which MAF works, and they are scattered throughout the world, from Australia in the south to Mongolia in the north, from Papua

New Guinea more than right round the world to Papua. We looked at work done by all four of MAF's four main operations, and were invited into the lives of pilots, chief executive officers, missionary wives and hangar cleaners alike through the diaries they kept.

Diaries are fascinating documents, and other people's diaries are especially so. There is something very intimate about reading the day-to-day details of another person's life. Even the trivial things, perhaps particularly the trivial things, give a depth of insight into lives in a way that nothing else can. And the diaries that span the work of MAF don't just give a snapshot of the life of the Mission, they allow its very heart to be seen; a heart that beats with the love of God and with his compassion for those in need and for those who don't yet know Jesus Christ as Saviour and Lord.

24.
APPENDIX — AIRCRAFT

05-297 Cessna 206

05-297 Cessna 208

05-297 Cessna 208_Amphibian

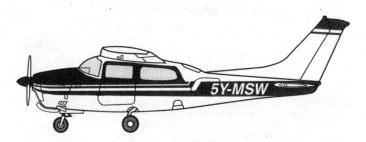

05-297 Cessna 210

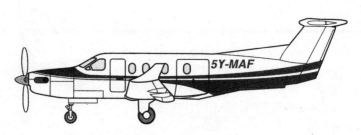

05-297 Pilaus PC12

25.

GLOSSARY

ACROSS	Africa Committee for the Rehabilitation of Southern Sudan
ADRA	Adventist Development and Relief Agency
AFS	Abyssinian Flight Services
AIM	Africa Inland Mission
ASC	Aviation Services Committee
ASD	Aviation Services Department
ASF	Aviation sans Frontières
BBQ	Barbeque
BSF	Bible Study Fellowship
CAA	Civil Aviation Authority
CAAB	Civil Aviation Authority Bangladesh
CASA	Civil Aviation Safety Authority
CEO	Chief Executive Officer
CMA	Christian Mission Aid
CMA	Christian and Missionary Alliance
CMS	Church Mission Society

CRMF	Christian Radio Missionary Fellowship
DRC	Democratic Republic of Congo
EU-CORD	European Christian Organisations in Relief and Development
FATEB	La Faculté de Théologie Evangélique de Bangui
FOM	Flight Operations Manual
GPS	Global Positioning System
GTM	Getma Transport Multimodal
HF	High Frequency
HIS	Horizon Situation Indicator
IECA	Evangelical Congregational Church of Angola
IMC	Instrument Meteorological Conditions
ISD	Information Services Department
IT	Information Technology
IV	Intravenous
JAARS	Jungle Aviation and Radio Services
LITV	Literal Translation Version
MC&OE	Maintenance Control & Organisation Exposition
MK	Mission Kid
MSE	Media Service Evangèlique
MSF	Médecins sans Frontières
MTN	Mobile telephone company in Uganda
NGO	Non-government organisation
NL	Netherlands
NRC	Netherlands Reform Church
NSSF	National Social Security Fund
OMS	(formerly Oriental Missionary Society)
OPS	Operations
PC	Personal computer
PNG	Papua New Guinea
RSA	Republic of South Africa
RTS	Return to service
SAMS	System Aircraft Management Software

SIL	Summer Institute of Linguistics
TCAA	Tanzania Civil Aviation Authority
TLC	Tender loving care
UN	United Nations
UNICEF	United Nations Children's Fund
UPS	Uninterruptible Power Supply
UTCAH	Technical Unit on the Coordination of Humanitarian Assistance
VHF	Very High Frequency
VOR-DME	VHF Omni-directional Range – Distance Measuring Equipment
VSAT	Very small aperture terminal (broadband by satellite!)
WFP	World Food Program
Wingman	MAF flight bookings computer program
YWAM	Youth With a Mission

26.

MAF Contact Details

Around the world, hundreds of people groups are still unreached. That's why MAF is part of an international fellowship of like-minded organizations working in cooperation. The following is a list of some of the organizations.

MAF Australia
Operating in 4 countries: North Australia, Papua New Guinea, Cambodia and Indonesia
Contact: Bill Harding
Address: PO Box 1099, Cairns, Queensland, 4870 Australia
Tel: 61-7-4046-1300 Fax: 61-7-4031-8664
E-Mail: MAF@maf.org.au
Web site: www.maf.org.au

MAF New Zealand
Contact: Rick Velvin
Address: P O Box 76-502, Manukau City 1702, Auckland, New Zealand.
Tel: 64-9-262-1725 Fax: 64-9-262-8449
E-Mail: maf@maf.org.nz
Web site: www.maf.org.nz

MAF Brazil (Asas de Socorro)
Contact: Rocindes Correa
Address: Caixa Postal 184 75001-970 Anapolis GO Brasil
Tel: 55-62-314-1133 Fax: 55-62-314-1450
E-Mail: ASAS@asasdesocorro.org.br

MAF Canada Operating in 2 countries: Angola | Namibia
Supporting: MAF- Philippines
Contact: Jeff Plett
Address: P.O. Box 368, Guelph, Ontario, N1H 6K5, Canada
Tel: 1-519-821-3914 Fax: 1-519-823-1650
E-Mail: jplett@mafc.org
Web site: www.mafc.org

MAF Korea
Contact: Rev. Young O. Kim
Address: Chung Jong Ro P.O. Box 28 Sodaemun-Gu Seoul Korea
Tel: 82-2-393-8068 Fax: 82-2-393-7286
USA Address: MAFK P.O. Box 6298, Corona, CA 91718
Tel: 909-737-4113 Fax: 909-737-7233
E-Mail: mafk98@aol.com
Web site: www.mafk.org

MAF Denmark
Contact: Filip Engsig-Karup
Address: Drosselvej 10, DK-8641 Sorring, Denmark
Tel: +45-8695-7084
E-Mail: national_office@maf.dk
Web site: www.maf.dk

MAF Europe
Contact: Mr. Chris Lukkien, CEO
Address: MAF Europe Operations Center, Henwood, Ash-
        ford, Kent TN24 8DH, United Kingdom
Tel: 44-1233-895500 Fax: 44-1233-895570
E-Mail: info@maf-europe.org
Web site: www.maf-europe.org

MAF Finland
Contact: Mr Heikki Hilvo
Address: MAF Finland, Helsinki-Malmi Airport, 00700 Helsinki, Finland
Tel: 358-9-3741-557 Fax: 358-9-3873-443
E-Mail: paavo.kilpi@gospelflight.fi
Web site: www.mission.fi/maf

MAF France
Contact: Denis Garcia
Address: 4 rue Château Maurice 25270 Septfontaine
Tel: 33-381-89-58-15 Fax: 33-381-89-58-12
E-Mail: maffrance@aol.com

MAF Germany
Contact: Peter Greilich
Address: Postfach 12 45, 31232 Edemissen, Germany
Tel: 49-51-76-92-23-08 Fax: 49-51-76-92-23-09
E-Mail: info@maf-germany.de
Web site: www.maf-germany.de

MAF Italy
Contact: Mr Luca Guadagno
Address: Via Ancillotto 20/22 E, Istrana, Treviso 31036, ITALY Tel: 39042273419
E-Mail: mafitaly@tiscalinet.it

MAF Netherlands
Contact: Adri van Geffen
Address: Postbus 65, 3840 AB Harderwijk, Netherlands
Tel: 31-341-564-488 Fax: 31-341-560-587
E-Mail: info@maf.nl
Web site: www.maf.nl

MAF Norway
Contact: Fred Karlsen
Address: Postbox 1608, NO-3206 Sandefjord, Norway
Tel: 47-33-48-07-80 Fax: 47-33-48-07-81
E-Mail: maf@maf.no Web site: www.maf.no

MAF South Africa

Contact: Butch Judge
Address: Postnet Suite 88, Private Bag X4, LANSERIA
1748, SOUTH AFRICA,
Tel. 27-11-6592880/1/2/3 Fax 27-11-6592885
E-Mail: MAF@mafSA.co.za Website: www.mafsa.co.za

MAF Sweden

Contact: KeA Arnlund
Address: Gamla Tanneforsvagen 17, S-582 54 Linkoping,
Sweden
Tel: 46-13-35--39-60 Fax: 46-13-35-39-65
E-Mail: maf-sweden@maf-europe.org
Web site: www.maf.se

MAF Switzerland

Contact: Andre Bucher
Address: c/o SMG, Postfach, Zurichstrasse, 106 CH-8700
Kusnacht, Switzerland
Tel: 41-1-910-73-91 Fax: 41-1-910-92-28
E-Mail: smgworld@compuserve.com
Web site: www.maf-swiss.org

MAF UK

Contact: Keith Jones
Address: Castle Hill Avenue, Folkestone, Kent, CT20 2TN,
United Kingdom
Tel: 44-1303-850-950 Fax: 44-1303-852-800
E-Mail: MAF-UK@maf-uk.org
Web site: www.maf-uk.org

MAF US

Contact: Kevin Swanson
Address:1849 N. Wabash Avenue, Redlands, CA 92374, USA
Phone: 1-909-794-1151 Fax: 1-909-794-3016
E-Mail: MAF-US@maf.org
Web site: www.maf.org

Entities operating in partnership with MAF-US:

ADS - Ecuador
Alas de Socorro

MAF Indonesia
Yayasan

ADS - Mexico
Alas de Socorro
Address: Apartado 20-COaxaca 68050, Oaxaca Mexico
Tel: 011-52-951-15079 Fax: 011-52-951-15079

SZV - Suriname
Surinaamse Zendings Vliegdienst (Mission Aviation Fellowship Suriname)
Address Doekhieweg 6 P.O.Box 2031 Paramaribo - Suriname
                 South America
Tel: 011-597-462101/011-597-432964 Fax: 011-597-497716
E-mail: info@szv-maf.com
Web site: www.szv-maf.com

Entity supporting the work of other MAF organizations

MAF Singapore
Contact: Peter J. Wigens
Address: 20 Jalan Insaf Singapore 2057
Tel/Fax: 65-259-5990

Christian Focus Publications
publishes books for all ages

Our mission statement –

STAYING FAITHFUL

In dependence upon God we seek to help make His infallible Word, the Bible, relevant. Our aim is to ensure that the Lord Jesus Christ is presented as the only hope to obtain forgiveness of sin, live a useful life and look forward to heaven with Him.

REACHING OUT

Christ's last command requires us to reach out to our world with His gospel. We seek to help fulfill that by publishing books that point people towards Jesus and help them develop a Christ-like maturity. We aim to equip all levels of readers for life, work, ministry and mission.

Books in our adult range are published in three imprints.

Christian Focus contains popular works including bio-graphies, commentaries, basic doctrine and Christian living. Our children's books are also published in this imprint.

Mentor focuses on books written at a level suitable for Bible College and seminary students, pastors, and other serious readers. The imprint includes commentaries, doctrinal studies, examination of current issues and church history.

Christian Heritage contains classic writings from the past.

Christian Focus Publications, Ltd
Geanies House, Fearn, Ross-shire,
IV20 1TW, Scotland, United Kingdom
info@christianfocus.com
www.christianfocus.com